ANTICIPATIONS OF THE FUTURE,

TO SERVE AS

LESSONS FOR THE PRESENT TIME.

IN THE FORM OF

Extracts of Letters from an English Resident in the United States, to the London Times, from 1864 *to* 1870.

WITH AN

APPENDIX, ON THE CAUSES AND CONSEQUENCES OF THE INDEPENDENCE OF THE SOUTH.

"If this be treason, make the most of it."
PATRICK HENRY—1765.

J. W. RANDOLPH,
121 MAIN STREET, RICHMOND, VA.
1860.

CONTENTS.

PREFACE.

Though the writer of the following pages has ventured to indicate the future results of supposed and stated causes, he does not claim to possess any gift of prophecy, or extraordinary political foresight. When speaking of the obscure and doubtful future as if it were the known past, he merely aims to present his general propositions and argument in a novel, and therefore a more impressive form, by using illustrations and examples of supposed actual occurrences, as the consequences of previous conditions—though the existence of these conditions may be doubtful, or even highly improbable. For the purpose of meeting all the current and popular objections of opponents, there are here supposed to occur, as early and principal consequences of the secession of a southern portion of these now United States, incidents which are not such as the writer deems to be either necessary, legitimate, or probable results. He does not believe, as being among such consequences, either that the then remaining northern states, (as the "United States," or in any other character,) will deem it expedient, or safe, to make war on the seceded states, or to invade southern soil, (unless the anti-slavery fanaticism shall have ripened to insanity, and also become general with the northern people—) or that they can successfully blockade southern ports, or be able (no matter how willing or anxious,) to excite extensive or important servile insurrection in the South—or that northerners can then even inveigle and abduct slaves with as much success and impunity as is now done, and will continue to be done, under the safeguard of, and by means of the facilities afforded by the present political union of the slaveholding with the non-slaveholding states. And if, by possibility, the northern people shall be so demented as to make war upon, and invade the separated South, and to seize upon and occupy any portion of the southern territory by an army, it is not believed that its defeat and destruction will be left to be effected by the slow though sure operation of blockade, with the results of starvation and disease. And, to fall farther back in the order of the supposed future events, the writer does not believe that the first inauguration of an abolitionist as President of these United States, and who will be necessarily elected by a majority strictly sectional, will be acquiesced in, and submitted to, by *all* of the southern states. Nevertheless, as this and the other named incidents, and calamities for the South, are all confidently predicted by "conservatives" and submissionists, and most of them are assumed as certain consequences of disruption of the Union, they are all supposed here, as either being effected or attempted, and are admitted as premises from which to argue, and to deduce their legitimate consequences, though from improbable causes. If these premises and postulates shall be objected to, and condemned by considerate readers, because of their being improbable—and some of them even morally impossible—the objection is fully admitted in advance. The excuse for their being thus adopted is that their truth has been so frequently and so generally asserted, both by northern aggressors and southern submissionists, that these opinions have been made to occupy false positions of importance in the public mind.

Further: Though it is here designed to deduce correct conclusions by sound reasoning, under the guise and through the medium of fictitious occurrences, the work ought not to be judged of as if sketched merely for amusement and entertainment, or as if the writer had been free to devise and shape the plot according to his unrestrained fancy, and to adopt such incidents and course of narration as he deemed most likely to engage the attention and interest of readers seeking amusement only. On the contrary, for reasons already adverted to, the supposed early and main incidents, used as premises, are precisely the grounds assumed and maintained by antagonistic reasoners—and all of which grounds the writer himself would be among the first to reject, and to protest against, as contrary to reason and probability. And even when deducing the results, both immediate and remote, from these premises thus forced upon his argument, the writer is allowed as little choice, or exercise for his imagination, as in the previous adoption of the premises. For, in acceptihg the premises, the obligation was necessarily incurred to reason strictly from them to their legitimate consequences and conclusions.

Again: Though thus presuming to anticipate and, in some sense, to predict future events in the general, it is only as such events will be the legitimate effects and consequences of the assumed and stated causes. And when stating, for example and illustration, particular incidents, or particular individual actors, and times of action, as consequences of the stated premises, the writer does not plume himself on accurate foresight of such minor or particular occurrences. Names of individuals are used as representatives of opinions or parties, and necessarily at hazard, as to their suiting the precise action presented. Some such of the many inevitable misapplications of names to incidents, (in advance of the facts,) have been already exposed by the passage of time in the few months which have passed since this writing was begun—and others will doubtless be seen before the publication can be made. But this is of no importance to the argument, and detracts nothing from the force of its illustrations or conclusions. These do not depend upon such immaterial issues as, for example, whether the wily, able and prominent Seward, or the obscure and coarse Lincoln shall be either the first or the second President of the United States, elected by the sectional abolition party of the North—whether such first election shall be effected in 1860, or not until a few years later—or whether the wrongs and the political subjugation of the southern states shall become intolerable, and so compel resistance and secession, at an earlier or a later time. One thing only of knowledge of the political future does the author claim, and by that test he is ready to be judged, and to abide the sentence. This is, that, on the grounds of such premises of facts as are here supposed to exist as causes, the effects and consequences are thence legitimately deduced, by reasoning *a priori*—and that, in the main and in general, and to all material purposes, the results would be such as appear in this narrative. And thus, by reasoning from supposed (and even though impossible) causes to the legitimate effects of such causes, the author trusts that he has maintained his main propositions—which are, that *a northern sectional party, and majority, directing the action of the federal government, need not exercise any unconstitutional power, or commit any "overt act" of usurpation, to produce the most complete subjection and political bondage, degradation, and ruin of the South;* and that whenever (before its prostration and ruin are consummated,) the South shall choose to resist such oppression and impending subjugation, *its means for safe and perfect defence, and for full retaliation of hostilities and injury, (if need shall be,) for achieving independence, and for securing the subsequent preservation of peace, and unprecedented prosperity—all will be as certain as can be any events of the future, or as the most ardent southern patriots would desire.*

June 5, 1860.

ANTICIPATIONS OF THE FUTURE,

TO SERVE AS

LESSONS FOR THE PRESENT TIME.

EXTRACTS FROM LETTERS TO THE LONDON TIMES.

LETTER I.

Preliminary Remarks. The First term of Service of an Abolitionist as President. Course of Lincoln's Administration.

WASHINGTON, D. C., Nov. 11th, 1864.

* * * * * * The last despatches from the Pacific States, through the magnetic telegraph, were delayed for some days by accidents which so frequently occur on the new Tehuantepec route. The complete election reports have now been received. As anticipated, California, Oregon, Washington, and also Sonora (the new Pacific free state, formed of territory last purchased from Mexico,) all have voted the ticket of the Republican party—as called by its members, or the Black Republican, or Abolition party, as designated by its opponents. William H. Seward of New York, is elected by a much greater majority than his predecessor, President Lincoln, obtained in 1860. Seward also now has the undivided votes of all the "free" or non-slave hold-

ing states. These, by the admission of seven new states since 1859, and the greatly increased population (evidenced by the last census) of the new states admitted between 1852 and '60, with the general growth of the party in all the northern states, have served to make Seward's entire electoral vote full two-thirds of the whole number. All the fourteen slaveholding states (Delaware being no longer one,) have voted against him as a unit, although there was not the remotest chance to elect his merely nominal democratic competitor. The present opposition to Seward and and his party, united and unanimous as it is throughout all the slavholding states only, is so weak, relatively to the supporters, that the thought of any future contest at the polls is more despised than feared by the now triumphant Abolition party.

At this point of time, when the issue of a new election is just ascertained, and the second term of power of this new and rapidly-growing Republican or Abolition party is about to begin, it may be of use to English readers to take a rapid glance over the more recent political events and tendencies of this country—of which the concerns, even when most important, are, by most Europeans, deemed of too little account to be carefully noticed, or to be long remembered.

In 1860, prior to the known result of Mr. Lincoln's election to the presidential office, the conflict of opinion, and the antagonism of the designed policy of the two great parties, caused violent agitation in the slaveholding states.—The outbreak effected by John Brown in 1859, and the general slave insurrection then designed, (though fruitlessly,) were obviously the legitimate practical results of a wide-spread conspiracy of northern men. The attempt, and its failure, and the speedy slaying, or later judicial executions of the criminals, found general sympathy among the Republican party and throughout the northern section. Though this long planned attempt to excite insurrection was promptly put down by Virginia, the state in which the attempt was made, and was altogether a failure as to its direct and designed results, nevertheless it caused much indirect injury to the slaveholding states, in weakening the security and tenure of their property in slaves, and in the great expenses thereby required and incurred for permanent as well as temporary measures of defence, against the recurrence of like invasions, with worse effects—or of more dangerous conspiracies, expected to be instigated or aided by northern emissaries and agents. The indignation of the southern people was expressed loudly in every state, and in almost every town and county thereof, and still more by the usually feeble direct popular voice than through the governmental authorities. The more southern and more ardent states seemed ready to adopt the extreme resort of seceding from the northern states, which had long been unjust and oppressive, and now showed themselves also as malignant enemies. But opinions among the southern people were then, as they still are, greatly divided, and even among those who are zealous for resistance. Many were advocates for immediate secession, whether of all, or of but a few States concurring in the measure. The grounds presented were the foregone and repeated and great oppressions, and unconstitutional wrongs, inflicted by the northern States—and that the power of the North was steadily and fast growing, and that it would become strong enough to attain the asserted great object of the Black Republican party—the abolition of negro slavery in the southern states —and the consequent utter ruin of the property and the prosperity of the people of these states, if not of their social and political existence. Then the secessionists were divided as to the proper time and manner for secession.—Many were for seceding as soon as an abolitionist should be known to be elected president, (which first occurred in November 1860,) without waiting four months longer for him to be installed in the office, and so get into his hands all the power of the Government. Others were for still more early action—or, if that should be denied, they deemed longer delay proper. They argued, that if the southern states consented to go into an election for the presidency, and it was legally conducted and they were fairly and constitutionally out-voted and defeated, they ought not, and could not, honorably, then refuse to abide by the result, and to submit to the nominee of the stronger party. And that all they could properly do, after the election, would be to wait for the next occurrence of what, in the fashionable phrase, was termed an "overt act," or a palpable violation of the federal constitution by the new president, and thereby violating the rights of the South. Of such grievances there had been sundry in past times—and there would, doubtless, be more and worse inflictions as the northern party and section approached more nearly to the attainment of irrepressible and almost unlimited powers. Many others, and including all the real but unavowed submissionists, professed that they were as sensitive of southern wrongs as the more violent; but that they did not admit secession to be a constitutional and legal remedy, and they maintained that the act, though it might be justifiable and indispensable, would, nevertheless, be revolutionary in character, treasonable (if it should not be triumphant,) and also, and necessarily, an act of bloody warfare. Still, these objectors declared (some in sincerity, and most of them as a cover of opposite opinions and designs,) that they were perfectly ready to join in these extreme measures, and to meet all the inevitable and calamitous consequences, whenever a majority of the southern people and states were as ready as they were for the trial. There were also many southerners who, in their veneration for the Union, and fears of the alleged probable consequences of disunion, were ready to submit to any extent of usurpation and oppression from the North or from the federal government, rather than to dissolve the Union, or than to adopt any other measure of defensive state policy, which their timid imaginations conceived could, by possibility, operate to increase animosity between the two sections, or have the remotest tendency, in the case of increased wrongs, to facilitate or enable a separation of the southern from the northern states. None of these ever dared to avow such submissive sentiments. They claimed that they were "Union men," and their opinions to be "conservative;" and generally, in every transient subject of controversy between different wings of the more ardent friends of the South, these conservatives threw their weight, for the time, to aid the weaker of the two parties, or the shade of opinion supported by the smaller number, so as, successively to defeat every opinion or proposed policy that was most likely to aid the maintenance of southern rights, whether in or out of the existing Union. Whenever they professed the strongest zeal for some one course of policy for the defence of the South, it was merely to use that proposition, and its friends, to stifle some alternative course which had many more real supporters, and which, if not so prevented, might have been much more effectual for promoting the ultimate objects professed to be deemed inestimable and indispensable by all.

The avowed or true secessionists were more numerous in South Carolina, Mississippi, Alabama, and Georgia—and next in Louisiana and Florida. The other slaveholding states inclined more either to "conservatism" or submission to the North; and the slaveholding states bordering on the non-slaveholding more so than all others. This grew out of their more exposed and dangerous position, if war should ensue, and the border southern states be made the chief battle ground, as was predicted, to be ravaged and laid waste, time after time, by contending armies. Also, on the frontier lines, most exposed to contact with abolitionists, there was found the almost only infusion of their opinions to be found in natives of the slave holding states. Virginia, the principal border state, still retained much of her former influence over her more southern and more zealous sister states; and this influence was successfully wielded by the then conservative and submissive majority of the people of Virginia, to restrain the movements of other states, who, whether with the leading, or the equal advance, of Virginia—or, if Virginia had plainly avowed the intention to submit—would have seceded before this time, either with or without Virginia and the other border states. Thus, among so many conflicting opinions and deceptious influences, nothing could be done to maintain the rights of the South, and but little (in military preparation) to defend the states from from such violence of invasion and outrage as already had been sent from the North, and was expected to be repeated.

Mr. Lincoln was elected in November, 1860, by a small majority, over both the Democratic party and the still organized remnant of the old Whig party. Most of the former Whigs, however, had previously gone off to the support of either the Democratic or the Abolition party. The separation of the votes against and for Lincoln, was precisely the same with the geographical line between the slaveholding and the non-slaveholding states. Lincoln lost but few votes in the latter, and did not receive a single vote in any one of the slaveholding states. If choice might have directed otherwise in some few cases, public indignation would not have permitted a southern vote to be offered for Lincoln.

To the inauguration of the new president in March, 1861, there was not the slightest resistance. In his early procedure he was courteous to all, conciliatory in manner to his political enemies, and did not show any resentment against those who had been his loudest vilifiers. He seemed eminently "conservative" in all his measures. It is true that, according to the previous and long established proscriptive policy of this government, the using all lucrative offices to reward friends and supporters (the system at first begun and consummated by President Jackson, and followed up by every party and president since in power,) Lincoln put out of the offices within his disposal every incumbent attached to the Democratic party, and replaced them with partisans of his own, or of his party creed, whenever such subjects could be found, or could be safely introduced from abroad, in some rare cases. In the southern states, where none avowed themselves to be Abolitionists or Black Republicans (except along the northern border line,) he had at first none of his own partisans to reward. Therefore, when displacing the before favored Democrats in the South, from all offices lucrative enough to be worth accepting, he supplied their places with southern submissionists, who most nearly approached in their practice to what suited the policy of the President and of the northern section. In the meantime, all the men of the South who had assumed, in good faith, as their requirement for secession, the President's committing an "overt act" of unconstitutional usurpation, were waiting for and expecting the occurrence in vain. And all of the smaller number who had desired to secede before the inauguration of the President, having lost all power for separate or leading action, were now compelled to join the ranks of the waiters for an "overt act." But President Lincoln, probably directed by the advice of counsellors much wiser and more prudent and cautious than himself, seemed determined to use the loudly avowed doctrine and professed rule of action of these southern waiters upon his measures, to make sure of their own inactivity and helplessness, in indirect aid of the future impregnable power of his section, and his party. He carefully abstained from committing any act, or exercising any authority, that was not clearly, and by universal admission, within the President's constitutional powers. While, within these limits, he steadily aimed to sustain his own party, and especially to reward his zealous partisans, his general policy and administration were praise-worthy, and respected for probity, wisdom, and firmness. However he might favor the North at the expense of the South, yet, if viewing the Union as a whole, he served its general interest well, and maintained the dignity of the government abroad, and its respectability at home.

So passed the first term of office of an abolitionist as president. Nor was there any appearance of change of course after later elections of other senators, and the admission of more new states, had served to place a majority of abolitionists in the Senate, as had long before been in the House of Representatives. The opposers of the administration had become more silent and faint in denunciation or censure. The southern thorough submissionists were even jubilant, and boasted of their early foresight of Mr. Lincoln's conservative principles and national policy, and their well-placed confidence in the sound patriotism and the magnanimity of the northern people, "who, even" as was predicted by their southern apologists "when having power, and unresisted in its exercise, would not abuse it to the destruction of the glorious Union and Constitution, as had been charged by the disunionists." The loudest complaints of dissatisfaction with the President's moderate policy, were heard from the underlings among his early supporters—who could not understand why every advantage their party had gained should not have been used immediately, and to the full extent, to forward the great object, the abolition of slavery. The more violent of his former opponents also, whether immediate disunionists or waiters (so far in vain) for an "overt act" of unconstitutional usurpation, still distrusted Lincoln and his party as much as ever, and suspected the worst for their future rule. They ascribed the apparent moderation to profound policy, and the delay of the formerly expected course of undisguised despotism to the design to render the success certain, by presenting, at a later time, irresistible strength to the more and more enfeebled opposers. If these suspicions were well-founded, it must now soon become manifest. For the power of the abolition party and section is now almost supreme in every department of the government; and it will, for the coming term, be wielded by a far more able and adroit politician than President Lincoln.

The moderate course of policy, pursued through his administration by President Lincoln, had caused no less disappointment to his southern enemies than to his early and most fanatical partisans. On this account, as well as in accordance with the policy of "rotation in office," which is so much approved and usually observed in the northern states, Lincoln was not nominated for re-election, and a second term of service, by his party, but was set aside, and the undivided and greatly increased abolition vote was given to Seward.

LETTER II.

Sectional Parties and their necessary effects. No "overt act" needed for the subjugation of the South.

WASHINGTON, December 20, 1864.

* * * * * In this Congress, there is a majority of forty votes in the House of Representatives for the president and the North. In the Senate, the majority of Black Republicans, as yet, amounts to but two votes. But the dominant party can command more from northern Democratic members, in sundry questions of granting lands, or other benefits dispensed to northern interests, in which the states of these senators are deeply concerned. On March 4th, the fixed Abolition majority in the Senate, because of changed members, will be increased to at least four. But before this time, there has been a fixed and certain majority in both Houses entirely in the interest of the northern sec-

tion. Of course, the southern minority, in all party or sectional questions, will be utterly powerless to carry out any measure, or even to defend southern interests from any legal aggression or wrong. And there are but few questions now which are not sectional in their bearing. The oppression of the minority, by the majority, must necessarily follow the division, by a geographical line, of a confederation of states, (even though before free, and equal in political rights,) into two unequal sections, having different and opposed opinions of policy, and different interests. When the earlier party divisions of this government existed, founded on principles or opinions having no relation to locality, every state, and almost every county and parish, contained citizens belonging to both the great opposing parties. And however the strength of such parties might fluctuate in different states, or the one might grow and the other wane in the whole Union—and however, at times, their conflicts might be heated and violent—still there would be nothing to detract from the equality of rights and political power of each state and each citizen. But now, whether old party names are still preserved, or new names adopted, the country is divided, in point of fact, into two great sectional parties only, on the subject of negro slavery, and which are separated strictly by a geographical line. This line has already been removed, and (if present conditions are to continue) is doomed to change much more by removal farther southward, as slavery shall be successively driven back by outside pressure. Wherever that line shall be, the people on the different sides of it will be opposed and hostile to those on the opposite side, in opinion, sentiment, and supposed interests—because of the opposite conditions of conservatism of the institution of negro slavery, and fanatical hatred to its existence. This alienation and hostility extend to every other matter of general policy or occasional expediency in which the interests of the two great sections may truly differ; and also, though prejudice and ignorance, to many other subjects in which the interests of both sections would be best promoted by the same policy. The prospective and successive removal of the line separating these sections will be caused (as in the most recent change of Delaware,) by slavery being gradually extinguished in a previous border slave-holding state. Such extinction will not occur because of public opinion, in such localities, having become unfavorable to slavery, or because slave labor has there ceased to be profitable, or less profitable than free hireling labor. The change, whenever it shall take place, will be owing to other causes, and chiefly because of the increased and increasing insecurity of slave property near the border, compelling owners either to sell off their slaves, or to remove with them to the farther southern states, less accessible to Abolition agents, and their corrupting operations on the slaves. The vacancy of population thus made near the border will, in time, be filled by immigrants and hirelings from the North; and when the like changes shall have extended gradually across the whole territory of any state, as a matter of course, that state will cease to be interested in the maintenance of the institution of slavery; and its then anti-slavery population next will put an end to it by law, and compel the speedy deportation, or otherwise the emancipation, of all the then remaining slaves. This end has already been reached in Delaware, is fast approaching in Maryland, and next, Missouri, Virginia and Kentucky, under existing circumstances, must successively be subjected to the same course.

While the two great sections are governed and alienated by such opposite opinions and sentiments on the subject of slavery—and while the opposition to it in the North has run into blind fanaticism—there is this notable difference in the prevalence of these opposite sentiments. Though the northern section is far the more populous and powerful, and elects representatives, both state and federal, who are nearly all in favor of the entire abolition of slavery, still every northern city and county contains more or less of dissentients, who would respect and maintain the rights and the property of the South—and who would oppose, as highly injurious, and even to the North, the extinction of slavery in the South, even if it could be effected legally, and justly to the slave owners. These dissentients also are among the more sound thinkers and the most worthy citizens—and their number is increasing with time. But almost everywhere they are the minority of their election district, and their opposing votes, if given, amount to nothing in the selection of representatives. However, in some few of the border districts, along the border line, the majorities hold pro-slavery sentiments, and elect a few members of Congress of like creed, who oppose their great section upon this subject. On the other hand, the southern section, however divided by old party names, has scarcely any division of opinion on the question of slavery. The very few Abolitionists, in the slaveholding section, are either near the northern line, or are northern immigrants to the commercial cities. In most cases such persons are so few and scattered, that they do not venture to utter opinions which are so generally abhorred. Should civil war between the two sections be the unfortunate future consequence of this division of opinion, these respective different conditions will have much influence on the final result. The whole population of the southern section will be united in opinion and purpose, while every portion of a northern state will be weakened by the presence of a strong minority in opposition. But as an offset to this, and of much more weight and danger if well founded, the northern people count confidently, in the contingency of war between the two sections, that they will find ready recruits and allies in nearly all the slaves of the southern States. Whether there is any solid ground for this expectation or not, I shall not here argue.

Under such circumstances as are stated above, of a confederacy with representative government and equal representation, but divided into sectional parties having conflicting opinions and interests, it must be an inevitable result that the weaker section will be completely ruled by the stronger, and be as entirely without means left for defence or relief, as if the weaker section had no representatives in the legislature, or no right of suffrage; or, indeed, was a conquered and subject province, at the mercy of the dominant section. By the constitution of this confederacy, both the rights of the states and of their people are well guarded, so long as parties are founded on differences of political opinion, and are intermixed in every state and smaller portion of the general territory. But, when parties become wholly sectional, and also opposed (or supposed to be) in every important interest, the constitutional safeguards of the weaker section are worth nothing—and all the safeguards of free and representative government become mere forms, and the delusive mockery of their former substance and value. If, for, centuries past, England and Ireland had been equally and fairly represented in proportion to their population and wealth, in the same Imperial Parliament, Ireland would not have been the less oppressed than she has been. Her having one hundred or one hundred and fifty votes in Parliament to oppose to more than three hundred of English members, would have served for no purpose, except to bolster up the pretence that Ireland, being fairly and fully represented, was as free, and therefore as justly governed, as England. Indeed, under such circumstances of a fixed sectional majority, the larger the minority is, the greater will be the injustice and oppression to which it will be subjected. For the greater the numbers of a minority, the more will it resist, and the more violent and turbulent will it be in its resistance—and thus will it provoke increased hostility and severity from the majority, which might have been escaped by a course of timid and humble submission. Thus, the total absence of all real legislative power of Scotland in the British Parliament, since the Act of Union, served to prevent all serious resistance to, and invite kind feelings from, the acknowledged irresistible voice of England. Under the old "rotten-borough" system, Cornwall had more representatives in the House of Commons than all Scotland. Yet, as alleged by Burke (when arguing in defence of virtual representation,) there had been no important instance known of the interests of Scotland having suffered because of her want of more full and equal representation. Probably, for the reasons stated, if Scotland had had no representation whatever, (or only a single representative to state her wants and wishes, as have the new territories in the American Congress,) and had been, both ostensibly and really, a province subject to England, and without restriction of authority, the interests of the dependent section would not have been less cared for by the English Parliament and Government, then ruling without opposition, or question of their supremacy or omnipotence.

Such are the reasons for my opinion, that the present and fixed sectional condition of parties, in this country, operates to subject the weaker section, in political subordination and bondage to the stronger, as completely as if the weaker had been deprived of all representation in Congress, by the sharp and speedy operation of a Napoleonic *coup d'etat.* Whether my reasoning is sound or not, will now soon be seen. The northern section and the President have now a perfectly reliable majority in the Senate. On every question of conflicting interests, the South is powerless and defenceless in the making of laws. The United States judiciary is not yet entirely sectionalized, or abolitionized, though, by vacancies and new appointments, the majority of the members will soon be of that character. And before that time shall arrive, the only remaining safeguard for the rights of the weaker section is in the federal judiciary, and that defence is limited to possible judicial decisions, and the construing of the constitution in regard to the institution of slavery, and the rights of slaveholders. The former noted decisions of the Supreme Court, in favor of southern doctrines and claims, may now soon be reversed, by means of new judges. The President will have no need or inducement to commit any "overt act" of unconstitutional usurpation—and for the sufficient reason that, without any violation of the letter of the constitution, every desired advantage and object may be gained for the northern section—and the interests and institutions of the southern section may be placed as low as their degradation may best subserve northern interests or wishes.

LETTER III.

Army. Land Grants.

WASHINGTON, January 10, 1865.

* * * * * According to the act of last session the regular army has but lately been increased to thirty thousand men. The recruits were obtained almost exclusively from the northern states, and mostly from the great cities, where numerous individuals, both foreigners and natives, are always suffering from destitution, and, consequently, the obtaining recruits for the regular service is there most certain and speedy. The southern cities would, in comparison, supply very few recruits, and the southern rural districts almost none. But few of the new officers have yet been nominated to the Senate. * * * * * *

The re-establishment of the high protective policy has all along been earnestly desired by the North, and was more plainly and strongly recommended by the President's last annual message than previously. A bill for the purpose is in progress, and will doubtless be acceptable to the northern section.

Grants of vacant government lands in the new states and territories are eagerly sought by petitioners and claimants of various kinds, and grants are made lavishly by Congress. There is no limit or restriction on the amount of this waste, except that the character of every grant is such that a precedent for it can be cited in the former enactments of past administrations, of both the old party divisions. Such precedents, for these or any other measures, serve to silence many opposition politicians who would object to the constitutional authority for many of these grants, if their party, and in some cases, with the aid of their own individual votes, had not established the first precedent of abuse. In the present cases, almost every grant of land goes to a northern beneficiary, or is in aid of northern interests. Money is also voted lavishly for improving the navigation of rivers, harbors and ports, all in the northern sections. But the partial or unjust destination of such benefits does not impair their constitutional authority, and these measures also have sufficient authority in former precedents, both of Democratic and Whig administrations. Future grants will be no less sustained by precedents, and by constitutional authority, even should they be made to cover every acre of public land from the Mississippi to the Pacific ocean—and shall all be designed for, and devoted to, the most unjust and corrupt purposes, and all for the benefit of the northern section. * * * * * * * *

LETTER IV.

Protective Duty System. Fishery and Navigation Bounties. Free Government in Theory. Universal Suffrage and Demagogues.

WASHINGTON, February 17, 1865.

* * * * * The new tariff bill has passed both Houses, and received the President's signature. The duties imposed to exclude foreign fabrics and to encourage the like home productions, are as high as forty per cent. on the general average. Of course they will operate to raise the prices

of the protected products as much as may be required for fair profits, within that limit of forty per cent., and by excluding importations, (which, if made, would pay duties,) will detract from the general revenue of the treasury just as much as lower duties would have yielded. The advocates for this protective policy, who are mostly northerners, declare that it will be most beneficial to the southern states, by causing therein the establishment of manufacturing industry, which is now almost entirely deficient. But this effect has not previously been, and never can be, produced by federal legislation, offering rates of indirect bounties ostensibly equal to all, but, in truth, operating most unequally for the North and South. For, because of the difference of condition, and of comparative fitness, advantages and disadvantages, a protective duty of twenty per cent. may be abundantly high to establish profitably a certain manufacture in New England, which, if relied upon for support in the southern states, would lead to certain loss. And if the duty were raised from twenty to fifty per cent. by the increase, there would only be given more advantage over any southern competitor. For while the manufactured commodities might rise, if demand or other circumstances permitted, fifty per cent. in price, or for the price to vibrate between twenty and fifty per cent., still the advantages of the northerner will always enable him to sell, say ten per cent. lower than a southern competitor. And so the latter will be undersold and driven out of market, whether at the highest or lowest protection by a federal tariff. Such have been the general results of tariff-protected manufactures commenced in the South, which attempts have generally brought loss, if not ruin, to the undertakers. If it is desirable to establish manufactures in the South, (and certainly it is, if the South is to be made independent of northern supplies,) it can be done only by state legislation, and state encouragement of southern, and prohibition of the introduction of northern productions. If this were the policy adopted, the South would, indeed, pay all the cost of the system—but would receive all the benefits of creating home supplies, and building up home markets for agriculture. But, under federal protection (as called,) continued for fifty years, the South has been paying (as of all taxation) the much larger proportion of the cost, and receiving little of the benefit—and thus has built up many great home markets for the North, but none for the South.

Senator Clay's proposition to repeal the fishing bounties (received exclusively by the New England States,) which has been discussed for years, and neglected even under the preceding Democratic administration, is now hopeless of success; and, as such, has been abandoned by the patriotic and zealous mover and advocate of the proposed measure of reform. This system, which has already bestowed more than fourteen million dollars in bounties, for no good general purpose, is still to continue. For the like reasons, the attempt to put down the indirect bounty to the American coasting navigation, and the consequent virtual monoply enjoyed by northern vessels, was still earlier abandoned. It is now so evidently hopeless to carry through any measure of defence for the South, against the interests and grasping predaceous action of the northern section, that few such attempts will be made hereafter, and none can be successful. The southern members now scarcely take the trouble to oppose new financial aggressions from the North, either by argument or votes. Whether opposing or not, they have to submit to inevitable defeat. There is now no use whatever in sending members from the southern states to Congress, unless to effect such petty objects as the asking for some small local benefit, or the abating of some local grievance, which the northern section has no interest in refusing, or will accord, from some touch of mercy or magnanimity, to a former rival, now powerless, unresisting, and contemptible. Except for such rare contingencies, the sending of members to Congress is now entirely useless to the southern states, and only useful to the members themselves, in the very high salaries and perquisites they receive for their nominal and useless service. But all these evils to the South are produced and maintained (as may be many more and worse) without the least infringement of the restrictions and checks of the constitution, and therefore they present no "overt act" of illegal misrule, by either the President or Congress, and, of course, (according to the generally received understanding,) should be acquiesced in, as both fair and just, by the suffering sectional minority. It is said, and generally admitted, that under a free constitution—where all citizens equally have votes, and all portions of the population have equal and fair representation—all errors, and wrongs and evils may be corrected at the polls by the votes of the people—and that this is the only and a sufficient remedy—and they who do not thus redress all errors of their delegated authorities and officials, can have no ground for complaint of injustice or wrong, and ought not to have any other mode for seeking redress. Yet, whoever will properly apply this specious theory to the rough tests offered by the existing fixed sectional parties, may learn that, with all the forms of free government and equal rights, the southern states are as much subjected, and as much in political bondage, to the northern, as is Cuba to Spain, or as was Hungary to Austria.

The theory of this system of free government is beautiful and admirable. It is suited to attract and secure the high applause of every Englishman who is truly a lover of freedom, and who loves and values the more complex constitution of free government of England, not for the many and great inseparable defects and abuses, but because, taken altogether, it has afforded the best protection to freedom, and to the growth and maintenance of free principles, of any government that exists, or, perhaps, ever has existed in Europe. Long ago, to my then more youthful and sanguine imagination, the government of the United States of America seemed more pure and more perfect than that of England, and my high appreciation of its constitution and earlier operation drew me to visit, and to continue a long sojourner in, this new country. I have not failed to recognize in the whole people another branch of the English family, and in some respects showing improvement upon the old stock, and its home succession. I admire the many great and good qualities of the general population of these States, and more especially of the better classes of the warm-hearted South. But nearer observation, and the passage of time through the many years of my residence in this country, have served to dissipate my early illusions as to the perfection of this government in practice as well as theory, and its fitness to secure the long-continued possession of freedom, and of equal rights and benefits, to all its states and citizens. Whenever any important difference of condition, opinion, or prejudice, distinguishes great portions of a confederacy of free states, as in regard to negro slavery here, there will be danger of sectional division and hostility operating to counteract and overcome the best principles of the best devised constitution of government. But if sectional division had not been produced, and all its evil consequences, there would have operated another bad influence, which has infused its debasing and corrupting poison into the body politic. This evil is the extending the right and exercise of popular suffrage much too far, or to its farthest reach—the being universal. If able statesmen, virtuous patriots, and true lovers of free government, were to decide upon the form of government best suited to establish and secure the permanence of freedom and the greatest good of the whole community, they would not extend popular suffrage so as to include a large proportion of the lowest and most ignorant of the citizens, or those who, as a class, have not any important interest in the affairs and prosperity of the commonwealth, and who, if they even had such interest, have not the knowledge necessary to guard its preservation. This great political error has been committed, and now has been carried to the fullest possible extent, in every state of the confederation. But still there is and must be a notable difference in the amount and measure of evil so produced between the slaveholding and the non-slaveholdlng states and sections. In the latter, popular suffrage is truly universal. In the slaveholding states it is not less unlimited, according to the written constitutions, among citizens, and all of the white race. But there is still the lowest class—of slaves—who are necessarily without political rights; and thus the institution of slavery serves to withhold from the exercise of suffrage the greater number of bodies without minds which are unfit to control any political power. Thus, in South Carolina, where more than half of the population consists of negro slaves, popular suffrage, even though nominally and literally made universal, is, in fact, restricted to fewer than half of the population—excluding, as slaves, all of the lowest and most degraded classes, who, whether slaves or free, white or black, or in the North or South, are and must be incapable of understanding or caring to preserve the principles or the benefits of free government. Now, in the northern states, where free whites occupy the lowest places in the community, and all have votes, the evils of universal suffrage have already extended, and will still more extend with time, to the worst consequences of this abuse of free institutions—and very far worse than any practical results of the same designed innovation established in the slaveholding states.

Demagogues in a free country are precisely the same despicable creatures as are the most servile flatterers of the monarch in an unlimited despotism. They both flatter, for their own personal gain, the sovereign power, and the source from which flows all power and emolument. And while these sycophants and demagogues alike aim to flatter, cajole and corrupt their respective sovereigns—the monarch or the mob—none know better than they do the weakness, the incapacity, and the low moral standard of those idols whom they pretend to worship, but whom they really despise and cheat and rob upon every safe opportunity. Demagogues have been the greatest bane to the free government of these states, and it is much to be feared that they can and will destroy the benefits, and next the existence, of free government, even if the more prominent and obvious danger of sectional parties can by possibility be averted.

LETTER V.

Southern Aspirants to the Presidency suited to the Northern Market—and their Injurious Influence on Southern Rights and Interests.

WASHINGTON, February 24, 1865.

An Act has been passed to increase the rates of salaries of nearly all the officers of the government, civil, military and naval. The number of officers, also, is much enlarged.—The increase of salaries and of officers will nearly double this before large item of the expenses of the government. Nearly all of this addition, as of all the previous payments from the Treasury, will go to the North, as nearly every existing office, worth having, is filled by a northerner and an abolitionist; or, if the duty is in the South, and there would have been insuperable difficulty to bringing in a northerner, in such cases these offices have so far been bestowed on natives of the South, but only to such as are supposed to be submissionists in their political position. Some few northern abolitionists have been appointed to lucrative civil offices in some of the southern cities only.

The discontent of the southern states with the rule of the northern section and the abolition party, seems, to outward appearance, to have been lessening, or, at least, becoming less noisy and violent, as the ruling power has become more fixed and unassailable. When the first usurpations of the federal government were complained of, in the presidency of the first Adams, and mostly by the people of the southern states, though the subjects of complaint were not, in magnitude or danger, to be compared to the much later acts, the opposition then raised was sufficient, in a few years, to produce a political revolution, which swept away the wrongful measures, and also their movers and their abettors. But in latter times, although the subsequent and new acts of oppression on the southern section have been of ten-fold weight and enormity, they have been successively submitted to. In the early contest referred to, parties were arranged by political opinions and principles, and not by sectional divisions and interests, or prejudices of locality. The greater strength of the administration party was in the North, and that of the opposition in the South. Yet large adverse minorities, in both, prevented anything like sectional character in the then division of parties. But in the latter times, when the anti-slavery sentiment and fanaticism of the North had begun to spread, and was rapidly growing in power, though not yet dominant, there had occurred another change in the political condition of the country, which served to distract, enfeeble, or disarm southern opposition for defence. Rapidly as the southern states had increased in population, it was mostly by natural procreation. The importation of negro slaves had been long excluded by law. The poor free emigrants from Europe preferred to settle in the new free states, where hireling labor was in great demand, and highly remunerated. Thus the millions of foreign immigrants have nearly all been added to the population and increase of the non-slave-holding and northern states, serving to give to them a great and still growing superiority of population and political power over the slaveholding states. Under this change of circumstances, it followed that a southern aspirant to the presidential office (and latterly there has been scarcely any very prominent politician and popular leader who was not an aspirant, either openly or secretly,) could not hope for success from southern favor, even if all the South were united in his support. It was essential for the success of any candidate that he should have the support of many northern votes, and even of anti-slavery voters; and this northern support was far more difficult to be obtained for a southern candidate, and required, in the effort to obtain it, much more caution and skill, and adroitness of political tactics. This was the secret cause of the utter failure of every disposition of the southern people to resist northern oppression, and their final and complete submission, in every successive case, when nothing was needed for successful and peaceful resistance, and the maintenance of all rights of the South, but such common and determined political effort as the general sentiment of the people indicated, and offered and authorized to their leaders. But throughout this transition state, from the early condition of southern ascendancy and political equality, through the growth, to the final undisputed supremacy, of northern power, the southern advocates for effective defence had no leaders, or rather their trusted leaders were unfaithful to their trust, and were corrupted by their own personal ambition and greediness for the presidential power—and so were induced to work secretly to thwart the generous and patriotic objects of their followers, and to palliate northern wrongs to their section and to their principles—so as to avoid the danger of the candidates drawing on themselves (by a different, patriotic and zealous course) the hostility of the North, and so lose for themselves all chance for securing that northern support which was essential to their personal success and aggrandizement. Under such influences, operating on every man who was a popular leader, and who might have been a leader in the effectual defence and protection of the South, (and of equal rights throughout the Union,) it is not strange that the complaints of the South, the threats of resistance or of secession, loud and violent as they were—and all entirely concurred in, at first, by these political leaders and aspirants, so far as words alone would serve to delude and pacify their followers—all successively subsided into final and complete submission.

The existence and operation of this secret but controlling influence was first brought to my notice some years past, when there were several prominent and avowed southern candidates for the presidency, and perhaps a score of less conspicuous or secret aspirants, not less diligent and earnest in striving to attain for themselves, at some future time, the support of northern votes. I happened to be present during a political conversation between some southern gentlemen, who knew me to be an Englishman, entertaining sentiments of much respect and regard for this great confederacy and for its free institutions, and more especially for the southern section—but still loving and preferring my own country, and deeming the principles and institutions of English liberty to be more stable than those of this country. One of the small company, an old planter of Virginia, and a private citizen, advocated the speedy secession of the slaveholding states, as the only means for defence and security then remaining to them. But, at the same time, he admitted and deplored that this remedy would not and could not be resorted to by the southern states, and for such reasons as have just been repeated—and which he further illustrated in a manner which, for its novelty, made an impression on my mind, and induced my subsequently considering, and tracing to their ultimate ends, the alleged causes of southern inaction and submission. "Putting aside," said the old planter, "all operations of legislative favor to the North, and of injustice and injury to the South, in direct and indirect bounties to northern interests at the cost of the South, there have been inflicted on southern rights, in the matter of negro slavery alone, more wrongful assaults, and which have caused more loss and danger to the southern states, than would have been all the grievances of these former colonies, inflicted by the British government, even if multiplied twenty-fold. And during all this time of the progress of our later and greater wrongs, there has been as large a proportion of the best population of the southern states ready to resist and to defend their rights at all hazards, as there had been of the patriotic party in the colonies from 1765 to '76. What, then, is the reason that, when resistance to the oppressions of the mother country was so much more readily resorted to by our patriotic and brave forefathers, we have submitted, and will continue to submit, to far greater injuries, and still worse consequent dangers, inflicted by our confederate states, with whom our ties of affection are weaker than those of the colonies were to the mother country, and when our relative strength for resistance and assurance of success are very far greater than the like conditions of the colonies were in comparison to England? To my mind the cause is clear. The noble band of patriots and statesmen who taught and led the people of the colonies to struggle, first to defend and secure the rights of the colonies—and, failing in that, to assert their independence—were influenced by no motives except the love of freedom and of their country. If any one of them had dim aspirations to distinction, or to high future official position, these rewards could only be obtained at great hazard and certain loss, and by the most arduous service to be rendered to his fellow-colonists, and to the cause of justice and of right—and not by any degree of truckling submission to the besotted British king and ministry. But let us suppose the existence of very different conditions. Suppose that it had been the established usage for the government of the mother country to bestow the office of governor of each colony on some one of its more prominent inhabitants, and that to the governor belonged the appointment to all the subordinate offices and dignities in the colony. Suppose, further, that these gubernatorial dignities and powers, and the patronage appertaining to them, had been as attractive, and as much the objects of ambition, as the presidency of the United States. Still further, in reference to Virginia, suppose that, during all the time, and through all the wrongs of British rule, from 1765 to '76, that Patrick Henry, Richard Bland, Thomas Jefferson, Richard Henry Lee, and George Mason, and others of the prominent men of the colony, had all been earnest solicitors, at the hands of the king and his ministers, for the appointment of Governor of Virginia, and that each one was confident of his own superior claims, and sanguine of success—would it have been possible, under such circumstances, for either of these aspirants to incur the displeasure and hostility of the bestowers of the high dignity sought, by insisting on the strict observance of the rights of his countrymen? And if it could be that these base influences did not entirely control in every case, would they not still have some operation, and produce some contamination of cringing sycophancy to the office-giving power? If these influences had been in operation, there would not have been the shadow of a chance for the patriotic acts of these heroic men, or of the glorious consequences of their conduct to this country and to the civilized world. These supposed corrupting influences are precisely such as have been in operation through all our latter wrongs, our complaints, and our successive sequels of submission. It would have been sufficiently depressing to the South if this influence had operated on the most able and trusted leaders only. But each of these has many subordinate partisans and friends, some of whom for disinterested love of their favorite candidate, and others for their hopes of personal advancement and gain, to be obtained only through his success and future patronage, use all their influence to quiet popular exasperation, or to postpone movements for defence or secession, which, if going far at this time, will utterly destroy all prospect of the success of their friend and prospective patron. For certainly no candidate can be elected president of the Union whose own state would secede from it, or whose chief friends advocated secession—and without approaching that extremity of danger, no candidate can secure and retain northern votes, except by advocating the maintenance of the union through all contingencies—which is equivalent to still continued submission to all wrongs to be inflicted by the North, through all future time."

If there had been any ground (as there was not) even as early as in 1859 for any southern aspirant to expect to obtain northern votes, and by their aid to attain to the presidency, there certainly have been none since that time. If the corrupting influence of such ambitious hopes formerly seduced the leading men of the southern states to shrink from defending and maintaining their rights against the successive assaults of northern encroachment and usurpation, there certainly is no such reason or motive for inaction remaining now. The most greedy and blind, and therefore the most sanguine, of southern aspirants, must now be convinced that there no longer remains the least ground for hope that any southern candidate can ever hereafter be elected to the presidential office, against the still growing northern or abolition majority —unless he is a renegade to the principles and a traitor to the rights of the South, and as such is chosen by the northern abolitionists as the most suitable instrument for their own purposes. But even southern apostacy would not now be of any value to the already triumphant North, and therefore could not now hope for such reward. When the northern and abolition support, in the canvass of 1856, was given to a southern renegade, in the person of Fremont, the party was not quite strong enough for certain success alone, and required the aid of some southern votes, which they expected, but failed to obtain, by taking up such a southern candidate. But now they are strong enough not to need any aid out of their own ranks. The vote will hereafter be always strictly sectional, and the now all-powerful northern section will never again offer to any other candidate than its own preferred northern leader, the highest dignity and reward in the power of that section to bestow. Now, there is left no hope of northern favor, to chill the patriotism and warp the political course of any southern aspirant to the presidency, or to buy the thorough apostacy and treason of the basest. In the release, then, of these heretofore fettered interests and abilities, there has now been brought into existence a new element of moral strength to the southern states. But, unfortunately for their cause, that element did not begin to operate until the relative political power, and all other means of these states for resistance or defence, had been reduced lower than ever before. Still, even in this extremity, it is better to have the previous check to patriotic impulse removed, than it would be to have all other means for defence doubled, and to have still remaining that fatal clog and impediment to all effective action.

LETTER VI.

Beginning of President Seward's service. Direction and Policy of the Government Patronage. View of Negro Slavery and its Abolition.

WASHINGTON, March 13, 1865.

The ceremonies of the inauguration of President Seward, attracted as large an assemblage, and was as imposing a pageant, as any such previous occasion. But there was a remarkable difference in one respect. Nearly all the visitors were from the northern section and party. The few spectators from the South who attended were necessarily in Washington in public service—and of these, there were none who offered any tribute or evidence of respect to the President. The general absence and entire silence of the South, on this occasion, seemed to indicate the silent and subdued and sullen discontent of all the southern section and people.

The legislative session and existence of the last Congress expired on March 3d. But the summons of the President retained the Senate, to continue its separate session for executive business, and for considering and confirming the appointments to office by the new President. The term of service of sundry senators expired with the late session; and in every such case of new election from the northern section, the new member is an Abolitionist. The changes have served to increase the previous very small excess in the Senate to a fixed majority of six votes for the President, and for the policy and objects of the northern section. This majority cannot hereafter be reduced—but will certainly be increased by every addition of new senators from new states, hereafter to be admitted. Thus, the three legislative branches of the government, and the two which direct all the patronage of the government, are now made entirely sectional in service for the future. The judiciary is the only branch and power of government of which the majority is not yet devoted to anti-slavery doctrines and policy. And for the same change to be completed for the judiciary also, there will be required the deaths of three very old judges, and their places to be filled by appointment of Abolitionists, which is certain to be done. And if desired and deemed expedient, the judiciary may be at once abolitionized, by a law directing an increase of judges, even without waiting the short time required for death to make vacancies. With this slight and but temporary exception, the domination of the northern section and party is now complete. Virtually, and for all practical purposes, the southern section will have no more power or influence hereafter in the administration of the federal government, or in the direction of its policy and patronage, or even for self-defence against any wrongs whatever, inflicted by the dominant section, than if entirely excluded, by the terms of the constitution of government, from all share of representation in the Congress and of benefit from the protection of government. The only hope left, is in the sense of justice and the forbearance of the despotic ruling section and party. And all experience of political history has concurred in showing that communities, and even free and virtuous political communities, having despotic power over other communities, are always more exacting and more tyrannical, and effective in control, than an individual despot, even though the latter may not be influenced by any noble or virtuous impulse of conduct.

With the then certain prospect of greatly increased strength of the abolition party, the late President had become bolder in his policy, from the beginning of the last session of Congress. This was shown in his official recommendations, and the legislation affected in consequence. His successor has already indicated his disposition to pursue a still more vigorous course.

Among the enactments of the past session which will have important effect in increasing the population and power of the northern section, is the "homestead bill," which has been attempted in every Congress for seven or eight years, and which had been defeated heretofore by the Senate. This law gives one hundred and sixty acres of government land in the new territories and states to every settler, without restriction. This great additional stimulus to foreign immigration will add hundreds of thousands of Europeans every year—all of whom will disembark in the city of New York, and all will go to the new states or territories, which will certainly be non-slaveholding, and belong to and co-operate with the northern section. These immigrants will first benefit New York, by spending there, *in transitu*, much of their money brought from Europe; and, next, will move to occupy the lands bestowed on them as bounty for their settlement, and, by this new encouragement, fill up new states for the northern section with double the former rapidity. These foreigners will be mostly low and ignorant, and ready to imbibe the anti-slavery fanaticism and prejudices of the previous northern residents, whose opinions and sentiments only will they hear, and, of course, will adopt.

The called session of the Senate remained for more than a week, with closed doors, considering the new nominations to numerous offices submitted by the President, before any results were known. The southern minority, though having no power to prevent the final results, determined to "die hard," and express in full and strong terms of rebuke and denunciation, the iniquity of the general policy indicated. In this course, the southern members had every reasonable indulgence from the opposing majority, and the benefit of every established rule and usual courtesy of debate. But not a vote was thereby altered, nor was a single recommendation of the President, for appointment to office, rejected. Every new appointment, for official service in the northern section, without exception, was filled by a northerner and an abolitionist—and most, also for foreign service. The exceptions, for foreign service and most of the offices requiring permanent residence in the southern section, were filled by southerners of the so called "conservative," or, more truly, of the submission school—who, whatever had been their party names—Whig, Democrat, or any other—had deemed the union of the states, under any possible contingency, preferable to resistance to any amount of wrong—and who still shouted hosannas to the Union, when the great southern section and people had been completely subjected to the northern section, and was left without a hope for any mode of relief, which these union-savers would deem constitutional or expedient.

Among the first named class of northern appointments, and required by the recent displacement from office of all other than thorough Abolitionists, there were offices, of emoluments proportioned to their supposed political usefulness or past services, for every noted and active and influential Abolitionist. There were thousands of civil offices to be conferred—United States marshals and attorneys, collectors, judges, receivers of land offices, deputy postmasters, inspectors of customs, and tide-waiters, and down to gaugers, weighers and measurers—and many military and naval vacancies, which had to be filled, of old offices, as well as the hundreds of new commissions, warrants, or other connected places, required for the late increase of both the army and navy. Whether of the higher and more lucrative appointments, requiring the confirmation of the Senate, or of the more numerous lower offices, at the disposal of one or other of the cabinet ministers, (and, of course, controlled by the President's wish,) all appointments and promotions were directed by the same test and rule, to abolitionists only, when such persons could be obtained for the service in the locality. Among the appointees to the most lucrative and important offices were Greeley, Anthon, Wendell Phillips, Giddings, Sherman, and all of the most active and zealous partisans, who had rendered good service to the cause of Abolition. Every other one of the sixty-eight members of Congress, who (like Mr. Seward, but separately from him,) had signed the published recommendation of Helper's infamous and incendiary book, received appointments of value proportioned to their supposed claims. All the persons who had been supposed to be concerned in the John Brown conspiracy and outbreak in 1859, and who then escaped being convicted and hung, have received appointments to federal offices, either from the President and Senate, or from the heads of departments, (War, Navy and Post-office,) authorized to appoint their lower subordinates. Gerritt Smith and Fred. Douglass, the negro, for special reasons, were the only exceptions to such rewarded parties. The much greater number of southern country post-offices yield so little income, that but few persons would accept them, if required to change their residence as the condition. In all such offices no changes were made, no matter who were the previous incumbents, as no other persons sought, or rarely would have accepted, such poor rewards. But in a few places, where federal troops were stationed, or on ground belonging to government, and subject to federal rule only, as forts, dock-yards, arsenals, &c., in the southern states, there were appointed postmasters, and other officers, who were known abolitionists, and previously northern residents. Residents of the southern states, if such were to be found, were preferred for the offices in that section, and still more if natives. There were very few of the latter. Of these Caldwell, formerly the only Black Republican representative of Virginia (as Senator of the Wheeling district,) was appointed United States Marshal for Ohio, as he would not venture to serve in his own state. The notorious Helper was made one of the new Receivers of the Land Office—which is a very lucrative place for an honest man—but very far more so for a thief, as was sufficiently proved in regard to nearly all of these officials who were appointed to, or held, this office under the administration of President Van Buren. The Abolitionist, Hurlburt, who, merely on the only ground of the accidental place of birth, claimed to be a South Carolinian, (and who, like Helper, used that character to more effectually libel the

South,) also was rewarded by a fat office. It was not ventured to place a known abolitionist as an occupant of an office in a southern state, and where the state authority was in full force. Any such attempt would have aroused so much popular indignation, that neither the government, nor any officer, was willing to incur the risk. But there has been an approach to the like operation, in appointing abolition preachers as chaplains to every military post, and to every vessel of war entitled to one by previous usage.

In the higher appointments, Chase, of Ohio, was appointed Chief Justice of the Supreme Court. That place, vacated by the death of the late venerable incumbent Chief Justice Taney, had remained vacant some months, awaiting the now increased majority in the Senate. Trumbull, Doolittle and Corwin had before been appointed Judges of the United States Courts. Col. Fremont, the former candidate of the Abolition party, in 1856, for the Presidency, who was then barely defeated by accident, has been appointed to fill the vacant place of Commander-in-Chief of the Army. Banks, of Massachusetts is ambassador to France, and the noted Sumner, to the kingdom of Italy. Every foreign mission without exception, has been filled by some noted Abolitionist. The most important, in every respect, the mission to England, has been filled by F. P. Blair, of Missouri. His residence in London, as Minister of the United States, will rejoice the heart of Exeter Hall, and re-invigorate its anti-slavery fanaticism—and operate, in various modes, and powerfully, to forward the abolition sentiment and policy. Southern visitors to England and other countries, will hereafter neither seek, nor have offered, any attentions from the Ministers of their government; but, instead, will probably have their previous load of obloquy, as slaveholders, doubled by the known doctrines and declarations of the representatives of their own country and its government.

It is obvious that these thousands of northern and abolition officials will, indirectly, if not directly, operate to influence, and with great effect, public sentiment both at home and abroad. This would be the case, even if all remained silent, and did not attempt to be propagandists of their creed. And the rewards so restricted and directed, and so liberally bestowed, will point out the way by which every southern renegade and traitor may make profit by deserting his principles and the cause of his section. But there will be other and more active means for operating in aid of abolition by many of these officials, either in federal posts in the southern states, or in foreign countries.

As an Englishman and a Whig, educated under the influence of the arguments of Wilberforce, Fox, Brougham, Macaulay, and Sydney Smith, I early imbibed, and long retained, a strong hostility to the whole system of negro slavery, and an earnest wish for its being removed from the civilized world. But since, I have had opportunities, afforded by long residence and personal observation, of witnessing the actual working of the system in these southern states—and also of seeing the results of emancipation in Jamaica and Spanish America. The facts personally observed, and the results of diligent inquiry and extended investigation, have served to change my previous opinions in many respects, and to convince me that, even with the counterbalancing weight of all the exceptional cases actually existing, of injustice and cruelty of masters, the slaves in these states are the most comfortable, happy and cheerful of all the laboring and poorer classes of population of the world —and are very far better provided for, and more happy and contented, than either the agricultural, manufacturing or mining laborers of England. Further, the slaves are still more elevated in comfort, in security from oppression, and especially in morals and religion, above the condition of their ancestors in Africa, and of the present inhabitants of the same barbarous regions. I do not mean to argue the general question of negro slavery, or any of its particular advantages or disadvantages. But I would steadily oppose, if it could be effected, the emancipation of these five millions of slaves, if sure of their condition being thereby rendered as good as that of the previously emancipated slaves of this country, or of Jamaica, or even of the free laborers of Great Britain. Sure I am that either of these changes would be far worse for the slaves themselves; and, in addition, because of the aversion of negroes to continued labor, as hirelings, the measure would be most ruinous to these southern and cotton-producing States, and consequently of incalculable injury to the all-important manufacturing interest of England. These reasons, founded on practical consideration alone, are enough for me. Why they have not as much weight on the people of the northern section of the United States, who have still greater interests dependent upon the slave labor of the southern section, can only be accounted for by their great ignorance of the working of the system, and of its results, and their fanaticism, which has blinded both their reason and common sense. The general emancipation of slaves in these southern states, no matter how brought about, would involve these states in general ruin and misery. But these effects would but a little precede in time, and exceed in measure, the general ruin which would next be produced, by the same cause, to the northern states. Great Britian, by the cutting off the supply of cotton, would be the next greatest sufferer, and to an extent not equalled in the experience of that country in the last two hundred years. * * * * * * * *

After confirming these appointments, the Senate adjourned. The legislatures of nearly all the southern states had previously closed their sessions. Therefore there is no opportunity for the discharge of southern indignation through that outlet. But the general disapprobation of the South may be understood from the denunciatory opinions already expressed in the southern newspapers. But it is evident that the President has deliberately calculated the effects of his boldest measures. He has exercised only his unquestionable constitutional power—and a large portion of the southern people, including all of the Unionists, and many even of the Disunionists, long ago declared that the people and the states have no legal redress for wrongs authorized by the constitution.

But the profits allowed to political partisans and favorites in salaries of office, were very inconsiderable, compared to the enormous amounts paid by the government, or which have been permitted to be plundered from the treasury, by means of corrupt jobs, and fraudulent contracts for public services, or in purchases for the government at double prices, and sales of government property at half prices. In various operations of this kind many millions of dollars have been and will be paid every year under this administration. Of course the plunderers thus benefited are all northern abolitionists, and supporters of the administration. But the President's political enemies, who have figured under former administrations, cannot well attack and expose these vile abuses. For bad as they are, they are not much worse than, and are precisely of like character with, acts under former administrations of both Whig and Democratic presidents. Especially, the respective administrations of the Whig Presidents, Taylor and Fillmore, and of the last Democratic President, Buchanan, (particularly in the War and Navy Departments of the latter,) would furnish precedents of corrupt jobbing, and permitted plunderings of the treasury, and abuse of public trusts for corrupt purposes, that will match any of the like acts of the present abolition administration.

The enormous abuse of power, and the outrage of displacing every functionary of the government (however humble, and without there being any connection of his office with politics,) if not a partisan of the President's—and the appointing to office none but his political and personal supporters—is what most shocks my opinions as an Englishman, and a lover of free and pure government. Such a change of functionaries, in subordinate administrative offices, has never been attempted, or thought of, upon any change of the ministry in Great Britain; and if any new ministry were so debased as to attempt such a policy, it would excite universal indignation and disgust. There is enough operation of corrupt patronage in England, it is true, in regard to political and high offices. But no Walpole has yet thought, on his getting possession of the administration, of descending so low as to turn out of office every tide-waiter, deputy postmaster, or other low and merely executive functionary, in the kingdom. But this has been the regular procedure in this country ever since the corrupt policy was first inaugurated and carried out by President Jackson, of punishing political opponents by removal from every office, and rewarding supporters of the President by putting them in the vacated places. Democratic and Whig administrations have since acted fully up to this iniquitous and shameful rule; and, therefore, neither party, as such, has any ground, or plausible pretence, for denouncing either President Lincoln, or President Seward, for having done for the Abolition party precisely what had been done before by the administrations of both the preceding and alternately dominating parties. Mr. Seward has now certainly extended the action; but the principle of action is the same as that which directed the patronage of both Democratic and Whig Presidents and parties.

LETTER VII.

Operation of late Government Measures on Slaves in the South.

WASHINGTON, November 1, 1865.

* * * * * * The before quiet and smooth surface of political affairs in the South, was generally and violently agitated by the appointments to office, made on so large a scale, and so impressive in character, at the last session of the Senate. Great discontent was generally evinced by the people, and loud denunciations of the President and the federal administration. But there was but little apprehension, in any quarter, of any other and more serious resistance. The cool and sagacious President—who knew that he had chosen a safe time to make this bold stroke, and by the exposure to indicate his future policy—seems to dread no danger. Opposition to the late manner of ap-

pointment, and its general operation, is embarrassed by the former positions and declarations of the different opponents. The appointments to office were given by the federal constitution to the unlimited discretion of the President and a majority of the Senate, or, by law, to the different ministers of the President. There was not the least doubt of the action in these late cases being constitutional; and all of those southerners (including numerous disunionists) who had before maintained the propriety of waiting for an "overt act" of unconstitutional usurpation by the President, were estopped by their own former arguments from making this exercise of clearly constitutional authority a cause for state resistance in any other form than in remonstrances and threats. The always great number of the timid and submissive, (or, self-called "conservatives,") however loudly complaining, were not moved from their accustomed final conclusion of complete submission. The disunionists, "pure and simple," who recognized no other safety for the South than in separation from the overpowering and oppressive North, were ready, as before, to resort to that extreme remedy. But they were too few to do anything of themselves. The elements and strength of southern opposition had been previously and gradually much weakened by the long relaxation of resistance during the term of Lincoln's administration, induced by his moderate and mild measures, and seemingly designed moderate general policy.

The effects already produced, to some extent, and expected in ten-fold greater evil operation hereafter, are alarming to most minds in the South. Without referring to anticipations of the more dreaded future, there are enough of evil consequences already seen, as is alleged. The civil and military and naval officers spread through the garrisons and dock-yards, and especially the chaplains in all their stations, are operating more or less as preaching missionaries of abolition. They have it very much in their power, and many use the facilities directly, and still more indirectly, to indoctrinate slaves as to their rights and interests (according to the abolition creed,) and to poison their minds, and make them discontented and insubordinate. Wherever there is a United States chaplain on federal soil, and surrounded and protected by federal troops, or other sufficient force, he is a regular preacher, whether in or out of the pulpit, of anti-slavery doctrines, and of such theories as, when put in practice, must invite to servile conspiracy and insurrection. Every space heretofore ceded by any of the states to the federal government for light-houses, forts, dock-yards, armories and arsenals, and the whole of the District of Columbia, as well as all of the broad newly-settled or organized territories of the United States, have been, or will be, rendered asylums (either secret or open, according to locality) to receive, protect and forward slaves fleeing to the North. In addition, it is charged that every war vessel of the government, whenever stationed in a southern port, is converted into a moveable and inaccessible stronghold to aid the general assault on slavery. It is also a new practice to enlist on board all these war vessels, when in northern ports, a number of free negroes, (or, in many cases, slaves who had fled from the South) as sailors or menial servants. When these vessels entered southern ports, these negroes, as being in the government naval service, were as free in action on shore as other United States seamen—no matter what might be the state laws prohibiting the entrance of free negroes from abroad. And the anti-slavery feelings of the northern commanders of these ships caused them to allow every indulgence to their negro seamen; and they, as permitted, if not instructed, were often on shore, swaggering through the streets, with all the carelessness and insolence of manner of persons in government service, and assured of official protection. This air of equality, and their protection by northern officers and federal law, alone, and without other words or acts, would have taught a dangerous lesson to ignorant slaves. But such indirect teaching was not all. These negro sailors had every facility for associating with many slaves, and for indoctrinating them with abolition lessons. The escapes of fugitive slaves from the seaboard counties to the North, which had been previously much checked by state laws, certainly have received some new and strong impulse of late. In all the country surrounding and adjacent to the naval and military stations belonging to and used by the federal government, the losses of slaves, by flight, have been latterly much increased. And wherever ships of war have remained for some weeks, some such losses have always accompanied, or soon succeeded, their departure.

LETTER VIII.

Effects on the South.

WASHINGTON, January 15, 1866.

All the state legislatures are now in session, as well as the Federal Congress. The recent appointments to federal offices, and their alleged evil design and tendency, are discussed in every southern legislature, and with much zeal and violence of denunciation. But it has been so often the usage of the legislatures of southern states, and especially of Virginia, to pass strong and fiery resolutions and declarations, in opposition to alleged federal or northern usurpations and oppressions, and then quietly to submit to every such wrong, that no importance is now attached to any such wordy indications and threats.

The President and his confiding and obedient northern majority are content to act, quietly and without parade, and to let the noisy but impotent South resolve and threaten, to any extent of grandiloquent verbosity. The course so long pursued by some of the southern legislatures, previous to Lincoln's election, had ceased to command any respect or notice in the North, and very little even at home. Whenever, in later years, the legislature of Virginia was engaged in discussing southern wrongs from federal or northern aggressions, and passing resolutions of the most determined and warlike aspect, the proceeding was contemptuously spoken of by many as "playing the political game of bluster and back-out."

LETTER IX.

Other Abolition measures proposed and declined.

FEBRUARY, 7th, 1866.

* * * * * * President Seward, different from most of his predecessors, rarely indicates by public recommendations any particular measures which he wishes Congress to adopt. His objects are privately communicated through his most trusted friends in Congress, who cause the first moves to be made by some other members, so as not at first to expose the source of the proposition. In this manner, the influence of the President is not exerted less powerfully for measures which are adopted. And if any fail to receive sufficient support, the discredit of the failure will not be brought home to the President. I have been enabled to learn from sure authority, though through a secret channel, of some of those movements set on foot in the palace, before they were offered to the Congress. And latterly, I have thus heard of some very important propositions, urged upon the President by the most violent and fanatical Abolitionists, which his caution and prudence have caused him to discourage, and to induce their being postponed or abandoned by his friends, as measures of government. The fanatical Abolitionists are eager for the earliest enactment of every measure of federal policy that will go to cripple slavery. Some of these have been long before the public mind, and were threatened by the North, and deemed possible by the South. Such are —1st: The emancipation of slaves, and the entire suppression of the institution of slavery, and of protection to slave property, in the District of Columbia and in the United

States Territories, and on all other federal ground. 2d: The burdening and restricting, or entirely prohibiting, the trade and transportation of slaves between the different states now holding them. Those who were supposed to know and to speak the opinions of the President, advised the postponement, or, for the present, the entire abandonment of both these measures. It is true, they said, that either measure would operate greatly to cripple slavery, and to lessen the value of slave property, and the security of its possession. And the President, in common with all of his party, entertained no doubt of these measures being within the plain constitutional powers of the federal government. Indeed, this admission of constitutionality would be made by many opponents, and even by many true southern men, however much they would object to the measures, on the alleged grounds of justice, expediency, and safety of southern interests and policy. Neither was there any fear of the opinion and future decision of the Supreme Court, as it will now very soon be organized. But these measures, if enacted, and however effective to damage and endanger slavery, would operate but gradually and slowly, and require many years to produce very important effects in extinguishing slavery. On the other hand, they would excite universal complaint and clamor in the slaveholding states, and might arouse their zeal and array their disloyal feeling, to oppose, with better means for defence, more important future assaults on slavery. It was not doubted, by his chief friends and supporters, that the President had in prospect the future use of still more effective and speedy measures for the extinction of slavery. Thus the particular measures just named, and formerly regarded and feared by the South as the last and worst of northern assaults on southern slavery, were dismissed, although deemed both constitutional and available, by the chief abolition leaders, as being too weak and too slow for the thorough work needed and designed.

There has been growing an important change in the business procedure of Congress since the parties have become entirely sectional. Formerly, every important question was discussed for weeks, and numerous long speeches were delivered, and the argument, *pro* and *con*, exhausted, before a decision was reached. Now, in a question between the two sections, the votes are given always according to locality. If any speeches are delivered, they are from southern members, and only for effect among their constituents, and are not expected to have the slightest effect on the northern members. These do not either listen to, or reply to the southern speeches—but stop the debate by raising the previous question, as speedily as possible, and beat their opponents by the full vote of all the northern sections.—Thus, new measures are now introduced in Congress, and consummated in three or four days, which, under former administrations, would have required as many months for discussion * * * * * * *

LETTER X.

The Supreme Court Sectionalized.

WASHINGTON, March 22, 1866.

* * * * * The judiciary system was lately re-organized by act of Congress, and, as usual in all important questions, this was carried through by a pure sectional vote. The former districts have been newly arranged and increased in number, and also the number increased of judges of every previous grade and jurisdiction. This law required the appointments of twelve new judges. The appointments have just been confirmed by the Senate of twelve thorough Abolitionists, and all from the northern section, as no distinguished and competent lawyers of abolition interests were to be found in the South, and the southern "conservatives" would not accept the service. The majority of the Supreme Court, and most of the inferior judges, are now of the northern party; and this department, also, is now ready to favor abolition doctrines as far as may be permitted by the judicial construction of the laws and of the constitution.

* * * * * * * * *

LETTER XI.

Negro Citizens and Negro Officers of Government.

WASHINGTON, April 19, 1866.

The famous *Dred Scott* decision of the Supreme Court has already come under the review of the court as lately re-organized, and has been annulled in some respects. One of the reversals is of the former decision, that a negro or mulatto cannot be a citizen of the United States. This reversal will re-open old grounds of controversy between the southern and northern states, and between the southern states and the federal powers, in regard to the right of the southern states to prevent the ingress of the colored "citizens" of other states into their territory. Black "citizens" may now claim passports from the State Department to travel in Europe, and equal legal facilities with white citizens, from the American ministers at the European courts. With ministers as well disposed as are Blair, Banks, Hale, Sumner, Howe, and most others now in Europe, we may expect the more distinguished negro citizens, as Fred. Douglass, and the negro clergymen and other professional characters of the North, to be entertained as the ministers' honored guests, and to be presented by them at court. The legal affirmative of negro citizenship now removes all restriction on the conferring on them federal offices, civil or military. If the northern section shall so consolidate and guard its now legal and constitutional power, as to prevent forcible resistance of physical power or armed rebellion by the South, it may happen, before many more years, that northern negroes will be elected to fill seats in Congress, or appointed to many civil offices, or even military and naval commissions. But this must be yet far remote—for, as yet, such results would be as much opposed in the North, by the general feeling of hatred to the negro there prevailing, and also the jealousy felt by the lowest class of whites, as by the general good-natured contempt entertained for the negro character and intellect by all southerners. Still there is now no longer any question of the conferring any offices on free negroes being lawful. * * * *

The policy of this government, long adhered to, of refusing to acknowledge the independence and sovereign power of Hayti, and of Liberia, has been now abandoned. Congress has just framed acts for these purposes, and to authorize the appointment of ministers to both these negro "republics," and to negotiate with them treaties of amity and commerce. * * * * * *

LETTER XII.

Negro Ambassador, and Negro Diplomatic Relations.

WASHINGTON, April 20, 1866.

The Rev. J. Seys, long employed by the previous Democratic administrations as a salaried agent for Liberian affairs, and in different capacities, has lately been appointed *Charge d' Affaires* for Liberia. The place had before been offered to several other persons, but all of them declined the honor, which would so likely be fatal, through the pestilential climate, to the appointee.

The rabid abolitionist, Joshua Giddings, has been appointed minister to Hayti. He has chosen Fred. Douglass as his Secretary of Legation. This, it is understood, will enable Fred. to study diplomacy, and to succeed to the higher place of Giddings, when the latter shall be better provided for, according to his merits. * * * * *

The Haytien Government has lost no time to respond to the friendly approaches of this government. The Haytien minister is already in Washington, and has been presented to the President. The office is filled by the Duke of Marmalade. For though the government of Hayti is still called a republic, its ruler has not the less established himself as despotic monarch, with the title of Emperor, and has restored the former nobility, with large additions. The title of Count of Marmalade was one of Christophe's creation; the present possessor has been raised to the dukedom by the reigning Emperor. He is a stout, burly negro, of clumsy frame and awkward mein; of features intensely African, in shape and color. He wore, when presented to the President, a gorgeous military uniform, (as he is also a major-general,) with sundry stars and decorations of orders of nobility. His presence and appearance in this city caused a great commotion, from different causes. Southerners viewed his advent as the manifest indication and culmination of the general policy of which the invitation and reception of this mission was but a part. Northerners tried to receive the minister, and all of his offensive accompaniments, gracefully, if not joyfully. The thorough fanatical abolitionists were the only persons who were entirely pleased. They can now, to the fullest extent, by attentions paid to the negro ambassador, show their exemption from all prejudices of color, odor and race. The lower classes stared at the minister in the streets, with mixed wonder and admiration, and, in most cases, also indignation, at the conjoint character of a duke and a major-general in the person of an ugly negro. The lower classes, if abolitionists, were rejoicing—if southern in feeling, were denouncing or cursing both the negro duke and the abolitionists who introduced him. The upper class of free mulattoes, of Washington, were proud of the occasion, and hoped to profit by it in raising their own social *status.* But the lower negroes, both slaves and free, though greatly corrupted by abolition contact and influence, still had enough left of their old feelings of deference and loyalty to the white race, and of want of respect for all of their own color and race, to heartily dislike their fellow-negro, who was thus elevated so greatly above themselves, and also, as all of them thought, above any possible merits of any one of the negro race. But, offensive as is this state of things to the slaves, it is not the less calculated to do them damage.

A more difficult course still remains to be pursued, when the Duke of Marmalade shall be a guest at the President's dinner parties, and when the northern dignitaries of the city, and of the government, must exchange with him the courtesies enjoined by good society. The Duke is a bachelor (or at least has no legal marital obligations,) and is said to be immensely rich. No doubt his attentions will be acceptable to sundry fair daughters of distinguished abolitionists.

* * * * * * * * *

LETTER XIII.

Northern Opinion of Southern Disposition and Courage.

WASHINGTON, June 1, 1866.

As heretofore, and through many years, the legislatures of the more noisy southern states had long debates on the more recent federal and northern aggressions, and the prospective greater dangers, and passed piping-hot "states rights resolutions," promising resistance to the *next* ensuing wrongs by the North, "at all hazards, and to the last extremity;" and, as heretofore, they will submit to the next injuries, and again and again. At least such is the universal northern opinion, founded on all past experience. The loudest threats of the southern legislatures and people—their proceedings that would indicate measures for concert with other states, and resistance or revolt—all are treated with utter contempt by the northern people. It is their almost universal belief that the South cannot be driven to resistance—cannot exist without northern protection—and, so far from seceding, that the South "cannot be kicked out of the Union." Even the arming of Virginia in 1860, at the cost of more than five hundred thousand dollars, and of other states to less extent, was not then even suspected to be designed to resist the government, and to facilitate secession, but for defence of southern lives and property against the future insurrections of their own slaves, led by northern white philanthropists and desperadoes of the John Brown order. There may a great advantage accrue from this contemptuous incredulity of the North, if resistance should ever be attempted by the southern states. For nothing that they can plan, or threaten, will be believed or serve as warning, until actual and important deeds shall take the place of violent and boastful words. * * *

LETTER XIV.

State of Parties. Prospects of the Southern Section, and of Slavery.

WASHINGTON, November 7, 1866.

The condition and prospects of the South in reference to the slavery question, appear to me, though a foreigner, to be of awful portent. Yet there are but few citizens, even of the southern states, who seem to realize their situation.

As ought to have been generally forseen, as far back as 1856, by all who were not politically blind, northern emigration and northern influence have worked, and will always so work, with perfect success, to prevent any new state from coming into the Union with the institution of slavery—or of slaves being held to much extent in the previous territorial condition of new states. Texas, it is true, by the conditions of its annexation, may be divided into four states, if having enough population, at the will of the present state of Texas. But, for reasons of policy, that state has been unwilling to use the privilege of division, and is not like to do so, under any circumstances, likely to occur for many years to come. No portion of the new or now unsettled territories can, by any possible chance, become a slaveholding state. The number of the slaveholding states, therefore, may be considered as fixed at fourteen, until still more reduced by the necessary future receding of slaves and of slavery from along their northern border, and finally throughout the present border states.

The stations for army and navy purposes, the light-houses, &c., throughout the southern states, and, to less extent, the federal public buildings in the greater southern cities—custom-houses, post-offices, &c., are, or may well be so made, in more or less degree, temporary places of asylum for fugitive slaves and seminaries of abolition, of which every officer and functionary is the missionary preacher. For if the officer is so discreet and forbearing (being, of course, an Abolitionist in principle,) or so correctly impressed with his proper duties, that he avoids uttering a word against slavery and the rights of slave-holders, still, his very silence and inaction in reference to an institution which is everywhere surrounding, serve as a standing protest against the rightfulness or innocence of slaveholding. Thus, the influence of such a military or naval officer would operate on his subordinates—of civil officers, on theirs—and, still more than all, on the neighboring slaves. A preacher's silent influence against slavery would be still stronger, and the more so in proportion to his deserving, in other respects, and acquiring, the love and veneration of his congregation. But such influence would be exceeded ten-fold, when such officers and functionaries, placed in the slave states, and protected by all the power of the federal government, shall become active agents and missionaries of abolitionism, and urging the doctrines, and the consequent action, upon all the ignorant slaves whom they can reach with their instructions.

* * * * * * * * *

According to the provisions of the federal constitution, three-fourths of the several states, concurring with two-thirds of the Congress of the United States, may at any time alter the constitution, in any respect and to any extent, with a few exceptions; and certainly may thus abolish slavery, or make any other change in regard to the institution, and to the interests of the southern people therein. The slaveholding states are now fourteen, and (omitting any increase by the division of Texas) there never can be another new slaveholding state added from new territory. On the other hand, it is confidently expected by most persons, and scarcely doubted by any, if political affairs and relations continue undisturbed in their present course, that Maryland and Missouri will not require twenty years to change from being slave-holding to free states, which will reduce the slave states to twelve. With this reduced number of slave states, it will require the northern section to increase to thirty-six states, or without any such lessening of the slave-holding states, to forty-two free states in all, to to authorize and enable the northern section to change the constitution, in strict conformity to its own provisions and conditions for amendments, and so to abolish slavery.—Can any one doubt that such will be the result, when there shall be constitutional authority for this long pursued object? There will probably be enough additional admissions of states, formed of newly settled western territory, within fifteen or twenty years, to increase the free states to three-fourths of the whole number of states—even without counting upon the change of character and section of Maryland

and Missouri, or any other now border slaveholding state. But, should even this short time of postponement be deemed too long for the North to wait for the utter destruction of slavery, there are other and also constitutional means for reaching that end, as speedily as may be deemed safe and politic for the northern section. It is entirely constitutional for the desired. number of free states to be created, in any week, by dividing existing states, which would only require the joint consent of the legislature or a convention of each of the respective states to be divided, and of Congress. All the parties to be consulted being for forwarding abolition, and the great measure in view being the complete extinction of slavery, it can scarcely be doubted that the consent of all the requisite parties could be obtained. Yet, it seems that this ready method of reaching all that is desired for the objects of abolition, has scarcely been thought of, either by friend or foe to that policy.

Whether the northern section and abolition party (which is the same power) will wait (according to Mr. Seward's cautious policy,) for this, or for the slower natural increase of non-slaveholding states, and so effect the great end, of destruction to slavery, legally and constitutionally, or shall prefer to take some still shorter and unauthorized route to the same end—in either case, the northern section will be able to do all that it may choose. The South is already deprived of all means for defence by protection of the laws and the constitution—except a respite for a few years, from the final execution of the already decreed sentence of political death. There is no further help for the South, or its institution of slavery, from any means which would be deemed lawful to use. Secession, as the last resource and refuge, even if not then too late to be availed of by the then comparatively feeble South, may indeed be claimed as legal means by seceding states. But it will be pronounced and treated as treason and rebellion by the overwhelming northern sectional power.

But if resisting—whether as seceders or revolutionists and rebels—the southern people will retain, at least, one most important means for defence in their particular constitutions, and organized state governments.

* * * * * * * * *

The success of the northern or abolition party had been so complete in the first election to the presidency of one of their party, in Lincoln, and was so manifestly growing, that but little of organized party opposition was made to the next, and still more triumphant, election of Seward. The other great party, previously competing for the administration of the government and the spoils of its offices and expenditures, the "National" Democratic party, in losing all hope of success, had lost its greatest stimulus to action. The battle made by this party in the last campaign, for the election of a President, was merely formal, and offered in the vain hope of merely maintaining its numbers and organization for future efforts. But all the corrupt politicians of the Democratic party in the North, and their followers, in despair, have withdrawn from it, and have either gone over to the Black Republican party, or otherwise remain quiet and neutral, waiting for future changes and chances. The still fewer of honest, patriotic and intelligent northern Democrats who had always been willing to render justice to the South, are so few as to be scarcely heard of. The old Whigs of the North have mostly united themselves to the dominant party, which alone is now organized, and would seem to embrace the whole active population, as it certainly does the large majority of every northern state, and of almost every county, town and village of the great northern section.

In the South, there have been, also, great party changes, though there is not yet any new party organization and array, or new party name. The avowed advocates for disunion, or secession, have been greatly increased by accessions from those who still call themselves either Democrats or Whigs, cherishing these old party names from habit or prejudice, when their former subjects of controversy are dead, and their former objects are out of both sight and hope. Though not yet designated by acknowledged names, the only true party divisions now subsisting in the southern states is of those who, whether calling themselves Democrats, Whigs or "Americans," would strenuously maintain the rights of the South against northern aggression—and those who, under whatever party names, while denouncing northern aggression in the general, and loudly threatening resistance, "at all hazards and to the last extremity," to any future wrongs, have regularly submitted, in practice, to every past wrong, and will (if acting alone,) continue to submit to every future federal usurpation. All these are but the materials of which parties will be made and designated should a great political occasion and necessity require—and men worthy to lead will present themselves, when patriotism, courage and talent shall be the necessary and the only available qualifications for a leader of the people. Of such men there are doubtless many who have remained unknown in the obscurity of private life. But, as yet, none such have appeared. The old Democratic leaders of the South, having no longer in prospect the dignities and spoils of the federal administration, have ceased to show anything of their former energy and activity, and therefore have lost much of their former popularity and influence.

LETTER XV.

Administration Policy. Negro Ambassadors. Northern Negrophilists.

WASHINGTON, February 20th, 1867.

The action of the President, through his obedient party and Congress, and wielding now the undivided power of the whole northern section, seems to be directed to strengthening every out-work of his position. Every thing that can increase the receipts of the treasury, or the efficiency of the army and navy, in their present numerical strength—and every measure that will give more power and gain to the northern section, or pecuniary benefits to active partisans of the northern party, are especially favored by the care and enactments of the present Congress. The votes of the northern section decide everything in which there is the slightest conflict of interest, or of opinion, between the two sections. The presence of southern members in Congress, for anything but their own petty local business, is of no use—and in truth, not half of them now are ever seen in their seats, or, at any one time, are usually in the city.

The advent of the Haytien ambassador, and his presence at the President's receptions and public dinners, gave the finishing stroke to the previous general voluntary exclusion of southern members of congress from such places. Now, scarcely any southerner, who respects himself, is ever to be found in the presidential palace, or at a public reception of company, unless as a mere looker-on for curiosity. The thorough-paced office-hunter, in pursuit of his objects, would readily stoop to any personal degradation. But southern office-hunters have now no possible chance for a federal office, or other government favor, or corrupt job, and, therefore, even they no longer pay court to the President, or need approach within smelling distance of the Duke of Marmalade or the other foreign ministers of African race, of whom there are now six, of various dark shades of color, from different places in Spanish America, besides the Liberian minister—who was formerly a slave in Baltimore, next a fugitive to New England, then a colonist in Liberia, and now is minister to this government. His secret or indirect influence over the slaves of his native state, Maryland, ought to be important; and the minister is a sharp fellow. He is also a member of the Methodist Church North, to which division the Methodists of Maryland and the northern half of Virginia are still generally attached, and of which the ministers, by their discipline, are opposed to slavery.—From the number of negroes and mulattoes sent as ministers by countries of mixed populations, and races, it would seem that it had been intimated to their governments that ministers and diplomatic agents of negro race would be most acceptable to the United States Government. Many of the abolitionists, who are most prominent in the political or fashionable world, are using these means, as much as possible, to break down the existing barriers of prejudice against the negro race and blood. At their entertainments these officials of negro blood are always especially welcome and favored guests, and they are received into intimate and cordial private associations by all the thorough-going abolitionists. But the much greater numbers of northerners, like all the southerners, keep aloof from negro associates, no matter how exalted in place.

LETTER XVI.

Measures of the Government.

WASHINGTON, March 13, 1867.

* * * * * This being the last session of the last Congress, it was ended by the limitation of the constitution on March 3d. The most important measures enacted were the following: Some changes of the tariff of duties, by which still more protection and profit were given to northern manufactures, both by increased duties on like foreign fabrics, (and in every case where needed for their aid,) and also by removing all remaining duties on imported materials for manufactures. Ten millions of dollars were appropriated to building or repairs of fortifications, and fifteen millions to various public works for improving navigation, roads, ports and harbors, &c., all in the northern section. The fortifications to be strengthened, also, are all in the northern section, except Castle Pinckney, which is on a small and low island in the upper harbor, and very near to Charleston, and which holds the city under its guns, and completely commands it, in a military sense, supposing the garrison, works, and armament all to be strong enough. This fortress is to be enlarged, its defences strengthened as much as the nature of the marshy ground, and its limited space, will permit, and the whole to be put in the most effective condition, for the necessarily small area to be enclosed within the walls. The lower forts, Moultrie and Sumter, which, on opposite sides, effectually command the passage of the harbor, were already in good repair—and Fort Moultrie, as well as Castle Pinckney had latterly been kept fully

garrisoned. The President had recommended the addition of five new regiments to the regular army, so as to increase its strength to thirty-five thousand men; and also large additions to the naval force. There was no important opposition to either of the two latter measures from any of the northern members, and bills for both were passed, and were long under consideration. But, for financial reasons, and temporary difficulties, it was deemed best, by the President and his party, to postpone both these measures to the next session, when they will certainly be enacted.

This large appropriation from the federal treasury for "internal improvements"—that is, for such works as constructing roads, not required, and indispensable, for military operations, or constructing canals, deepening the channels of the harbors and rivers, &c.—was the earliest act of either this or the preceding administration, under abolition direction, that could be objected to by political opponents, as being unauthorized by the constitution. And even as to these recent enactments, no political party, as such, could, with clean hands, bring this charge—because both of the parties, previously and alternately in power, had committed like acts. There were but few individuals, of any party, who had been long in Congress, who had not aided by votes to establish precedents for the worst of these abuses. The Whig party had generally maintained the doctrine of the federal government having the constitutional power to construct such public works. And though the strict construction school of the more modern southern politicians had denied the right, and vehemently protested against all exercise of such federal powers, as being without constitutional warrant, still these and other like "strait-jacket doctrines," (as derisively designated by a distinguished southern Democrat,) were maintained by a fraction only of the great Democratic party, and were not received, or at all respected, by the northern members of that party, in Congress or elsewhere. When such measures were before Congress, and for northern improvements, the objections of the strict-construction southerners of the Democratic party, for a long time back had been generally voted down by their northern fellow Democrats, combined with the minority of Whigs, or of Abolitionists, before the latter sect had grown to be a majority, and the ruling power.

Another such exception to the general rule of the forbearance of exercise of unconstitutional power by this administration, would have required to be made, in this narrative, if these events had occurred between twenty and forty years earlier. This is in reference to duties imposed on foreign commodities, not for the legitimate object of thence deriving revenue to the treasury, but to protect, and to bestow indirect bounties on home manufactures. To this long established policy, constitutional objections were formerly strongly urged—and still are entertained by many. But they had long (and before the Democratic party lost its supremacy,) ceased to be presented in opposition to the various successive enactments of protective features of different tariff laws. And by this cessation of opposition on this ground, and also by the southern strict-construction portion of the then dominant Democratic party having concurred in voting for numerous enactments of this character, (embraced in general tariff bills,) it may be correctly assumed, that, practically, all opposition to the constitutionality of this policy had been yielded by all—and, therefore, that no charge of infraction of the constitution in this respect could be sustained by any party, because all had either aided in such measures, or had acquiesced in their lawfulness, by being silent as to their being infractions of the federal constitution.

In this view, however obnoxious the administration might be to the charge of violating the restrictions of the constitution, in both these respects, no such charge could properly be brought, and no such case made out, through general and logical reasoning, by any opposing party. Therefore these cases, no more than any others, were such "overt acts" of constitutional infraction, or usurpation, as many southerners were waiting for, and which would demand and justify resistance of the South to the oppressive acts of the federal government.

LETTER XVII.

End of Slavery in the District of Columbia. Condition of the South. Fugitive Slaves and "Underground Railroads."

WASHINGTON, July 23, 1867.

Though no law of Congress has been enacted to abolish slavery in this federal district, it has been virtually effected. The great influence of numerous abolition missionaries and agents in this city, including all the northern members of Congress and office-holders, together with the presence of foreign officials of negro race, with other incidental causes, all have served to render the slaves here discontented, and disposed to insubordination. All who choose to flee to the North had ample facilities, including the personal aid of men in government offices, or in Congress—and very many availed themselves of these means for escape. The owners of others, who were not willing to lose their slaves, sent them to the southern states for sale or employment. Many others, more indulgent, and also themselves impressed with anti-slavery doctrines, or to gain favor from the administration and the party dispensing all the favors of government, either emancipated their mutinous and almost worthless slaves, or accepted from them very low prices for their legal sale and emancipation. From all these causes, this city and the District of Columbia are now no longer slaveholding. The free negroes are increasing by fugitives from the South and immigrants from the North, who are dangerous neighbors to the surrounding slave population of Maryland and Virginia. Besides all the more private instruction, every Sunday there are sermons preached by northern preachers, including among them the chaplains to Congress, in which the iniquity of slavery and slaveholding, and indirectly the incitements to servile insurrection, are set forth and urged with all the zeal and vehemence that could be looked for in Boston or New York, formerly, from a Parker, a Beecher or a Cheever. If the subordination of the slaves of Maryland and Virginia can be maintained under these and all other hostile operations of abolitionists, there must be, (as southerners maintain,) in the negro race, dispositions to cheerful contentment, and of affectionate loyalty to their superiors, that cannot be found in any lower class of the free white subjects of any government of Europe. * * * * * * * *

The complaints of the people of the southern states have been much increased by the governmental action of the late session. The strength of the northern section and of the administration will be thereby greatly increased. And while there has been no direct violation of the provisions and checks of the constitution, since the sectional northern party attained to undisputed supremacy, yet, constitutional powers have been so used, that not a shadow of political power, or a benefit from the government, is left to the subjugated and degraded southern section. Still, the thorough submissionists of the South, while in words loudly protesting against all their wrongs, maintain that they have the sanction of the constitution, and that so long as the constitutional safeguards are respected, the people of the South have no right to resist legal burdens, or to oppose the imposition of hardships, except by their votes. The waiters, real or pretended, for an "overt act" of constitutional infraction, to justify resistance or secession, have at last learned that the dominant and oppressing party had no need to supply them with any such "overt" ground or justification for resistance, and that the adminstration has cautiously avoided all approach to furnishing any. These former waiters have now abandoned their useless ground; and those who are sincere have gone over to the advocates for secession, and those who assumed that ground for disguise are, as they always should have been, among the submissionists, in practice, to every successive federal aggression and wrong But it is very difficult, and almost impossible, for any people to be aroused to resistance to its government by reasoning on their rights and wrongs, when no immediate or personal injury has been felt as severely oppressive. It requires something practical, of individual tyranny and of individual sufferings, to arouse the sluggish popular mind. In this way, the violent and bloody inroad of John Brown, and the consequent sacrifice of the lives of but three or four citizens, quickly as the outrage was suppressed, caused more southern excitement than all other legal wrongs inflicted previously by the North. But that effervescence was not more violent than it was transient. In six months nothing of its effects remained, except the previous enactments in Virginia, and some other of the more southern states, to arm and train portions of their militia. Owing mainly to that provocation, and the supposed danger of the recurrence of such conspiracies and assaults of northern abolitionists, the military condition of the South had been greatly strengthened. These and other such measures for military or other state defence were opposed at the South by conservative and submissionists, as preparations and means for subsequent disunion. But it is remarkable that the northern people did not charge, nor seem to suspect, any such design. They ascribed all the military preparations to the fears of the southern people of insurrections of their own slaves; and the greater these preparations were, then and since, the more were they deemed evidences of the weakness and timidity of the southerners, and of their inability to resist their own slaves, whenever the North might choose to encourage their insurrection.

* * * * * * * * *

As might well have been anticipated, from the causes operating, there has been great increase of the number of slaves escaping from the South to the northern states, and to Canada, in the last year. These losses have been especially great near to this federal district, and to all the military and naval stations of the government. The losses, and the greater danger apprehended for the future, have still more increased the soreness and exasperation of the southern mind. The organized associations in the North, for inviting the escape and the transporting of fugitive slaves from the South to the North, which have been so long in active operation, have continued to increase in numbers of members, in amount of funds, and in effect. The seduction and removal of fugitive slaves employ numerous secret agents. Many are resident in the South, who secretly incite the flight of the slaves, and arrange the manner of their escape. Other agents provide modes of conveyance—first to, and next through, the nearest free state—and thence to Canada, if deemed necessary for complete immunity of the slaves, and also of their aids and guards. Whatever may be the various modes and routes of such conveyance of fugitive slaves, whether by railroads, vessels, or private carriages, it is commonly expressed that the escape was made on the "underground railroad." And never were the business and success of this "railroad" so great as within the past six months.

LETTER XVIII.

Abductions of slaves in great numbers.

WASHINGTON, October 4, 1867.

Within a few days reports reached this city of simultaneous "stampedes," or concerted abductions of slaves in larger numbers than have ever occurred before. From one neighborhood of the eastern shore of Maryland, there escaped 231 slaves. The plan had been long and well arranged. A swift northern steamer, under some pretext of needed repairs, had arrived a week before, and was in the Patuxent river. All the arrangements for escape had previously been made. On the night of a Saturday, the engaged slaves, from three different farms, and by various private routes, reached the landing place. At midnight all were on board, and the vessel floated off with the ebb tide, until far enough to use steam, without attracting observation. As the absence of slaves through a Sunday, in most cases, is but little noticed, the steamer had a start of more than twelve hours before the true state of the case was understood by the owners of the slaves; and it was not until Monday morning that any pursuit could be even attempted. It was then in vain. The steamer had passed through the Capes of Virginia on Sunday, and was not afterwards seen until her freight was landed in Boston, where both the negroes and their deliverers were protected, or sent on to Canada.

The other case was in Jefferson county, Kentucky. On the same Saturday night, by preconcert and direction of resident agents, the fugitives assembled at sundry different points of the Ohio river, all within a mile of each other, and embarked on boats of sufficient capacity, which had been sent for the purpose. The boats were rowed to the same landing-place on the opposite side of the river, in the state of Ohio. There the fugitives and their aids were safe, except from pursuit by the Kentucky people. To avoid this danger, light wagons, with good teams, and relays at every twenty or thirty miles distance, had been provided on the route. The party was soon in motion on the road, and reached Canada in safety. The slaves, who were thus carried off, were 157 in number. All the arrangements required for these two successful expeditions were provided at the cost and under the general direction of the northern organized association for aiding the escape of southern slaves. This is deemed, in the northern states, a work of piety and benevolence, as well as of political policy; and many of the most respected individuals, including clergymen and ladies, are zealous and liberal members of the association, or "Underground Railroad Company."

* * * * * * * * *

The late abductions of slaves, unprecedented in numbers, and for the boldness of the operations, and their occurring at one time, seem to indicate to the southern people much more wide-spread plans, and perhaps for the insurrection, as well as for the abduction of slaves. Everywhere there is increased diligence, and new measures of safeguard and for the detection and capture of northern emissaries. The mustering and equipping of companies of volunteer militia have received a new and strong impulse. The Governors of all the slaveholding states have encouraged these preparations so far as their powers extend, independent of the legislature.

In these, as in all other such cases of abducted slaves by northern citizens, it would be idle and entirely useless to make legal requisitions for the criminals on the Governors of their states. Not only the offenders of this class, but all who have attempted to excite servile insurrection, or have induced and aided robberries and murders of southerners by their slaves, and who, of course, fled to the northern states, have been there protected by the state authorities, as well as by popular sympathy. Since Mr. Seward, when Governor of New York, (in 1839) refused to deliver to the requisition of the Governor of Virginia, three known abductors of slaves, and Governor Kirkwood of Iowa, and Governor Dennison of Ohio, in 1860, refused to deliver the escaped murderers who had aided the Harper's Ferry atrocity, there has been no case of any perpetrators of these crimes being delivered up by a northern state for trial, to the requisition of a southern state. Thus, the most frequent and dangerous northern offenders against southern laws, though required by the Constitution of the United States to be surrendered for trial, are systematically screened from punishment by the violation of both the oaths and the duty of the northern state authorities. And since the first election of an abolitionist as President, and the northern section has ruled the Union, the federal government has, in these respects, followed up fully the previous examples of the northern state governments.

It might seem, from the stated disposition and movements, that there is more alarm in the South than is justified by those two cases of wholesale abduction of slaves, or by any plausible suspicion of more extended conspiracy or hostile designs of the northern abolitionists. But any danger of servile insurrection, especially to fathers and husbands, is, of all calamities, the most alarming, for its possible bloody, merciless and horrible results. A negro insurrection in the southern states never will or can occur, unless induced and stimulated by white plotters, or influence. And even if so incited, an insurrection cannot miss being suppressed, and its actors punished, in a very short time. Therefore, if considered as an incident of the history of a country, or in a military aspect, nothing can be more fruitless, feeble or contemptible than a negro insurrection, even with all the aid and furtherance thereto, to be bestowed by northern philanthropy. These general truths are recognized by every southerner. Yet, when an alarm of insurrection comes, with all the usual uncertainty, vagueness of reports, and enormous exaggeration of statements, every head of a family at once thinks of the possibility of the near vicinity of the outbreak, and of all that are precious to him being among the victims. For, as there is no reason for the beginning, or chance for the success of insurrection anywhere—and as, wherever incited, it must be the effect of extraneous inducement and stimulation, applied to the gross ignorance of the slaves—it is nearly as likely to break out in one place as another, and where it would be the least expected, and the most quickly and certainly suppressed and avenged.

* * * * * * * * *

LETTER XIX.

Constitutional *Coup d'Etat.* Retrospect of the condition of the Southern States.

WASHINGTON, December 18, 1867.

Congress was no sooner at work than the army and navy bills, postponed last session, were brought forward again, and will soon be enacted. The only opposition to them is of the entire southern vote. But as that, being a fixed and certain minority, counts for nothing, the passage of both bills could not be more certain if the whole southern vote was for them. The effect of these acts will be to add 5000 men to the present greatest strength of the army, and to double that of the navy, as soon as the recruiting can be effected for the one, and the additional war steamers built for the other. * * * * *

The legislatures of the states of New York, Ohio, Minnesota, Kansas, California and Michigan, were all in session with closed doors in the first week of their present term. This mysterious coincidence of very unusual procedure is now explained. These legislatures all had a similar proposition before them, and all have consented to enact the measure, with the necessary assent and confirmation of the Congress of the United States. This measure is the very important one of dividing each of these large or populous states into two states. The first private suggestion of this scheme doubtless proceeded from the President. And to him have been sent the enactments of the several states, which, with his recommendation of consent and concurrence, he has laid before Congress. The object and effect of the proposed divisions will be to double the present representation of these states in the Senate, so as to give twelve more senators to the northern section, and, of course, all of them of the abolition party. These will make in all forty-two abolition states, being three-fourths of the whole number of states. Two-thirds of both Houses of Congress may call a convention to propose amendments to the federal constitution, and such proposed amendments will become part of the constitution, if ratified by three-fourths of the states. If the proposed several divisions of six states are now made, the northern section will thereby be rendered as supreme in power, to change and to make the constitution, as it has been for some years in regard to all other legislation and government of the United States. With this suddenly increased political power, every article of the constitution (with some few exceptions,) and including the entire abolition of slavery, will be in the power of the northern section; and this, or any other changes required by the northern section, can be consummated as soon as state conventions can meet to ratify, by three-fourths of their number, the amendments recommended by two-thirds of both Houses of Congress. The same preponderance of numbers of northern states could have been obtained in eight or ten years longer time, by the regular and ordinary increase of northern population, and the admission of new states. But the constitutional *coup d'etat* now in progress, if carried through, will enable all the ends of abolition to be effected within twelve months. To effect this great object, these six states, all great in population or extent of surface, have been content to submit their state pride and dignity to the acquisition of other advantages—double representation in the Senate, and the gain of every desired power for the northern section, and for anti-slavery opinion.

No doubt this scheme had been known to all the leading men of these six states, and of the abolition party, long before it was brought before their legislatures. The advantages to be thus gained for their great sectional objects were well understood, so that very little opposition was made in either of the legislatures, and the approving votes were speedily given. It may be presumed that there will be still less delay required in Congress, and that in a few days this revolutionary, but still entirely constitutional measure, will be completed, except for waiting for the formal ratification by conventions of these six states. To permit these to act, may require six or eight months more of time. As the northern part of Michigan (lying between Lakes Michigan and Superior) is not alone large enough for a state, it is proposed to add to that territory the adjoining portion of Wisconsin—for which the consent of the latter state also will be required, and no doubt readily granted.

This bold stroke seems to have been entirely unexpected, and is a surprise to nearly all who had not been in the secret. But it was not so to me. For it is in perfect agreement with the whole policy of President Seward. This has been to respect the restrictions of the federal constitution in every particular of the letter, and even in regard to doubtful powers; but to avail himself and his section of every unquestionable constitutional power, to establish the supremacy of his section and party. If, then, he could (in this manner) attain every object of his policy, and in the earliest possible time, by these strictly constitutional means, what was more likely than that he would resort to this course? * * * * * * * *

A few days served for both Houses to act upon and give the congressional consent to the divisions of the six states. A separate act is in progress to call separate conventions of all the states, to consider the alterations of the constitution, which will be proposed by three-fourths of the future enlarged Congress. There can be no question that the entire abolition of negro slavery will be thus recommended, and that this tremendous change, whether for good or for evil, will be effected before another year shall pass away.

It will be well for your readers, who feel an interest in American politics, to take a retrospective glance at the changes which have occurred to these states, under their free constitution of government, which seemed to secure equal rights and benefits to every citizen, and to every state. It has been shown, in my former letters, in the record of successive political acts, that as soon as the states were divided by a geographical line into two unequal sections and parties, having different interests, opinions, and political doctrines, the weaker section necessarily became subjected to the stronger, in every question of interest between them. While every citizen, of the weaker section still retained and exercised his constitutional right of voting for representatives—and while the representatives had their equal votes in Congress, yet they were necessarily and regularly out-voted by the representatives of the states of the stronger section, and entirely ruled by them. Consequently, all laws affecting the conflicting interests of the sections have been made to benefit the stronger as much as possible, at the cost, and at any loss and disadvantage, of the weaker section. All offices and trusts and emoluments, and corrupt contracts and profitable jobs, in like manner, have been confined to individuals of the dominant section and party. Thus, with all the forms of perfectly free government remaining, and every restriction and safe-guard of the letter of the constitution having been respected as sacred, the smaller population of the weaker section had been entirely deprived of every benefit and safe-guard of government that could be taken away without infraction of the constitution. Finally, and still by strict constitutional procedure, the constitution itself is to be changed by the will, and to suit the opinions and prejudices, of the stronger section; and the great and essential interest of the weaker is now inevitably to be overthrown, and all its prospects of future prosperity and safety, if not of political existence, to be irretrievably destroyed at one stroke! Yet the people of the weaker section are still called free by those of the stronger, and asserted to be still enjoying equal political rights, and will be so understood, even after the final acts of the series shall have been consummated!

Add to this, that the military and naval forces of the general government are about to be greatly increased in numbers and efficiency, and that they will be entirely officered by abolitionists, as well as controlled and directed by the dominant sectional party. * * * *

LETTER XX.

Agitations in the Slaveholding States, and movements in some of them.

WASHINGTON, December 26th, 1867.

The legislatures of all the southern states are now in session. The last measures of the federal government fell on these bodies and the states they represented like a "clap of thunder in a cloudless sky." The most torpid or submissive were somewhat aroused, and the patriotic and the ardent were excited and exasperated far beyond the measure of any effects of all previous provocations and outrages.—None dared to oppose, to the general outburst of indignation of the disunionists, the old argument in mitigation, that "the northern party and the President had used only their constitutional rights and privileges—that the southern people still possessed all of theirs—that the ballot box only had given success to their northern opponents—that the battle had been fairly contested, and that the defeated party ought to abide by the result." These positions and arguments were just as sound now, as they had been when first used to ward off resistance to the earlier oppressions of the northern section. But they were not available in these extreme and now certain consequences.

It seems inconceivable that the dominant party has not feared to make their opponents, however submissive heretofore, desperate, by this extent of oppression, so manifestly designed. The infatuation can only be accounted for in the presumed weakness and timidity of the South, and the supposed utter inability of slaveholders to make successful resistance by arms. As to the rightfulness of all the measures oppressive or threatening to the South, no question or doubt seems to be entertained by any of the northern section. It was enough that the letter of a free constitution had been observed throughout, and that every question had been decided by a majority of votes, which, as generally understood in the North, is the only true democratic principle, and that its complete recognition and observance constitute the perfection of free government.

* * * * * * * * *

The legislature of South Carolina sent commissioners to the legislatures of Georgia, Alabama, Mississippi, Louisiana and Florida, inviting them to send other commissioners to a designated place, to confer on their present condition and prospects. The like invitation was also sent, in writing, to all the other slaveholding states. But there was so little expectation of concurrent action from any of the more northern and border slaveholding states, that it was deemed best not to wait for their dilatory replies, or to be embarassed by their probable inaction.

The report of these southern movements, and of the agitation and zeal extended through all the southern states, produced but little effect in Washington on the northern party. Contemptuous comments were generally made, and the whole commotion in the South was deemed and treated as nothing more than a repetition of the old game of "bluster and back-out," which had been so common in past time, and in which, it was said, Virginia and South Carolina had especially distinguished themselves. Burlingame, one of the United States senators of Massachusetts, and Hickman, a senator from Pennsylvania, in conversation with others of their party, said that it would be a good thing if the southern agitators would rebel, and require to be suppressed by the military force of the federal government—as there would be no difficulty in the suppression, and the punishment of the actors—and that heavy contributions raised from the rebellious states, and the confiscation of the property of all the principal traitors, would serve as the best and a much needed lesson for all the South, and the best means for securing future tranquility and obedience to the constitution and laws of the Union. The southern members of congress say but little, except among themselves. Those of the most excited states probably were not surprised by the late political movements in their states. It is the ordinary habit of southerners, and even of the southern members of congress, when most oppressed by the superior legislative power of the northern section, to be open and loud in their expressions of complaint, and of denunciation of their adversaries, and to be bold, and arrogant, and contemptuous in manner and expression. Now, the southern members are silent and cautious, and whatever may be their opinions or intentions, they are not made known by themselves to the public. Nothing has been done, or deemed requisite, by the federal administration; and the agitation at the South has not been in any manner alluded to in any act or proposition of the President or of Congress. The latter body, as customary in latter years, adjourned on the 24th of December, for a recess of ten days, for relaxation; and for many members, who are sufficiently near, to spend the Christmas holidays at their homes. As the attendance of southern members has long been of no sort of influence on the enactments of congress, most of them are now always absent. Many of them had not attended since the beginning of the present session; and all who had attended, and had not gone sooner, left Washington for their several states as soon as the Christmas recess was voted. * * * * * *

LETTER XXI.

President Seward for a second term Secession of six states, and consequent political movements and military preparations. Operations at Charleston.

WASHINGTON, January 21, 1868.

It is a remarkable result of the now overwhelming superior strength of the northern section, and of its unanimity of sentiment, that there is no organized opposition for the next presidential election on the part of the South—and that no aspirant to the office, (which is now more exalted and important than ever before,) whether from South or North, has made any open movement towards becoming a candidate, in opposition to the present incumbent. President Seward has now no rival in his character of exponent of northern sentiment, and the executor of the northern will. And by his hold on this strong ground for preference, he will again have the unanimous vote of all the states of the northern section—and will be elected President of the United States without opposition, for a second term of service.

* * * * * * * * *

There has been received here lately reports of important incidents and indications, and of intense interest to all hearers, and serving, at last, to startle the northern party from its previous calm of fancied perfect security.

The several legislatures of Georgia, Alabama, Mississippi, Louisiana and Florida, have concurred with that of South Carolina, so entirely and speedily, that it is evident that there must have been preconcert and a good understanding of views, among the leading men of these six states, for some time before any open movement was made. These several legislatures were in session, with closed doors, until the termination of December 24th, at which time it was known, by telegraphic dispatches, that Congress had separated, upon an adjournment for ten days. Then the common resolutions and enactments of these states just before adopted, were first made known to the public. All the legislatures have declared for the immediate secession of their several states from the heretofore existing federal Union, and their being united in a new confederacy. They have further concurred in ordering the election on January 15th, of members for a general convention of the seceding states, to be composed of one member from each of the previous congressional districts of each state—to assemble at Atlanta, in Georgia, on the 20th, to ratify the declaration of secession, and to adopt the necessary changes of the former federal constitution, to suit it to the changed circumstances

—and to order the elections necessary for the new federal government, which may be agreed upon and established by the convention of the seceding states. Further, by the concurrence of the legislatures of all the seceding states, a provisional federal administration was authorized, to exercise both legislative and executive powers—indeed dictatorial powers—for the short time of its existence. This body will be composed of all the late federal senators of these six states, with the addition of four other members from each of these states, elected by their respective legislatures. This provisional government will continue in power until superseded by the general convention, which will retain the like power until the succeeding organization of the constituted government, and the inauguration of its administrators. As most of the same most influential citizens will probably be chosen members of all the bodies making these successive political authorities, there will be no danger of conflicting counsels, or of interrupted or irregular procedure. The whole arrangement will secure both mature and energetic action from the beginning, and throughout. But in advance of the joint acts of secession and of new organization, though manifestly in anticipation of both, there had been still earlier and very important action by South Carolina alone.

The fortifications of the United States, to protect the ports and seaboard cities from naval attacks, have been constructed on a gigantic plan, in remarkable disproportion to the generally small number of the regular army, and the number of effective garrisons which can be distributed among these many forts. Thus, Fortress Monroe, in Virginia, to be fully manned, would require a garrison of four thousand men, which would have taken more than half of all the regular army of the United States, as the number stood then, and for many years together. Because of the want of men, most of these extensive and strong fortifications have for many years been left without garrisons, and in some cases without even the smallest military guard. The substitute, in such cases, would be some trustworthy old sergeant, who, with his family, resided in the fort, to take care of it, as if private property. In this condition, and charge, was Fort Sumter, though a new and very strong fortification on the right side of the harbor of Charleston, and much stronger than Fort Moultrie, on the opposite side of the passage way. The guns of these two forts completely command the passage—and either one alone, if well served, would stop any hostile fleet, and inflict as much damage on the assailants as was effected by the brave Moultrie and his raw soldiers, on the British ships of war, on June 28th, 1776, from the old Palmetto fort which then stood not far from where Fort Moultrie stands now. Fort Sumter is constructed on an artificial island, (raised by depositing stone on the outer edge of a shoal,) and the outer walls are everywhere washed by the surrounding water. The channel is there deep, and passes very near to the fort. But from the fort to the main land, for rather more than a mile, there is a continuation of the same shoal, and the water is too shallow to be navigated, except by small boats, with crews well acquainted with the bottom—yet too deep, and too variable in depth, to be forded. Excellent as was this fort for its military purpose, it was a lonely and disagreeable place of residence—being as much secluded as a floating-light vessel. Therefore, this strong and well armed fort was left unoccupied, except by its one guardian, and the whole garrison was in Fort Moultrie, which is on the main land of Sullivan's Island, (and which stretches along the upper part of the harbor and the ocean). There both the officers and men had society in the residents of the adjoining village of Moultrieville—and hourly communication with Charleston, five miles distant from the fort, by ferry steamers. Moultrieville, on the border of the ocean beach, is inhabited mostly, and for the summer and autumn only, by citizens of Charleston and the neighboring country, who resort there for health. The residents who remain throughout the year are but few. But at all times, there is good society, and the place is a very pleasant residence. The garrison of Fort Moultrie then amounted to three hundred men. During the troubles between South Carolina and the federal government, during President Jackson's administration, Castle Pinckney had been kept garrisoned, not to protect Charleston from naval attack from the ocean, but to serve as a bridle upon the city, and upon the state, of which Charleston is the great commercial capital, and the most important and the only considerable and usual outlet of the trade and navigation of the state.

In anticipation of the events to be announced on the evening of December 24th, the Governor of South Carolina had authorized and ordered the commanding militia officer in Charleston, to take secret and proper measures to capture Fort Sumter in the night of December 24th, and at the same time to commence the investment, on the land side, of Fort Moultrie, with a view to blockading it, if not proceeding to besiege or attack it more vigorously. To arrest the single guardian in charge, and so to take possession of Fort Sumter was easy enough. But it would require a considerable number, and of the best soldiers, all being entirely raw, to retain possession, in defiance of any regular military and naval force of the United States that could soon be brought to attack either of these forts, if seized upon by South Carolina. Half a dozen bold and trusty men, residents of Charleston, and neighbors and friends of the old sergeant who was the sole occupant and guardian of Fort Sumter, made an appointment to visit him on the Christmas eve, and to spend some hours with him in the customary merry-making of that time. Using this deception to prevent the possibility of their old friend resisting, and so incurring any bodily damage, the single guardian was arrested, and the fort taken possession of. Twenty companies of volunteer militia, the best disciplined in Charleston, had been called out on duty at dark. As this procedure was not unusual at Christmas, and always took place for the slightest rumor of insurrection, (and which false and foolish rumors came in latter years almost as regularly as Christmas,) the calling out of all these companies caused no alarm, and attracted but little notice. For the officers and men of each company knew only of their own company being on duty. These twenty companies, including the corps of cadets of the state military school, were separately sent off, the smaller portion, by water, to garrison Fort Sumter, and the others to begin the investment and blockade of Fort Moultrie. Before daybreak the next morning, Fort Sumter was occupied by a garrison of five hundred men. They had learned when taking charge of the defence of the fort, and greatly to their joy, that they had the honor to be the first soldiers in the service of the now seceded and independent state of South Carolina. Care was taken to strengthen both the garrison and the fortification as soon as possible, and to render them safe from any probable attack.

* * * * * * * * *

Sullivan's Island is, for the greater part, a low and flat bed of sand, raised by the ancient action of the winds and waves, to the elevation of a few feet above the highest of ordinary tides. The remainder of the surface, in the rear, and northward from the harbor and ocean side, is of marsh, through which passes a crooked strait, navigable for small boats only, but too deep, and the bottom too miry, to be forded any where—and which strait separates the island from the main-land, there also bordered by a broad extent of low marsh. The island is about three miles long; and, where the fort stands, is less than half a mile across, and all of firm sand, from the margin of the main shore of the harbor, to a small bay in the rear called the "Cove," which unites with the wide water of the harbor rather more than half a mile above the fort. At half a mile below (and eastward from) the fort, the island is not more than one-sixth of a mile, between the harbor, or the ocean beach, and the upper extremity of the Cove, in the rear. The sand, which forms all the higher and dry soil of the island, is so loose as to be liable to be moved and shifted by the winds—by which natural operation, sand hills would be raised against the walls of the fort, and high enough to over-top the parapet, if the accumulations were not often removed.

A force of twelve hundred militia, reached the rear of the island soon after midnight. Taking every care to prevent noise and thereby alarming the garrison, the militia, divided into two bodies, occupied the island at about half a mile distant from, and both above and below the fort.

Plenty of intrenching utensils had been brought to employ six hundred men, and some thousands of bags to fill with sand. Some hours later, when the first begun work was well advanced, there were brought a much larger supply of tools and of bags, and also seven hundred negro men to labor in the trenches. Before the night was over, the volunteers had been increased to two thousand. The sentinels of the fort were all within or on the ramparts, and probably they were not very vigilant during that night of general festivity. The unavoidable noises made by the march and the labors of the militia were not noticed, or distinguished from the usual and expected sounds of the noisy Christmas merry-makers in the adjoining village of Moultrieville. Even the accidental discharge of a musket of one of the soldiers in the trench, was naturally supposed to be the rejoicing salute of some drunken reveller in the village. The soft and loose sand was moved, to construct the embankments, with but little labor or noise. Before day-break, and before causing any alarm to the garrison, embankments of loose sand, faced and strengthened with filled sand-bags, laid like masonry, had been raised at both positions, strong and high enough to protect the men from the cannon of the fort. There was no other danger to fear. For, if the garrison had sallied out of the fort, they would have been too few to attack the militia, even while the latter (as at first,) were without artillery. The first raised embankments were designed to be subsequently extended so as to make completely enclosed water batteries, to be mounted with heavy cannon bearing on the harbor—and lines thence to extend backward, and from one to the other, so as to surround the fort, on the land side. As blockading the fort was all that was designed, there was no need of the surrounding intrenchments being nearer than was entirely safe for the investing army.

The next morning a low-lying mist at first obscured the newly erected earth-works. As the sun became visible above the horizon, the usual morning gun was fired at each of the forts. At Fort Sumter then arose on the flag-staff, and was spread out on the strong breeze, an extemporaneous flag made of white sheets, in the centre of which was seen the Palmetto Tree of South Carolina—for which there was inserted the small flag of one of the volunteer companies. As soon as the flag reached its highest place, it was saluted by six discharges from the heaviest cannon of Fort Sumter. After short intervals of time, the like salute was repeated twice. The appearance of the Palmetto flag and the firing of the triple salutes to the flag and to the southern confederacy, gave the earliest notice of the changed condition of things to the commander and the garrison of Fort Moultrie, and even to all except a few military and civil officers of the city of Charleston. And now the drums were beaten in the intrenchments on Sullivan's Island, and the several small company flags were hoisted above the parapets, and a salute was fired of muskets, and by a single piece of light field artillery, which had been brought by one of the latest arriving companies. The embankments and the troops they covered, were already secure from any hostile operations of the garrison.

Reports of the immediately succeeding operations have been received here, but as they are doubtful, and somewhat contradictory, I will wait, according to my usage, for reliable information, and perhaps later events. * * *

LETTER XXII.

Earliest Proceedings of the new confederacy. Military Defence. Inaction of the United States Congress, and the causes.

WASHINGTON, January 31, 1868.

The provisional general government met at Atlanta, and was organized and in operation by January 3d. Every previous member of the Senate of the present Congress of the United States, from each of the seceded states, was present to serve in his new position—and also the additional twenty-four new members, elected by the six state legislatures. Mr. M., of South Carolina, was chosen president *pro tem.* and Mr. Y., of Alabama, vice president, and speaker of the assembly. The state legislatures were zealously at work to do everything that could forward the arming, organizing, and strengthening the militia—and readily aided to carry out all the measures proposed by the provisional government. Since her preparations in 1851, South Carolina had not ceased to be the best prepared state for military defence. And the other seceding states had not yet lost all the previous military preparation which the abolition conspiracy and outbreak, under John Brown, in 1859, had then induced. Five thousand volunteers have been called into active service, besides the garrisons of Charleston and its vicinity, which, by exchange and substitution, have been made as efficient as can be of raw troops. The cadets of the Charleston Military School, under their own officers and organization, make part of the garrison of Sullivan's Island; and, boys as they are, they are among the best soldiers of the state. There are but a few of the best trained volunteer city companies that can compare with the young cadets in capacity and zeal for the service required. Fifty thousand other volunteer and minute men, in all the six states, are ordered by the provisional government to hold themselves in readiness to march when called for.

* * * * * * * * *

Congress, of course, could do nothing before the re-opening of the session after the Christmas adjournment. The greater number of the northern members were eager for inflicting summary vengeance on the southern "rebels;" but the views as to the best manner for their coercion were much divided. A considerable number, though a minority, of the northern members were doubtful as to the policy, and feared that the success of the attempt to conquer the revolted states would be very uncertain. They argued that even if the conquest should be effected, it must cost much more in blood and treasure than any benefit thence to be derived would be worth. And when conquered, what then could be done with the rebellious states? To re-admit them to constitutional equality would effect nothing, as punishment for the offence, or in remuneration for the great expenditure of blood and treasure. They could not be held as conquered and subject provinces, except at intolerable cost. By any result of war, deadily hatred would be produced between the contending parties, which no lapse of subsequent time could extinguish. Most of the representatives of the western states on the upper waters of the Mississippi river, were averse to warlike or aggressive action on other grounds. Their trade, through the Lower Mississippi, and their only navigable outlet, had not yet been obstructed, and (as had been given out) will not be, without open war takes place. But if the seceding states shall be invaded or assailed, then the trade and navigation of the northwestern states will be entirely cut off, and cannot be again opened before the state of Louisiana and her allies shall be completely subdued.

While these different opinions, and the different modes of coercion, were debated, the executive power was used to march regular troops from the various northern posts to Washington and elsewhere, to be ready for use, and to provide munitions of war, so far as enabled previously, or to be enabled subsequently, by Congress. Ships were ordered to be fitted out, and all preparations made for their sailing, with the intention, as supposed, to blockade the seaports of the seceding states. * * * * * *

The provisional government of the southern confederacy has made several important decrees. All debts due from their merchants and other citizens, to people of the North are sequestrated in the hands of the debtors, until ordered otherwise by the government. And all debtors, who may desire to discharge such debts, may pay them over to the general government of the new confederacy, which will become responsible for the debts. The long established course of trade has caused the greater share of commodities consumed in the South to be brought from the North, and the regular usage is, also on time. The consequence has been that while the South was the best customer, and also a safe debtor to the North, there was general, and continual, and large indebtedness, which, though regularly and punctually discharged, was immediately renewed for new purchases, made for the next business season. Thus the usual and permanent amount of debts due from the South did not fall much short of the whole amount of annual purchases made from the northern Atlantic states. The amount of these debts, now due from the six seceding states, to the merchants and manufacturers of the North, and mainly to the cities of Boston, New York and Philadelphia, is computed at more than $40,000,000. All this is sequestrated for the present. If remaining unpaid to the North for but six months after being due, it will cause incalculable commercial distress, and numerous bankruptcies of the before stronger firms and business companies. The retaining of this large amount by the debtors, or, if received by the government, will operate as a forced loan of so much, for the benefit of the southern community.

The operations of the post-offices and collectors of customs, and of the railroads, telegraph and express transportation lines, vessels, &c., are not to be obstructed, so long as carried on in the manner proposed. But the receipts of both post-offices and collectors, until ordered otherwise, are to be accounted for, and to be paid over to the new southern confederacy. The federal officers before in office, if southerners, and deemed legal and trustworthy, and also responsible for their required payments, are to be continued in office. But such as are otherwise, and all northerners or abolitionists employed in any capacity by the former federal authorities, have been dismissed, and new appointments made.

Police measures are ordered to insure the watching of all transient or suspicious northerners, of but recent residence, on entrance into the South—and to expel them when deemed proper—or to require security for their loyal conduct to the South, if remaining.

The troops of the United States, in forts or garrisons within the seceding states, and any war vessels already lying in their harbors, are not to be molested in any way, or treat-

5

ed in hostile manner, provided they abstain from all action hostile or threatening danger to these states or their people. But, if acting as enemies, they will be treated as such, and every available war measure will forthwith be put in operation against them.

Should any invasion or hostile and warlike attack be made by the northern or federal power, every means for defence or retaliation will be resorted to, including the sequestration or destruction of all northern shipping then in these states, and all northern merchandize or other property.

These decrees of the provisional government were made public before any legislative action on the subject could be agreed upon by Congress, or before anything of military coercion had been attempted to be carried into effect by the sole power of the President.

* * * * * * * * *

LETTER XXIII.

Offensive Measures in Progress against the Seceding States, and their Plan of Defence, and general Political Procedure.

WASHINGTON, February 19, 1868.

The General Convention was duly elected, and met in Atlanta, on January 20th. As soon as organized, the Convention resolved that only such few changes of the former Federal Constitution should be now made as were required to suit the new circumstances. Accordingly, the former Constitution has been adopted as it stood, with but a few

and mainly formal exceptions. These recognize the present number of confederated southern states as six—with arrangements to admit any other slaveholding states which may hereafter seek admission to the southern confederacy, and which shall obtain the consent of the southern congress. The election of members of Congress, and of president and vice-president, are made to suit the changed number of states. The seat of the southern federal government is fixed for the present, at Atlanta. Other than these mere formal changes, not affecting the principle or operation of the former federal constitution, there was no change of its provisions made. Only in one important respect, in the manner of electing the president and vice-president, the constitution was restored to its first designed operation, and which had been perverted and abjured from a very early time of the former Government. The framers of the constitution unquestionably had intended that the members of the electoral college should be elected by the people—and, it may be inferred, severally by districts—and that the electors should be truly empowered, according to their judgment, to elect the president and vice-president. But, after the first election of Washington, this discretion has never been exercised, and the electors have been mere blind and powerless instruments, and their appointment and service a mere form and farce. The framers of the constitution had wisely designed to leave this duty to the electors, for two sufficient reasons, first, that the people could not possibly know whom to choose for president; and next, if knowing how to select, could not possibly concentrate opinion, and exert the popular will. The new southern convention aimed to remedy the long continued perversion and abuse of the constitution in this respect. The congressional districts are also to be the electo-

ral districts, and each one is to choose one elector: and the additional two electors to which each state is entitled, are to be elected by the respective legislatures. The electors are to have, and exercise, their discretion in electing the president and vice-president, and careful provisions, not necessary to be stated here, have been adopted to secure the maintenance of this power, and its inevitable exercise, to the electors exclusively. Still, it is required that the electors of each state shall vote together, as the majority of the electors of each state may prefer, so as not to divide the entire vote and strength of any state. If the electoral votes of any state should be equally divided between two candidates, (as ascertained in a separate and preliminary session,) then that equal portion which had been elected by the greater number of popular votes, shall be deemed the majority, and shall determine the vote for the whole state. This plan will enable the people to best exert their choice, and which they are qualified to make, of a capable and worthy district representative. And the choice of the president will be made by the representative electors, and who will be qualified to select a chief magistrate.

The original federal constitution, which was thus adopted unchanged in principle and in its important features, is a more equal, just, and altogether better form of government for these slaveholding states, whose circumstances are so nearly similar, than it has been for the first confederation for which it was designed. In the recent adaptation, the provision fixing the slave representation at three-fifths as much as of whites, is not objectionable to any interest, as it was deemed by both the northern and southern sections of the United States, for opposite reasons. Also, as no very small state (like Rhode Island or Delaware) is in the south-

ern confederacy, there is no very unequal representation in the Senate. Still, the recent hasty adoption of the constitution of the United States was induced by the existing necessity for speedy organization, and is considered but a temporary measure, to be reviewed and more maturely acted upon hereafter.

The constitution was adopted in the course of a few days, and elections ordered in every state and district, first to ratify or reject the constitution—and, for the contingency of ratification, at the same time to elect members of the House of Representatives, and district presidential electors. The several state legislatures, immediately after, elected the two state electors for each state. The new Congress soon met, and also the electoral college. Mr. M., was elected president, and Mr. C., of Alabama, vice-president. Most of the former members of both Houses had been elected to fill the same stations in the new Congress. Mr. Y., of Alabama, was elected to the Senate. Sundry other very able men, of ardent patriotism and devotion to southern interests, were elected to one or the other of the two Houses. The new government was mainly composed of the same individuals, and included all of the most worthy, who had made up the previous provisional government, which ceased to exist as soon as the new government was inaugurated.

These changes and arrangements had been completed by the southern confederacy before anything had been determined upon by Congress for the coercion of the new independent southern power, or before more than preliminary steps for military and naval action had been taken by the President in the exercise of his independent authority. The differences of opinion among the northern members served to give to the remaining slaveholding members of the body some, and important legislative power, of which they had been totally deprived as long as the North had been undivided as previously. The members from the remaining slaveholding states now held the balance of power between the different modes of military, or coercive, or other policy, severally advocated by the different northern states. And by this remaining southern vote being always added to the weaker northern portion, or given to postpone or embarrass all hostile action by Congress, it was long before anything could be done by new legislation.

In the meantime, the President has ordered vessels of war to proceed to blockade Charleston, Savannah, Mobile, the mouth of the Mississippi river, and every other important port of the southern confederacy, which can be safely and effectually blockaded. Any action of troops, or their march to the revolted states, is postponed until Congress shall take measures to make such action irresistible, by appropriating money and providing all the other necessary incidental requisites.

As soon as the sailing of war-vessels from northern ports was known (through the magnetic telegraph,) southern troops were marched to the principal provincial towns and harbors which were most important, and sure to be blockaded. But it was still the policy and earnest effort of the southern government to avoid all hostile collision with the northern troops and ships, and especially all bloodshed, as long as possible. The vessels in these ports, owing to the previous course of navigation and trade, were nearly all belonging to the North. All these then remaining in the ports were seized, and brought together in the several ports, and dismantled, so as to prevent their sailing, and also, were so placed that they could be easily and quickly burned or scuttled, if required. A sufficient guard of militia was maintained to enforce these regulations.

* * * * * * * * *

LETTER XXIV.

State of Popular Feeling in Virginia, and of Political Affairs. Prospects Ahead.

.RICHMOND, February 26, 1868.

For nearer observation of the events most likely to be interesting, I am on my way to Charleston. I had obtained from southern friends and members of Congress, still in Washington, from the slaveholding states, letters of introduction, which will serve as vouchers for my friendly disposition and sentiments, and facilitate my observations.—On the route I stopped at Richmond, and shall remain some days.

The legislature of Virginia is still violently excited.—The most ardent spirits, and most of the members of ability, were for immediate secession—and, as not having gone with the six states in that measure, they wish now to follow their lead, and offer the adhesion of Virginia to the adopted constitution and policy; though, by holding back, Virginia has had no voice or influence in shaping either. The more ardent states had long before waited for Virginia to be their honored and trusty leader in resistance to northern oppression. But all hope of such aid and direction having ceased, the more southern states, when they deemed that longer delay would have been certain destruction to them, proceeded to act without Virginia.

The advocates for secession are still but a minority.—The majority of the legislature includes sundry shades of opinion. A very few (from the northwestern counties) are abolitionists. Many more, and from every portion of the state, are submissionists in any and every contingency.—Others will resist, as they say, when there remains no other hope; but still cling to the glorious (former) union, and denounce the rebellion of the South. In addition, the present legislature is a very weak body, and does not fairly represent the people either in intellect or patriotism. The intellectual standard of the representatives of this formerly great and honored state has been gradually lowered, from the time when the old freehold suffrage state constitution (the oldest written constitution of free government that existed) was first impaired, in 1829, by alterations which were not amendments. But the later changes, in 1851, were very far worse. The convention then assembled to make amendments, had not been demanded by the popular will or wish. It was required and carried through mainly by demagogues, and the new constitution was shaped so as to put all political power into the hands of demagogues. The election of governor, of judges, and other high officers of government, by the votes of the whole state—or, in some other cases, by electoral districts too extensive for the people's knowledge of the candidates, or even for the concentration of popular opinion and wishes—produced, as a necessity, and established, the infamous "convention" or caucus system of nominations, imported from the corrupt State of New York—which system serves to throw elections into the hands of a few cunning and concealed demagogues, or tools of principal office-hunters, and to cheat the people of their proper and rightful influence, as well as of all means for their correct and honest guidance. Worthy men, disgusted with the working of the vile system, have gradually withdrawn from all endeavors to promote fair elections and honest purposes. The certain operation of the caucus system, is always to degrade the standard of average and general intellect, and of patriotism and worth, of all representatives.

* * * * * * * * There is no unfriendly feeling existing between the seceding states and the remaining slaveholding states. And along the new lines of division between the two, the people on both sides are entirely homogeneous in character, sentiments, and interests. The southern border counties of North Carolina and the eastern of Tennessee and Arkansas not only have no inimical feeling to the adjacent people of the new confederacy, but hold them, as previously, as neighbors and friends, and who, in numerous cases, are family relations, and would rejoice if their respective states would unite with the seceding states in resistance to northern oppression. Along and near the northern border lines of the slaveholding states, there is a strong and general feeling of enmity between their population and the neighboring northern people. But, these being still under the same general government and laws, there can be no reason or inducement for permitting the border enmities and feuds to ripen into armed and bloody hostilities.—Thus, for the present, the border and other adjacent slaveholding states serve as the most important means of protection and security for the seceding states, in preventing all border troubles and dangers, and offering a safe-guard to the

seceding states from hostile invasion by land, by the interposition of some five hundred miles width of territory, which will be neutral at least, if not directly friendly, to the South; and most probably in the future, an armed as well as broad barrier for its protection. It is generally supposed that Virginia (if not all the other border states,) though not yet ready to join the seceding South, will not permit the march, across her territories, of federal troops to invade the southern confederacy. In the nullification troubles of 1833, the brave old Governor Floyd, boldly assumed and avowed this position, to protect South Carolina; and the iron will of President Jackson, and his malignant hatred to South Carolina, her great statesmen, and her policy, had to hold back and to yield to the expressed determination of Virginia. The present legislature of Virginia will not be likely to direct so bold a course—but will scarcely dare to oppose and forbid it, if the former example of old Governor Floyd should be imitated by the present Governor S., which is most probable. The latter is a true southern patriot, and an able statesman.

The legislature, however, had previously increased the efficiency of the militia by the organization and equipment of many new volunteer companies, whose services have been offered within the last year, in consequence of the increased progress and danger of abolition attacks. Of these, and of other companies of ordinary militia, twenty thousand have been designated as "minute men," who are required to be ready to march, whenever called upon, at the shortest notice—and that is counted on to be within the day of the notice. North Carolina and Kentucky have adopted similar measures for military defence. Another law, recently passed by Virginia, forbids, under heavy penalties, the transportation of troops, or arms and munitions of war, on any railroad line passing through the state, except for the state, or by authority of the governor. This will exclude one, and the most speedy and efficient, means of assault by the federal power on the revolted South.

But if the legislature of Virginia is slow and inefficient in acts, it is, as always heretofore, loud and violent, and denunciatory of federal aggression, and especially of the recent indications of designs of crowning usurpation. As often heretofore, the strongest resolutions of *future* resistance have been passed, to be put in action whenever the manifestly designed constitutional abolition of slavery shall be attempted. As the conventions of all the northern states cannot act to alter the constitutions short of some six months, that much time will be allowed for further postponement of action. But in April there will be new elections for the legislature of Virginia, and the advocates of secession here expect that the present imminent danger of all the South and its institutions, and the zeal of the people, will induce the calling into public service the ablest men and best patriots of Virginia, nearly all of whom are now, and long have been, in private life.

There is one strong evidence of the popular feeling, which, in more ways than one, must draw Virginia and the other border states more certainly to sustain the southern confederacy. There have been offered to President M., by individuals and by companies, the military services of more than ten thousand volunteers from the border states, and nearly half of these are from Virginia. All of these are men of the best material for such service—all stimulated by the spirit of adventure, of patriotism, and of bitter hatred for the North. Very many are young men of the best family connections; and some entire companies of calvary have equipped themselves with horses, arms and uniforms, at their own expense. They passed out of the state as civilians, and assumed their warlike character and equipment only after entering the borders of South Carolina. Neither that state nor any other of the new confederacy had any need of men—they wanted only arms, munitions of war, and money. Still it was deemed good policy to accept the services of the organized volunteer companies offered from abroad, for the moral effect and reaction that will certainly be produced on their countrymen at home. In a few months more, if things continue as they now promise, there will be fifty companies of Virginian or other border volunteers defending the new confederacy, and maintaining southern rights and independence. There will scarcely be a neighborhood or a large family connection of the commonwealth of Virginia that will not have some beloved members and representatives engaged in this cause, so dear to all southern patriots. And this state of things will operate powerfully to enlist the popular interest and feeling of this state, in favor of the Virginia volunteers, and of the cause for which they will be contending.

* * * * * * * * *

LETTER XXV.

Beginning of the Blockade of Southern Ports. Military Spirit and Action of the South. Operations at Charleston.

CHARLESTON, March 15, 1868.

* * * * * * President Seward certainly has exhibited a degree of courage in conducting political invasions and assaults which most other and even more powerful rulers would have shrunk from attempting, in dread of the resistance to be provoked, and the possible consequences of resistance. But civil and military courage and conduct require very different qualities—and it seems to me that there is already enough evidence that the President is very deficient in that promptitude of thought and action which is essential for military conduct and success—and his deficiencies are not supplied by the abilities of the Commander-in-Chief, Gen. Fremont. Instead of hastening to attack the seceding states (if hostile military operations were designed,) before their new organization was completed, and while they were in the necessary weaker condition of change from one government to another—as the iron-willed despot Jackson would certainly have done in like circumstances—President Seward has as yet done but little besides urgently applying to the Congress for more military and naval forces, and more means, and the more perfect equipment of the previously existing or authorized armaments, and for munitions of war, and for authority to call for, and means to equip, volunteers and other militia—and especially, and as a condition precedent to any important and new military action, for funds sufficient to defray all the early expenses

counted upon as needed. Because of the political circumstances which have been already stated, nothing of importance had yet been done in these respects, by Congress. And the only measure which the President had deemed within his means, was to use the then existing and available small naval force, to blockade and threaten the ports and seaboard cities of the seceded states. This had been done early in February. One or two ships of war, only, made up the force sent to blockade each of these ports, or mouths of great rivers, with the exception of Charleston. Here, owing to the more warlike state of affairs, and of the two ports being still held by the northern troops, and they being besieged by the forces of South Carolina, more extensive and strong measures were ordered. Still earlier than the other vessels, designed merely for blockading other ports, these arrived in the outer harbor, and anchored below the bar, a squadron composed of a ship of seventy-four guns, two heavy frigates, and two sloops-of-war, with some smaller transports and freight vessels—bringing reinforcements and supplies for the forts, provisions, and cannon of the most recent improvement and extensive range, and also mortars, shells, and powder. Neither of these ships-of-war, with the armament on board, can pass over the bar—and even if any were of light enough draught to be able to pass over, they could not, under the fire of Fort Sumter alone, navigate the intricate channels.

All the efforts made to send supplies to Fort Moultrie in the smaller vessels, have been so far frustrated by the vigilance and the round shot of Fort Sumter and the lower temporary earth-work battery of Sullivan's Island. Every thing for the defence of the city will depend on the continuing to keep out these supplies, and effectually preventing communication between the squadron and the two forts still held by the enemy. Unless attempting to attack Fort Sumter, (by the vessels of war, previously lightened of their guns, &c., to cross the bar,) or the city, by aid of a strong additional land force, (neither of which attempts is likely to occur soon,) the naval force can effect all the objects of mere blockade of the port, at their present anchorage—and, might, as well do so, with one or two small armed vessels only.

Acting upon President Jackson's former policy, in the then expected troubles of 1833, notice has been given by the commander of the blockading squadron that the payment of customs on imports, from all inward bound vessels, will be required to be made to the United States collector on board of the flag ship—but that there will be no other obstruction to vessels complying with that requisition, except to such as belong to the revolted states, which, as under all other circumstances, will be seized as prizes of war. The foreign ships, then in port, were free to carry out cargoes—but none that should pass in later, during the continuance of the sea blockade. The vessels in the port of Charleston, some thirty only then remaining, were nearly all the property of northern owners, and which had been bound for New York or other northern cities. If these had been permitted to sail, they would all have carried cargoes of cotton to the northern manufacturers. As was before stated, these northern vessels were detained and dismantled. Here, and elsewhere, there are scarcely any vessels, except small craft for river navigation only, belonging to the southern states.

Since the occupying of Fort Sumter by the state troops, every vessel, and even the smallest boat, passing either up or down the harbor, has been required, and compelled, to pass close under the guns of that fort, and to stop for inspection or examination, before being permitted to proceed. This rule could be strictly enforced upon all foreign or sea vessels, and therefore was implicitly obeyed. As to small boats, which might sometimes have eluded the vigilance, and risked the fire, of the fort, and of the guard-boats, (especially in the night,) there was no danger at first, because such boats, with supplies for the forts, could have been sent only from the neighboring territory; and the patriotism and public spirit of all the inhabitants were better sureties against such aid to the enemy, than all the strong military means used for prevention. After the arrival of the blockading squadron, still more careful safe-guards were used; and so far effectually, against the several attempts which have been made by the ships' boats to reach and reinforce Fort Moultrie. These were all discovered when in progress, at night, and the boats were fired upon by all the cannon bearing on them, so that the further effort was manifestly fruitless, and highly dangerous, and the boats were compelled, in every case, to return to the squadron.

Before the arrival of the blockading squadron, there had been no stoppage of the navigation, trade, or free departure of any northern ships, provided they complied with the regulations stated above, and avoided every thing like hostile conduct, and especially any attempt to communicate with the enemy in Castle Pinckney or Fort Moultrie. Northern vessels had only been required, as of all other foreigners, to pay duties on their imported cargoes, and all the other legal port charges for foreign vessels. But in anticipation of the system of general port blockade by the enemy, the southern government had enacted a law, which was to go into effect for every port only as soon and as long at it should be blockaded by the vessels of the northern power. By this law, which had been previously proclaimed, an embargo was imposed on every such blockaded port, to operate on all northern vessels. But all European vessels, offering sufficient evidence, or security, that their cargoes were designed for Europe, will be free to depart, if they can elude the vigilance of the blockading vessels. Ports not yet blockaded were to be also free from the embargo. The object of this policy was to retaliate for the hostile action of the United States Government, and to cut off the essential supplies of cotton needed for the northern manufacturing states, which otherwise, notwithstanding a pretended general and strict blockade, would be permitted to pass to the North, and there only, under licences. The retaliatory procedure was also thought likely to furnish grounds for difficulties and quarrels between the blockading enemy and the European powers, for whose manufacturers abundant supplies of cotton are indispensable. It was also enacted, and published, that any vessels that submitted to pay customs to the collecting officers of the United States on board the blockading ships, would be still required to pay full duties at the southern custom-houses, if landing their cargoes. Of course all ships will avoid entering a blockaded port, unless in evasion or defiance of the blockade.

It is the general opinion in the seceded states, that any effort, made to attack or invade them, by the northern federal power, must fail of success, even if not bringing disaster and great loss to the invaders. Still, from the hostile disposition shown by the administration, and the people of the North, it is fully expected that the southern confederacy will be invaded both by strong land and naval forces. And as United States troops still hold the two forts in the neighborhood of Charleston, and are there in great peril, if not speedily and effectively succored, it is confidently believed that the first blow of the invaders will fall upon this city. Still with all the military and naval preparations, and even here, where the opposing parties are brought so near together, there has been, and still is, an evident wish, on both sides, to avoid as much as possible, extreme measures, in actual conflict in arms, and blood-shed. For whenever blood shall have been spilled, and all angry and revengeful feelings thereby thoroughly aroused, there will be then left little hope for early peace, except through the complete defeat of one or the other party, and perhaps through the incalculable damage of both. Policy therefore has directed the course of unusual forbearance which has been here pursued, on both sides. But there were other causes operating. Most of the officers of the forts had been stationed there for some years. A large proportion of them were gentlemen of intelligence and pleasant manners. Some had wives and children with them. The officers and their wives, though all northerners, had made many intimate acquaintances and some warm friends among the residents of Charleston—and the ladies had passed much of their time as boarders in the city hotels, or as guests in the houses of their friends residing there. Similar friendly connexions, to some extent, existed between the soldiers of the garrisons and many of the lower classes of citizens. And all these circumstances operated to soften the asperities of war, and to limit the injuries inflicted, by both the hostile parties, to such only as were essential for their respective main objects.

On the first morning of the investment of Fort Moultrie,

as soon as the presence of the assailants had been announced from their as yet unfinished batteries, their commander, Gen. J. sent a flag of truce to Col. T. to demand (*pro forma*,) the surrender of Fort Moultrie and Castle Pinckney to the authority of the State of South Carolina. As expected, the prompt answer was a decisive refusal, and accompanied by the demand of the immediate evacuation of the island and Fort Sumter, and cessation of all hostile action against the United States forces and military works. This answer was speedily followed by a cannonade from the fort on the sand embankments, to obstruct their extension or completion, and in the hope of frightening and driving off their raw defenders, before the means for their defence could be strengthened. This firing caused but little damage to the embankments, and only such as could be easily and speedily repaired—and no loss of life to the covered troops. The cannonade was indeed an agreeable accompaniment of the other operations, and kept up a semblance of battle, and of danger, which the Carolinian commander, Gen. J., deemed very useful, as serving to accustom his raw soldiers to the sound, and also to the general inefficacy, of cannon, when fired against earthen banks—and to keep up a continued pleasant excitement, to relieve the dullness and monotory of blockade service. Except this cannonade—which was not continued very long, because of its manifest inutility—and the firing, from Fort Sumter and the sand batteries, on the vessels and boats which, either to aid the enemy, or in ignorance of the prohibitory orders, were sometimes seen in the channel or other more shallow waters leading to Fort Moultrie, or other forbidden waters—there has been no firing, or hostile attack from either side or the other—and no persons killed or wounded, except a few of the sailors of one of the boats of the blockading squadron, which was shattered by a round shot, when making one of the several fruitless and defeated attempts to convey supplies to Fort Moultrie.

The two forts, Sumter and Moultrie, were within range of each others largest guns, and might have battered each other, to the considerable damage of both. But neither would have thereby incurred any more danger of being captured by the other's garrison—nor would any advantage have been gained by either fort that would compensate for the waste of its ammunition. Therefore, by tacit agreement, there was no firing between the hostile forts. Neither were any soldiers of the opposing fortifications fired upon when exposed upon the ramparts, or any where within their own fortifications. But if any of the garrison of Fort Moultrie showed themselves without the walls, or if any of the besiegers advanced the least in front of their parapets, they were immediately fired upon. Of course, as was designed, the blockaded garrisons were thus confined closely within their walls, and made to suffer the worst effects of such confinement. The rigor of this procedure, designed for combatants, and to compel the earliest surrender, was not extended to unnecessary cases. The ladies of the enemies' garrisons, (by permission of Gen. J., and with his assurance of their safety,) were invited, with their children, by their friends in Charleston to come and reside with them as welcome guests. And in some cases, and in all where either a mother or a child was suffering from sickness, these friendly and hospitable invitations were accepted for the family. To the ladies who still remained to share with their husbands the hardships of confinement in the blockaded forts, and to the sick soldiers of the garrisons, there were often sent presents of fruit, and other delicacies highly gratifying to the suffering beneficiaries, but which could not extend the ability of the garrison to hold out longer.

From the beginning Gen. J. has confined his operations against the enemy to strictly blockading the garrisons, and preventing all communication between them, and also with the enemy's ships, after they arrived below. The ardent and brave, though inexperienced volunteers, under his command, were eager to be led to the assault of Fort Moultrie, and deemed it highly discreditable to them, that with such great superiority of numbers, they should be confined to the slow operations of blockade. But the discreet and judicious commander had thought otherwise—and his action, according to his correct judgment, had been approved both by the state government, and that of the southern confederacy, since the latter had been inaugurated, and had assumed the conduct of the war. With the force of the southern army, maintaining the blockade, (though reduced to 1500 men on the island since the intrenchments and sand-batteries had been completed, and the latter supplied with heavy artillery,) Gen. J. could probably have succeeded in taking Fort Moultrie by escalade or assault. But it would have cost the lives of many of his command, valuable as citizens even more than as soldiers—and all such unnecessary losses he was most anxious and careful to avoid.

For the general course of warfare—of offensive operations directed against the two forts, and of defence against the blockading ships and for the city generally—there is no omission of vigilance, and nothing is trusted either to the weakness, the forbearance, or the inactivity of the enemy The strictest guard is everywhere maintained, and, where needed, on the water by guard-boats, as well as on land. Every preparation or safe-guard, necessary for defence, has been made. Besides the strong garrison in Fort Sumter, and 1500 men in the batteries and behind the extended earth works on Sullivan's Island, and 3000 in the city, all the men of military age in Charleston and its neighborhood, and many also of younger boys (at their own will,) are frequently exercised under arms; and of these, 1000, in turn, are every day under arms, and more strictly drilled, so as to make that much of regular, though daily changing, addition to the garrison volunteers always under arms. Every thing is of military character. Even the younger ladies are generally learning to use fire-arms—and it has become a fashionable amusement for them to meet, in associations, to practice shooting at a mark, with revolvers and light fowling pieces. All of the young females are zealous to be distinguished as good marks-women. And many are already so skilful, and ready in the use of fire-arms, that they boast that, if required by an invasion, they can add some thousands to the effective defenders of the houses and the ramparts of the city.

There might possibly be one kind of damage, and that the most terrible and distressing, inflicted on Charleston, by the stronger military and naval forces which the enemy could assemble for attack—and even (and more surely,) by the present garrison and armament of Castle Pinckney alone. This is the bombardment, or burning, of the city—which might be certainly and easily effected, without any means for prevention, by bomb-shells thrown from the close adjacent castle. And perhaps the like destruction might be effected on others of the southern sea-port cities, either by bombardment from ships of war, or by the hasty incursion of a land force, to retreat as soon as the designed object was accomplished. But such acts of sheer brigandage, and instigated by hatred or vengeance, however injurious to the sufferers, could yield no benefit, even of compensating booty, to the most successful incendiaries and destroyers. And such atrocious acts would excite unextinguishable hatred, and thirst for revenge, in all these southern states, against the people and the government resorting to such means of warfare—and which resort would also bring upon them the reproach and detestation of the civilized world. Should this mode of warfare be attempted, however calamitous the results may be to the southern confederacy, they will serve to double its active strength and the measures for retaliation, and the number of its defenders and allies.

The water blockade, alone, and its direct effects, will cause much loss to the trade of Charleston and the other ports heretofore used for the import and export trade. Also there will be but little money received, by either government, for duties on imports. But though the channels of trade will be diverted, and the smuggling of imports will be extensively substituted for legal trade and the payment of duties, there will still be nearly as much cotton shipped as previously, from the many small and shallow harbors and sounds, rarely used heretofore; and there can be no suffering for want of enough supplies through the same channels, of foreign productions, and articles of necessary use, of every kind.

LETTER XXVI.

Obstacles to the operation of the Blockade. Effects on both South and North.

CHARLESTON, April 6, 1868.

The system of blockade has been extended to every ordinary port of the southern confederacy, and to the mouth of every considerable river. Still there are many shallow ports, and navigable inlets, and connecting passages, which may be resorted to, with the use of steamers and other vessels of light draft. These expected conditions were made known to the consuls of foreign governments, residents in these cities, as early as the independence of the southern confederacy was declared—with the further information that foreign vessels of suitable construction could thus discharge and receive cargoes without risk or difficulty. Arrangements had been forthwith made for and by merchants of England, France, and other commercial countries. Some small vessels have already arrived, and have discharged cargoes of which part were of arms and gunpowder, for the government. It is understood that these small vessels will run only to the free port of Bermuda, or otherwise to St. Thomas', or to one of the French West India islands, where their cargoes of cotton will be transferred to large ships, for Europe, and from whose cargoes of European commodities, previously there landed, the smaller vessels will be re-laden, and return to some one or other of the numerous shallow harbors or inlets of the South, which are not, and cannot be, closed by the few war vessels of the United States; and it may be doubted whether it can be done effectually by any amount of blockading force.

There is a remarkable topographical feature of this southern coast which is now of the greatest importance, and which will enable the people to be protected from any thing like close blockade. From Virginia to Florida, there extends along nearly the whole sea margin, and parallel thereto, a succession of narrow passages of unobstructed water, usually admitting, in different parts, vessels drawing from four to eight feet of depth. Sundry narrow inlets, at distances apart of many miles, offer difficult passages thence to the open ocean—where the shore is entirely exposed to storms, and the coast proverbially dangerous to ships. These interior passages, or sounds, are very near to the ocean, and separated therefrom in most cases by low and narrow strips of sand banks, or low islands, and high sand hills, where the islands are broadest—and sometimes shoals scarcely visible above or below the surface of the water. This remarkable general feature offers a nearly connected passage for small vessels, safe from ocean storms and from enemies on the coast, with different inlets for entrance or departure, as many and as open as needed for convenience, and as few and as difficult, as desired to prevent hostile attacks or obstruction. No large vessel would risk lying off any part of this dangerous coast, through a heavy wind blowing toward the shore, or even in threatening weather. It would be extremely hazardous for the boats of a hostile off-lying ship to enter the sounds, because of the very variable water and difficult and shifting channels of the deeper water, and also because of the exposure to ambuscades on the numerous islands and sand banks. Again, elsewhere, as from Mobile to the mouth of the Mississippi river, and thence westward to Texas, the coast is generally indented with inlets, bays and sounds, or passages open at both ends, or elsewhere, affording safe entrance and shelter, and points for landing cargoes for small vessels having good pilotage, but of which the entrance would be too hazardous to be attempted by a stranger or an enemy. Of these different kinds of entrance, or of continued and safe passage-ways, there are scores, if not hundreds, along this southern coast, which will serve to render a strict blockade impossible. By the attempt, trade will be partially obstructed, and the inland channels of trade often diverted. Old and established marts and ports will lose greatly, and new ones, and transient interests, will gain by the changes. The southern government's custom-houses will have to be moveable, and the collectors ambulatory—and doubtless, half the dues to government will fail to be collected. But there will be not much effective prevention of either exports or imports between these southern states and Europe, or the West Indies. The chief obstruction will be of the cotton and grain needed for the northern states, which the existing war must shut out to great extent, and operate to divert to Europe. Thus, as it seems, the damage of the blockade will be chiefly inflicted upon the all-important manufacturing and commercial interests of the Atlantic northern states.

There is still another peculiar and yet general feature of the southern coast and its principal harbors and ports, which, though a great disadvantage to navigation in time of peace, became a powerful auxiliary for defence in the recent conjuncture. The outlet of every great river, where near to the ocean, is obstructed by a bar, which prevents the entrance of merchant ships of ordinary draught, and all vessels of war not of small size, or constructed especially for shallow waters. The harbor of Charleston will not admit the safe and easy passage of ships drawing as much as eighteen feet of water. The water on the bar of the mouth of the Mississippi is much shallower—and that of nearly all the other great sea-ports and principal harbors is no better. Pensacola only, has as much as twenty-one feet water, on the bar, at high flood tide. Most of these bars also are variable in height, and shifting in position, under the various influences of river floods and ocean storms. These general obstacles to commercial and peaceful navigation, are still greater impediments to war vessels of a hostile power—whether for attacks on the cities above the bars, or for blockades which can only be attempted below the bars, and in some cases off the coast. These, added to all the other difficulties before referred to, serve to render, and must always render, the attack of these southern sea-ports impracticable for large ships of war, and very difficult even for those of medium sizes—and the effective and continued blockade of the harbors, almost impossible.

The internal trade, by land or river routes, between the seceded states, and the adjacent or border slave-holding states which have not seceded, has not been in the least obstructed, by any action of the southern confederacy—and so far, the commercial and other intercourse of these different sections, of like interests and sentiments, but now under different governments, has not been sensibly altered by the recent political change, or even by the present condition of actual war commenced by the northern federal government on the southern.

But very important consequences have followed the blockade of the mouths (and other outlets) of the Mississippi, and the embargo, in reference to the north-western states, and their previous and present policy. Previous to the imposition of the blockade, there had been but inconsiderable new burdens or inconveniences added to the trade of the upper or north-western states with New Orleans, or any part of Louisiana or Mississippi, on the river and its lower navigable branches. The duties on foreign commodities remained as before the secession, the previously existing United States tariff having been adopted by the southern confederacy, at first, together with the United States code in general. The people on the upper waters, having nothing but agricultural products to sell, on which there were no duties under the tariff, and being received still as friends, found no seriously injurious change in their accustomed southern markets. The European commodities there bought, and obtained in exchange for their products, were increased in price only by the same rates of duties which had previously been imposed on them. Thus, the great trade of the north-western states at first continued undisturbed. And it was the fear of causing its complete obstruction that induced the members of Congress from all these states to hesitate at, and dally with, the warlike propositions of the President—and indirectly, or by inaction in Congress, to discourage all schemes for the military coercion of the southern confederacy. But now their profitable trade was completely destroyed, and by the act of their own general government. As there was no longer any outlet abroad for the exports of these north-western states, and only the limited home demand of the southern states on the Mississippi river, of course the supply of their products greatly exceeded the then demand, and prices soon fell ruinously low. Thus all the commercial evils to be expected from the existence of flagrant war with the South, were already incurred by the north-western states.

LETTER XXVII.

Active hostilities and invasion of the South proposed. Losses and suffering in the North.

WASHINGTON, April 15, 1868.

The energetic military policy desired by the President, had already been delayed and obstructed for some months, by the previous conflicting interest of the north-western states, and by the southern members of Congress (from the still adhering states,) uniting in aid of all the different impediments presented to early action—and these two different interests, of the north-western and the remaining southern states, thus out-voting the north-eastern states. The new commercial position of the north-western states, in the practical exclusion of their products from market, and their consequent reduced prices, and the immense losses incurred for as long time as hostilities may continue, induced the representatives of that great region now to concur in the most effective measures of offensive war, for the purpose of speedily conquering a peace, and compelling the entire subjection of the South. The reunion of these recently opposed portions of the whole northern section, restored the former overwhelming superiority of the North in the

Congress. The remaining southern votes, reduced by the secession of six southern states, were now a still more contemptible minority than through all the latter past years, with but the very recent exception, permitted by the accidental and temporary division of the northern section and party. The President was now invested with the authority, and the means, for all the military and naval forces which were deemed necessary, and was provided with funds, (by loan and issue of treasury notes,) for the early expenditures. Besides large additions ordered for the navy, the President was authorized to increase the regular army, if deemed necessary, to 60,000 men, and to call on the states for militia, or to accept the services of volunteers, to any number not exceeding 250,000.

In the north-eastern states, and especially in all their great cities, there have been already great losses, and which are added to daily, suffered by the rich, and in every branch of trade, manufactures, and navigation interests—and there is general suffering of the unemployed and destitute poor classes. The sequestration of forty millions of debt due by the seceded southern states, was the first and great cause of loss, which brought bankruptcy to hundreds of the heaviest dealers, and heavy losses to thousands, especially in the cities of Boston, New York, and Philadelphia, and throughout the New England states. Next came the beginning of the subsequent entire cessation of the purchase of northern fabrics, and of the employment of northern vessels, by the seceded states. In addition, the supply of cotton for the use of the numerous northern factories had been diminished by one-half, compelling the discharge of half the hands before employed, and permitting only reduced wages for those still retained. But this reduction of operations, if it had not been compelled by the deprivation of the raw material, would have followed the loss of their former southern market for the fabrics, and the loss of the large sequestrated portion of their trading capital, without which they could not have bought cotton in former quantity, and paid the former amount of other current expenses of their business. There are now thousands of unemployed poor in every great northern city, suffering with want, and destitute and hopeless, who are too many to submit to die of hunger. They must be given food, or they will take it by force. * * * * * * *

LETTER XXVIII.

Measures for Defence, and Progress of War Events in the South.

WASHINGTON, April 17, 1868.

In addition to the peculiar topographical and natural features of the southern sea coast, which, of themselves, afford such strong means for defence against hostile invasion, their defensive operations and effects were much increased by some political influences, which had previously been entirely adverse to the southern states, and were among the results of the partial and oppressive rule of the North. One of these was the previous general neglect, and in some cases, entire abandonment, by the federal government, of the fortifications formerly constructed to protect southern sea-ports. This enabled the seizing, in every such case, by the very early action of the several southern states, (as before narrated of Fort Sumter, and generally with much more ease,) of nearly every still retained fortification—and the selection and occupation of the best sites for other new structures, which sites had been formerly fortified, but since dismantled and abandoned by the federal government. Of the latter description, among others, were forts St. Philip and Jackson, which, on opposite sides of the Mississippi, served to guard the entrance and ascent of that great river. The forts which had not been dismantled, or entirely abandoned, but which were easily surprised and taken possession of in the first movements after the secession, were not only in good condition for defence, (except for wanting garrisons,) but also were generally well provided with cannon, and in some cases with other material for either military or naval warfare. All these sites, after being seized and occupied by southern forces, were forthwith strengthened by new and sufficient earth-work and other fortifications—and these labors were speedily performed by thousands of slaves who were readily obtained and employed for this purpose, and of whom any greater number could have been had, if needed. This resort is another very important means for defence, possessed by these southern states.

But all these means for defence might have been of little service, if the necessary talent to direct the use had not also been provided, and that too by another constitutional act of northern oppression on the South. By the policy, before stated, of the federal administration, of driving southern officers from the military and naval service, nearly every one had before resigned his commission in the United States service. These officers, not only as southerners and patriots were equally ready with others to defend their country, but many were still out of employment, and all were sore and smarting under the unjust and insulting treatment to which they had been subjected by northern domination. Hundreds of such officers, from all the slaveholding states, had hastened to offer their zealous services to the southern confederacy; and, when there was no vacancy suited to their former rank, they were ready to act in any subordinate station. Every camp and garrison had the aid, in command or for instruction, of excellent officers of this description, who, by their experience and knowledge, soon supplied much that was necessarily deficient in raw troops. Especially useful were the officers of engineers and artillery. Under their direction, and with the unlimited resources of slave labor, the essential fortifications were rapidly constructed, and their cannon, if too few, were soon served by the best skill of gunnery. Fort Moultrie and Castle Pinckney at Charleston, and Forts Barancas and Pickens, which guarded Pensacola and its important Dock Yard, were the only old fortifications still held in the South by the northern power.

With such excellent aid of good officers, the southern congress have ordered the organization of a small regular army, mostly of artillery. As fast as recruited, so far, these regulars have been sent to man the forts, or new fortifications, or to replace volunteer militia acting as artillery men. This most important service, and especially in constructing fortifications, requires the highest order of talent for the command and direction, and of skill, experience, and discipline, in the subordinate officers and the gunners and a few other soldiers. But most of the inferior duties may be soon performed by any ordinary laborers—and when behind strong walls, as little of the courage and discipline of soldiership is required, for the greater number, as of intelligence and military experience. Practical evidence was afforded of this by the commander of Fort St. Philip, who, before being supplied with a sufficient garrison, drilled the negro slaves, who were used as laborers, to aid in part in serving the cannon. And with their mere mechanical aid to the intellect and skill of others, the gunnery was soon excellent. The numerous slaves employed as laborers on the fortifications, are necessarily subjected to some of the forms of military organization; and thus, and otherwise, are accustomed to something of the "pomp and circumstance" of military display. They enjoy it greatly, and soon become as zealous partizans, and as hostile in feeling to the northern enemy, as any citizens—and might well be relied upon as soldiers, unless incapacitated by their natural and constitutional cowardice. But even this worst fault of a soldier is not very important in their station, and behind walls—and perhaps is compensated by the more implicit obedience and perfect subordination of negroes to the authority of white men, as masters or commanders. If necessity shall ever require it, one-half of the garrisons of forts in the South may be made up of negro slaves—and who, however efficient in that department, would thereby learn nothing of military knowledge for the field, or to enable them to act as principals, or which could lessen their subordination and value as slaves. The zealous feelings of patriotism evinced by negro slaves need not excite any wonder or incredulity. The most ignorant and even the most oppressed subjects—as French conscripts and English impressed sailors—who have the least personal interest in their country's success or defeat, are notoriously thus disposed. It has been long ago said, and truly, that the common sailors of the English navy were the most patriotic class in all England. Yet then the greater number were impressed men, and all unjustly and hardly, if not cruelly, treated by their country and government, and who enjoyed less comfort and fewer privileges than the negro slaves of the southern states.

There are also many of the former officers of the United States navy, who, as southerners, were driven from that service, who are not less useful in the service of the southern confederacy than the officers of engineers and artillery. In Charleston, and at other places, armed flotillas have been formed, and mainly composed (in the tide-water ports,) of the sequestrated northern merchant vessels. These armed vessels have been fitted out, and are commanded by experienced naval officers, of high grade of ability. These vessels are well suited, in their positions, for harbor defence, or to harrass blockading squadrons.

In some such post or other, of regular or volunteer service, and whether of proper or reduced rank, in command or as instructors, or, if not in their former line of service, in some other, nearly all of these excellent officers are now zealously serving the southern cause. And probably no newly recruited troops anywhere, even for regular service, are as well officered and instructed as are most of the volunteers of the South now in the field, and in consequence of this source of instruction, added to that furnished in the state military schools.

Though the southern states have very few sailors, all of these few were ready to serve on the flotillas—and the services of as many more as were needed were urgently offered by the foreign sailors, and even by many of those of the northern states, who had composed the crews of the northern sequestrated vessels and who had since been retained as prisoners on parole, or in easy confinement. Some of the former masters, and other officers of these vessels, though northerners by birth, have applied to the authorities to be commissioned as privateersmen, in the service of the southern confederacy. The resorting to this general policy is yet under consideration. Should extreme measures of the invading enemy make it expedient and proper, the resort to privateering by the South will be a blow of tremendous force, which cannot be retaliated on them, as they have no shipping or property on the ocean to be captured or destroyed. In this view, the former monopoly of all foreign and coast-wise navigation by the northern states, (built up by the government bounty system,) unjust and costly as it has been heretofore, is now one of the greatest means of safety for the southern states, and also for the most effectual offensive warfare against the northern states. For, in a war of privateering and attack on commercial vessels, it is not the country having the richest commerce and most numerous merchant marine, that is the most powerful, but the reverse. The southern states, having no commercial shipping, have nothing to lose by naval captures. But, they can authorize and commission hundreds of private armed vessels, which will find many and rich prizes in the thousands of northern merchantmen that are still sailing on every sea, and to every port of the commercial world. And as the exports and imports of the southern confederacy will be transported, (during the continuance of the war,) exclusively in European vessels, which will easily evade the blockading squadrons, and may even forego the use of all the blockaded harbors—then the whole carrying trade will, as now, belong to Europeans, and will not be subject to capture at sea, in any case, or beyond the distance of a few miles from the ocean shore of the southern confederacy.

The trade, as of all other amicable relations, between the seceded and the border slave-holding states continues as previous to the secession, except that no commodities are allowed to be bought from these states which were manufactured or produced north of the slave-holding states, or, if brought from abroad, which had paid duty to the northern federal treasury. The increased demand, to supply all the southern consumption, of southern manufactures of cotton and wool, &c., has greatly increased the business and prosperity of all southern factories, and to equal extent, has damaged or lessened the sales of northern fabrics, and northern importations from the old world.

LETTER XXIX.

Political affairs in Virginia. Military preparations and movements of northern troops. Obstacles to invasion of the southern seaboard.

WASHINGTON, April 28th, 1868.

The legislature of Virginia, has adjourned, after some action suited to recent and prospective political affairs, but which was so much exceeded and overshadowed by other proceedings of mere words—in strong "southern rights resolutions," violent denunciation of northern aggressions, and threats of resistance ("at all hazards, and to the last extremity,") to the next *future* act of aggression that shall occur, and especially to the consummation of the indicated design to abolish slavery—that what was done is lost sight of under the loud-sounding of the "brave words" proclaimed. But, though, according to the long usage of this legislature, (and the policy established by the influence of the federal office-seekers,) all that was done and said, was for future application, and nothing for already passed wrongs, still there were some legislative measures which may be important. These were, the better organization and arming of the militia, and especially of volunteer companies and "minute men," in reference to their most speedy and effective service when called out. Rail-road companies were prohibited, under stringent penalties, from conveying any troops, or military armament, through Virginia, except those of the state, or by special authority of the governor. And though there was no direct enactment made, or even proposed, to prevent the marching of United States troops through the state, to assail any seceded southern state, yet there has been such expressions of opinion on that subject from the people, that it is understood that Governor S., will deem himself fully authorized to prevent the passage of federal troops, in any manner, over the soil of Virginia, for such a purpose. This determination has been unofficially, but clearly, made known to President Seward.

The more effective action, and stronger determination of the legislature of Virginia, were not appreciated, nor regarded as of any importance by the northern people, or their general government. Therefore, no attention was paid, either to the acts or the words, except as to the opposition to the passage of northern troops. It was deemed politic and expedient to respect this feeling and professed determination, lest a different procedure by the federal government might awaken popular feeling and patriotism, and serve to unite Virginia heartily with the seceded states. As to every other recent resolution and threat of the legislature, and its ordered military preparations, all were deemed but as repeated and scarcely varied performances of the long played game of "bluster and back-out," for which Virginia had acquired an unfortunate celebrity, and, by the northern people, was supposed incapable of carrying out any more effective policy for defence. For this reason, the firmer attitude lately assumed by Virginia, did not operate to alter any previously designed measure of the federal administration, unless as to the matter of troops passing through the state.

It is reported that the veteran regular troops, stationed at various posts in the remote western territories east of the Rocky Mountains, were long ago ordered to move eastward, and must now be far on their way. They will descend by steamers and other boats, according to local convenience, either the Missouri or Arkansas, to concentrate on some point on the Mississippi river, where they will meet a large force of militia, provided under the late law of Congress. 10,000 militia have been called out for this purpose from the states of Ohio, Indiana and Illinois. Also requisitions have been made on Kentucky for 1000 militia, and on Tennessee for 2000, to be encamped in the latter state on the bank of the Mississippi river. It is conjectured by some of the southern members of Congress now in Washington, that these requisitions are made on Kentucky and Tennessee, mainly for the purpose of testing the public sentiment in these border slave-holding states, and to know how far they may be relied upon for loyalty and obedience to the federal government, and when called upon to act in opposition to the revolted states. Kentucky and Tennessee, notwithstanding their many complaints against the action of the North, and the federal government, had not ceased to assert their continued devotion to the Union, and their rejection of the southern doctrine of the legal right of state secession, and their abhorrence of illegal and revolutionary state-resistance to the federal government.

Of the larger portion of the regular army, before distributed in various forts and stations in the Atlantic and mostly in the northern states, 3000 regulars are stationed in Washington, and 5000 in Baltimore, most of both corps being of infantry. In Philadelphia there were 7000, among whom were nearly all the cavalry and artillery of the whole forces. More than half of these 15000 soldiers are new recruits, enlisted in the northern cities.

The destination of these troops which are now in the east, as well as of those ordered from the far west, is evidently for the southern seceded states—but the route of the troops now in the eastern posts is doubtful. For these, the passage by sea would be speedy and easy to the southern sea-coast. But land forces are not needed for the blockade service—and, if placed as garrisons in forts on the coast, they would be of but little use, unless to be employed for offensive operations, and systematic invasion and occupation of the country. That course might be more or less successful, in overcoming the opposing force of raw militia, and seizing and holding neighboring positions to be attacked in succession, as desired. But such service, in a country so much intersected with deep rivers with miry bottoms, and large swamps, would be very uncertain in results, and hazardous, even in merely a military point of view. But, further, the coast lands of the farther southern, and of all the seceded states, and of the low country of South Carolina, especially, (except in large cities and places on the open ocean beach,) are, even as early as in May, unhealthy for the old residents, and will soon be pestilential to strangers newly arrived from the northern states—and they will continue as unhealthy as late as to November. I am not in the confidence of any officer of the army, or of the government—but I infer, confidently, from these considerations, that the route of the troops designed for invading the southern confederacy will not be by sea, or, by any other route, at any earlier time, to the low lands of the southern Atlantic or Gulf states.

LETTER XXX.

Surrender of Fort Moultrie.

WASHINGTON, May 1st, 1868.

The slow but sure operation of the blockade of Fort Moultrie has at last been completed. When the scant stock of food of every kind had been almost exhausted, and without any hope remaining of new supplies, after many deaths caused by disease, and when half the remaining garrison were sick from the severe privation of their situation, Col. T., was compelled to surrender Fort Moultrie, without terms of capitulation. Of course, the garrison became prisoners of war, and the armament, &c., of the fort, prize to the captors. Castle Pinckney, happened by accident to have been much better supplied with provisions at first. On this ground, and also because of its undoubted means for great injury to the city—which, however, were not used previously, and which the commander will scarcely now dare to attempt —he holds out for more favorable terms of capitulation. These demands have been refused—and a surrender at discretion only will be admitted. Probably this state of things, and the inconvenience or danger of Castle Pinckney alone still obstructing the free use of the upper harbor, and threatening the city, will not be much longer submitted to; and that more speedy means than starving out the garrison will be resorted to.

Fort Moultrie was immediately garrisoned by the victors. Then the command of both channels, and the whole passage was complete, and the defence deemed secure against any naval attack.

LETTER XXXI.

Commercial Difficulties of the South, and their compensations. Northern Sufferings, Mobs, and Sanguinary Riots.

WASHINGTON, May 14, 1868.

The very important events which have occurred since early in May, were all at first so doubtful, and were also so continuous and connected for some weeks, that I preferred not to comment upon them, until I could (as I always aim to do in these letters,) be sure to report the facts correctly. At no time do I seek to state reports of occurrences very early, as they are almost always at first but partially correct, are generally grossly exaggerated, and sometimes wholly false. The unusual postponement of my present notes of latter events, will enable me to treat of them more methodically, and in connexion, for each of the important separate scenes or subjects, of which the principal occurrences have already been learned by your readers who feel any interest in these affairs.

The suffering of the many unemployed poor of the northern cities, and of the manufacturing villages and country, and the much more extended complaints, continue to increase. Only the beginnings of troubles have yet been felt—they are such that the continued progress, and the still growing weight and suffering to be produced, can well be foreseen; while there is presented no prospect, or means, for relief, short of the renewal of the former friendly relations with the southern states, and the main customers and employers of northern industry—or otherwise the complete subjugation of these states, and their unresisting submission to northern control and domination for the future. So far, the attempted blockade of all the southern ports has had but little of the designed stringent effects. The duties collected for the northern government by the floating custom-houses, have been very inconsiderable. Foreign goods are now sent to the South in small vessels, and enter some of the many shallow harbors which are not, and cannot be, regularly blockaded—and these pay duties to the southern confederacy, if there is a custom-house established, or otherwise are smuggled in at other unfrequented landing places, without paying any duties. The cities and former commercial marts are indeed much damaged by the loss of their former trade. But numerous other before unusual landing places, and the routes for transportation to them, receive nearly as much new business and profit. The commodities exported and imported, between the southern confederacy and Europe, are not lessened more than one twentieth below the former amount of all the exports and imports—and all the increased charges cannot equal another twentieth of the whole expenses. And much of this new expense will go to establish a most profitable new trade, and great trading capital and business, in the free port and *entrepot* of Bermuda, and others of less importance in New Providence, Martinique, and St. Thomas. And though these two-twentieths of loss would alone be very heavy to the blockaded states, it is nearly compensated by new and incidental benefits. One of these is found in the general patriotic feeling and spirit which encourage and enable the people to bear privations of former enjoyments of mere luxuries, not only without complaint, or pain, but with emulation and pride, and actual gratification. It is now deemed an honorable and laudible sacrifice to patriotism, to cut off every use of imported commodities, and especially of all of northern production, which can be dispensed with, or of which the use served to gratify only the love of display and ostentation, or effeminate luxury. The pride before indulged in enjoyments or expenses of these kinds, is now better ministered to, in sacrificing luxury and display to the cause of patriotism. When *public opinion* and *fashion* will permit, people can be, as those of the South now are, as comfortable and as happy, with plain and cheap clothing and food, and at half the expense for their living, as if at double the expense, and with every gratification for mere luxury and show. Thus, a people so constrained by a foreign enemy, and meeting and preventing the inflictions by economy and patriotic self-denial, may even be gainers by their losses. But further—while thus voluntarily dispensing with every supply from the hostile northern states, the result of that condition is to offer greatly increased demand and better prices and profits, to every manufacturing establishment in the new confederacy, or in the other neighboring slave-holding states, with which states products are still exchanged without impediment from political divisions. Much of the cotton of the southern confederacy, by rail-roads, is sent to the sea-ports of North Carolina and Virginia, and thence shipped to Europe, or partly to the northern states. In the meantime, new passages for transportation to safe, though shallow ocean-harbors, are continually being opened to use, and increased in number. There are now several such used in side-outlets from the lower Missisippi, (as through Achafalaya, Lake Pontchartrain, &c.,) besides the main channel of the river—and all of which cannot be kept always closed, or even watched, by the most vigilant blockade to be effected by the small navy of this country.

Added to the loss of trade of the northern states, is the want of employment for their shipping, in place of the virtual monopoly formerly enjoyed of all the southern carrying-trade. And worst of all, are the effects now felt by the merchants and manufacturers of the North of the forty millions due them from the South, and sequestrated by the government of the new confederacy, for as long time as the war shall continue.

It is reported that as many as one-fourth of all the usually laboring and self-supporting poor of the great northern cities, and throughout the manufacturing rural districts, are now paupers and beggars, and supported gratuitously by the rich, or those able to contribute. And the 30,000 to 40,000 able-bodied men of this class, who burden and terrify each of the great cities of Philadelphia, New York and Boston, are not meek and humble, but sturdy and insolent beggars, who already presume upon their numbers, and supposed physical power, and will not be denied abundant means for support in their state of idleness. Large contributions, made by all persons who are able to contribute, and which, by the existing circumstances, are not voluntary, but compulsory, do not lessen the complaints and murmurs, and in many cases threats, of those who enjoy them—or induce any expression of gratitude or satisfaction. Everything that may be required, or extorted, to supply the unemployed or willingly idle poor, is deemed by them as simply their right—and that thanks and praise are due to themselves that they are thus content to live on little of the offal food, or surplus wealth, of the rich, instead of their seizing an equal share of their superabundance of riches. There are daily assemblages, or processions of the unemployed poor, in the cities where they are most numerous, to show their numbers and strength to the rich, as a significant warning. On one late occasion such a "hunger procession" of 40,000 men, marched through the wealthier streets of New York, and took especial care to exhibit their strength in the Fifth Avenue of sumptuous palaces, the chief place of residence of the "merchant princes" of that great and rich city.

To hunger processions there soon succeeded hunger mobs and riots, in which food only was seized at first, but in which the actors soon proceeded to plunder other moveable property, and especially money and other valuables. There was general consternation among all honest people. The regular, and much increased police force being found insufficient, the volunteer militia, the best disciplined and most respectable of the cities, were called out by the mayors, and the rioters were dispersed only by volleys of musketry and artillery, and after the loss of many hundreds of lives. Requisitions for military aid, and defence, were made by the city authorities on the governors of their respective states, and by them on the President of the United States to lend the services of regular troops, and marines, where they were stationed near. The previous withdrawal of all the then embodied United States soldiers from the great northern cities, for distant service in the West and South, seemed to have encourged the first movements of the suffering and dangerous classes. By such vigorous and bloody means, only, were these rioters and plunderers repressed—and forced to sullen and angry submission to the laws. But there was no speedy restoration of the previous feeling of security of property, or even of the lives of property-holders.

These disorders were soon renewed, or broke out in new places, of which Lowell was one. There is already produced, through all the great northern cities, and all the manufacturing parts of the northern states, a line of distinction between the rich and the poor, as separate parties and interests. The poor look upon the rich with malignant hatred, as their worst enemies and oppressors—and the rich, and indeed the small property-holders, look on the poor with feelings of great uneasiness, alarm, or terror. The cessation of riot and plunder is merely a suspension of associated predatory power, and of armed outrage, obtained by the employment of military force—and employed here in as great strength as has yet been required in the southern states, under either the pressure of the present war of threatened invasions or any fears of attempts for servile insurrection. In addition, at this time of war in the southern states, and with a much stronger enemy that threatens the exciting of insurrection of the slaves, there are few southern planters who lock their doors, or bar their windows, at night—and there are none whose houses and property and families, are not, (as always,) through every night, in the trusted charge, and entirely at the mercy, of their own slaves—and in trust of whose care, and loyalty, the owners sleep as free from either alarm or doubt, as they do in reference to possible injuries from their own best friends and near relatives.

Further—there is a very general suspicion in the northern cities that it will not be safe to call into service, to repress riots and to shoot down the rioters, plunderers and incendiaries, any bodies of the ordinary militia of the cities, lest many of these should be as much inclined to side with the plunderers as with the wealthy and plundered parties. The uniformed volunteer companies of the cities, only, have yet been used, which are mostly composed of men of some property, or business, and of respectable position and reputable connections. Further—the lowest and most desperate and villanous of the destitute and lawless class, are every one voters—and, as a class having a common feeling, they exercise great legal influence on elections, and in the building up or pulling down of every political dignitary. Therefore many persons of the higher classes will be disposed to truckle to this mob-power, and, if not absolutely to excuse or defend its enormities, or at least to avoid subjecting its guilty members to the full extent of deserved punishment. It is very certain that if ever the destitute of the great northern cities shall choose to sack and burn them, and, after plundering, to massacre the property-holders, there will be no sufficient restraining power to prevent, either of the city, or the state. And now, if a force of the United States military, numerous enough to be respected and feared, is not kept in or near every city thus exposed to the destitute and desperate classes, the safety of the property and the lives of the wealthy inhabitants will be at great hazard. Under these late circumstances, there can scarcely be any more of the new recruits to the federal army sent soon as reinforcements to the southern states. And it is generally thought that if the recent movements of troops (of which I have yet to speak,) had not been already made to invade the South, it would be much better to have their defensive protection in the Atlantic northern states.

The continued recruiting for the regular army had served to take up thousands of the destitute individuals who composed the desperate and dangerous class of the northern cities. The authorities of the northern cities have latterly begun a course of policy designed to stimulate the enlisting of their dangerous residents, and so relieve the better population of something of their police expense, and their danger. It would be cheaper for the city to pay an extra bounty of fifty dollars to one of this class, to induce him to enlist as a regular soldier, than to continue to support him as a pauper, even if not hereafter as a rioter and robber by open violence. This procedure has been adopted by nearly all the cities—and to the great forwarding of the recruiting service. However, these large contributions were ascribed entirely to patriotic zeal, and nothing was said of the true motive.

LETTER XXXII.

Preparations of Virginia for resistance. Movement of United States troops. Features and difficulties of the north-west routes.

WASHINGTON, May 20, 1868.

Immediately after the defensive enactments of the last General Assembly, the Governor of Virginia had sent orders to the Major and Brigadier Generals of Militia, and also to the Colonels of all the regiments, to be vigilant and careful in forwarding the discipline, and preparation for service, of the militia under their respective commands, and especially of the volunteer companies and minute men. It was also then ordered that if any United States troops, without having the authority of the Governor, should attempt to pass over the territory, or on the rivers of Virginia, they should be stopped, and turned back, by any military officer of the state having means to enforce the order—and such officer was authorized, if his command was disobeyed, to use any available measures of war to compel obedience.

The federal administration did not doubt its ability to march its troops through Virginia, by any desired route—or, if necessary, easily to conquer and humble the state, despite of all the resistance that might be either threatened or attempted. But the first and great object of the President was to invade and subjugate the already revolted states, and as soon as possible. And, until that was done, he wished to avoid forcing any other state into open revolt, and increasing the number of actual enemies—or the changing the scene of war from the territory of the more southern states to that of Virginia. Therefore he did not choose directly to disregard and oppose the avowed determination of that state in this respect, and hazard its armed resistance, by marching troops upon its soil, and in open defiance to its prohibition. But it was not deemed objectionable, but, on the contrary, very desirable, to evade and frustrate all the obstacles threatened to be opposed by the authorities of Virginia; and, if it could be effected, to pass troops, by surprise, over her territory before it could be opposed, or even known to any parties who could oppose obstacles to the movement. It was thought that this might be easily done over a railroad, by proper arrangement and concert with its authorities, they being entirely favorable—and the troops could be thus transported across the state, and beyond its farther boundary, before any effective effort could be made to obstruct them. If this could be effected, the success would entirely defeat, or frustrate the designed opposition of Virginia, without permitting it to be commenced in action. And no further action, in the case, was expected from the foiled and humiliated state, when further opposition and hostile action could bring no redress. The attempt, to be made on the Baltimore and Ohio Railroad, was further encouraged because the law of Virginia forbidding the transportation of troops on the railroads of the state, was found to be defective in its application to this road, which, though running partly through Virginia was the property of a Maryland corporation. The company, at any rate, would incur only the payment of a heavy pecuniary penalty, which the United States government would discharge—and the functionaries would escape the heavier personal responsibility and corporeal punishment, which the President and other officers of a state road would incur.

On the morning of May 8th, without any previous notice

to the public, all the 7000 regulars, stationed in Philadelphia, were moved off, upon special trains, on the railroad to Pittsburg on the Ohio—taking along the horses for both the cavalry and field artillery, and the guns, and wagons. Of this body of 7000 men, 2000 consisted of cavalry and 800 of artillery. Secret notice and orders had been given to the railroad authorities only, so as to bring together a sufficient number of trains for the entire transportation at one trip. All necessary arrangements of the troops had been made in the course of the preceding night, and the movement had been made from the camp, and was fully in progress on the route, before the intention was known in the city, or to the public. With precautions and arrangements still more carefully concealed from the public, in the afternoon of the same day, 2000 of the 3000 in Washington, and the 5000 from Baltimore were brought together on the railroads from these cities, on special trains, which, having joined near Baltimore, proceeded together westward on the Baltimore and Ohio Railroad, with all possible speed, and without any stoppages that could be avoided. The trains entered the territory of Virginia, near Harper's Ferry, after dark. The journey being thus begun without any notice or publicity, and the part in Virginia mostly made in the night, and by special trains, this important movement was made without its being understood even along the route, so long as night concealed the trains.

It is now necessary to describe other circumstances, for the purpose of explaining subsequent occurrences—and especially to indicate the remarkable topographical features of the broad north-west region of Virginia embraced between the summit ridge of the Alleghany mountains and the Ohio river. Almost every part of this region is not only mountainous, but much of the surface is extremely steep, and the valleys are deep, and usually so narrow as to offer but little width of level bottom. Very many of these valleys are merely mountain gorges, and their bottoms, defiles, narrow and winding; and in some cases they continue so for miles in length, and also bordered on both sides by very steep mountain sides, rugged with huge projecting rocks, and overspread by tall and dense forests in their original state. Almost every bottom is the passage-way of a rapid stream, of sizes varying from rivulets in the smaller, to rivers of considerable volume in the larger valleys—and all of which either meander throughout their courses, from the dashing against, and being repelled by, the steep mountain side, or precipice, on one side, to the like meeting on the opposite side—or otherwise entirely filling the bottoms of the narrower gorges and defiles. The country is generally fertile, even on steep mountain sides. There is but a small proportion of the land yet cleared, and still less is under tillage, as grass is usually the preferred growth. The distance from markets, and the scarcity of good roads, and still more the scarcity of labor, have prevented much extension of tillage, except on the border of the Ohio. The proximity to the anti-slavery states, Pennsylvania and Ohio, and the facility of escape to them, have caused slaves to be very insecure property here. Consequently, there are but few slaves, even compared to the very sparse white inhabitants, who are more generally graziers of cattle on the uncleared mountain lands, than tillers of the soil—and the poorer class are much more addicted to hunting than to obtaining a living by either tillage or pasturage.

Because of the small number of slaves held in this region, and of the small proportion of persons who own any, it has been heretofore believed by many southerners, and by all northerners, that the people generally were hostile to the institution of negro slavery—and that, in any contest thereupon, they would be much more inclined to side with northern than southern views. This erroneous belief had much weight to induce the federal administration to send troops through this portion of Virginia, in which, if unexpectedly delayed, they would be among a population supposed entirely friendly to the federal government, and to the North. This opinion perhaps was generally correct as to the narrow northern extension of Virginia, vulgarly termed the "Pan-handle" which lies between Pennsylvania and Ohio. But the people of much the larger portion of the great residue of this region, are sound and true southerners.

The only natural practicable routes for travel, and these always difficult, and which served as the tracks for the subsequently used and wretched paths and roads, were along the bottoms of the valleys—and crossing the mountain ridges only at depressions, or over the more gentle acclivities. The few later turnpike roads, all constructed at the expense of government, and the still later railroads, in pursuing straighter routes, and crossing the mountain ridges, and the streams in the valleys, have had to encounter and overcome formidable difficulties. The Baltimore and Ohio Railroad in its course through Virginia, and especially from the Alleghany ridge for many miles westward, is a succession of passages along the bottoms of narrow valleys, bordered by steep, rugged, and forest covered mountain sides—or, more usually, the track is elevated high up the sides of such steeps, and running on a narrow excavated shelf, bordered in many places below by precipices, barely far enough from the track to permit safe passage. Deep artificial cuts, and high and long and narrow-topped embankments, for the track, in other places vary the character of the difficulties, and the liabilities and facilities for obstructing the road-way. But worst of all, for the passage of a hostile army, are many subterraneous tunnels, excavated for the road-way through the crossing high ridges, or projecting spurs of mountains.

The Baltimore and Ohio Railroad from Baltimore to the Ohio at Benwood on the Ohio, (a few miles below Wheeling,) is 375 miles. A branch connected with this track, the North-Western Railroad, 104 miles long, diverges from the main route at Grafton, about 85 miles from the Alleghany summit, and runs to Parkersburg on the Ohio, 91 miles below Wheeling. Besides these two railroads to the Ohio, there is a state turnpike, and an excellent road, from Romney in Hampshire to Parkersburg. This, for most of its route, from Cheat river westward, is not anywhere far from the North-Western Railroad, whose use, since its construction, has nearly superseded that of the older turnpike road. The natural features of the routes of these two roads, and the many facilities for their being obstructed, are much the same with those already stated of the main route.

So much for the general features of all these roads, and the many facilities for obstructing the passage, if attempted by even a feeble enemy. But the United States administration, and the military commander, Gen. W., feared no obstacles, not only because of the supposed loyalty of the inhabitants to the general government, but still more because the passage, from Baltimore to the Ohio river, had been so well arranged and prepared for, that it could be completed in twenty hours—and all the earlier and doubtful portion of the journey, through Virginia, would be made in the night, and would not be made known in advance of the passage of the trains to any but a few of the higher functionaries of the railroad company, and not even to them earlier than three days in advance. Upon these different grounds, this route was selected for the invasion of the state of Mississippi—and the movement was commenced in the afternoon of May 10th, as before stated.

LETTER XXXIII.

A Guerilla Officer, and his Preparations for Service.

WASHINGTON, May 22, 1868.

Among the hundreds of southern officers of the United States army and navy who, some years ago, were excluded from active service and all command, and from full pay, because they were not abolitionists, was J. M., then captain of artillery. He was a graduate of the West Point Military Academy, an admirable officer, devoted to the duties of his profession, and especially to the artillery department of the military service. He was too poor to resign his commission, as most other southern officers had done when thus degraded in position. But he was also too indignant and impulsive to submit in silence. He imprudently uttered his opinion of the conduct of his superior officer, and the administration, in such offensive, though true words, that he furnished grounds for damaging him still more. He was tried by court-martial, for disrespect to his superiors, and insubordination, and cashiered. He then returned to his native town of Wheeling, and was soon offered, and was glad to accept, the office of superintendent of transportation for the western end of the Baltimore and Ohio Railroad which duty he had since well performed. M. had always been one of those far North-West Virginians, who, being entirely opposed to northern abolition sentiments and action, were made the more violent in this opposition, and hatred, because of being surrounded by so many abolitionists—who made up a very large proportion of the 20,000 inhabitants of Wheeling and of the country portion of the narrow "Pan-handle." None were more ardent in southern principles, and in patriotism, than the true Virginians who were thus placed in contact with the almost only abolitionists of Virginia, or of all the slaveholding states. To the highest degree of this feeling of M. was added the influence of his strong resentment for his own ill-treatment and disgrace, all causing intense hatred for the Abolitionist party, and the northern section. Added to this, the man who had been the colonel of his former regiment, and the mover and cause of M's trial and sentence, and also an active tool of the government in carrying out the general iniquitous policy then adopted, was now Gen. W., and commander of the army at Baltimore and Washington.

The cashiering of M., for the known cause, served to add still more to the high estimation of his friends and all who knew him and approved his sentiments. Though his abolitionist neighbors fully returned his hatred for them, even they did not prevent the general award by public opinion to M. of the well deserved character of a gentleman of great worth, and a man of great mental and physical ability. He availed himself of the high consideration of many of his townsmen to gratify his military taste and zeal. He had raised a volunteer uniformed artillery company, of which he was appointed captain, and which he delighted to drill and train, and had brought to a high degree of discipline and skill. This company being full, the example was followed in the forming of another, of which both the officers and privates emulated and approached the merit and the success of their predecessors. Subsequently, M. was appointed colonel of the regiment, which included three volunteer rifle companies, as well as the two of artillery. In zealously and ably performing the duties of this higher military rank, he did not the less continue to serve, with diligence and delight, as before, and so far as his private business and duties permitted, in training and instructing the artillery companies.

The general of the militia brigade in which M's regiment was included, was also a resident of Wheeling. Gen. B. also was a good and zealous officer, though without any experience of actual service—and who reposed great confidence in Col. M. They both, in common with all other officers of like rank, had very recently received the private orders of the governor before stated, and which had especially commanded that the entrance or passage of any other than state troops, and without authority from the governor, should be stopped, if possible—without bloodshed and peaceably, if the prohibition should be obeyed, but, if disregarded, after notice, the proposition to be enforced by any needful force and military action.

Very soon after the military order, M. as superintendent, received from the president of the railroad company, in Baltimore, secret orders to such purport as was necessary for his preparing for, and facilitating the safe and certain transportation of so numerous a line of special trains, from

Baltimore to the Ohio, that he was sure that the design must be to transport a United States army. Here was a difficulty presented to the mind of the heretofore faithful functionary of the railroad company, and to the patriotic military officer of the state. His different duties were placed in painful conflict. To be faithful to one, he must be treacherous to the other trust. He did not long hesitate to decide for complying with the higher duty, and, in his military capacity, to serve his state and obey its authorities. And this he could not do in this case, to any effect, unless he availed himself of the power which he possessed over the affairs of the railroad company. To this course he brought his determination, though with much compunction. He provided every thing required by the superior functionaries at Baltimore, and sent on all the required trains. But after making all these arrangements, then, as a military officer, having also direction of the western portion of the railroad, he made such other arrangements as he deemed best adapted to fulfill the governor's order to stop and turn back the United States army—but still with such precautions as would prevent, as much as possible, damage to property or life, provided resistance to the orders should not be attempted. In that event, he designed using any measures of offence, and of destruction, which the laws and usages of war justified, and which the effecting his objects might require. To public duty was added the incentive of private hatred to urge the defeat of Gen. W's bold adventure.

Col. M's inferences, and his plans, were communicated to his superior officer, Gen. B., only, and in confidence, and met with his full approval and concurrence, and received his authority for any measures for which it might be needed. Provisions and ammunition and all necessary munitions for the service in view, were secretly provided. The first company of artillery, (lately M's own,) and the three rifle companies were paraded immediately after day break on the morning of the day in the afternoon of which the army trains were to leave Baltimore. It had been given out the day before that a military parade, and excursion on the railroad were designed, for which every man was to come fully equipped for camp duty for three days. This notice had prevented surprise being caused by the movement, or the appearance of mystery. The four field pieces of the artillery company were placed separately on as many strongly floored cars, constructed and used for transporting earth and stone for repairs and improvements of the road. The sides of these, and also beneath the carriages of the cannon, were piled a large number of thick planks, which had been prepared for flooring bridges. The four military companies, with their arms, and also 100 spare muskets, and the needed tools, provision, ammunition, &c. were placed on as few other open and light cars as would contain their mixed freight —of which the men were seated in close order on temporary benches, made of the like thick planks. The only locomotive engine which had been left, drew this train, and which was soon on its way, with Col. M. in command. Very early in the morning, and in advance of the train, he had sent on a trustworthy subaltern on foot, to cut the telegraph wire at a short distance from Wheeling, and to do the like farther on, when overtaken by the train. Gen. B. had as early caused the secret cutting of the wires on all the other telegraph lines leading from Wheeling—so as to prevent their being used for at least twelve hours thereafter.

At the last station on the designed extent of the journey, Col. M. had the locomotive engine placed in the rear of the short train of cars, so as to propel them ahead of the engine, for the short remainder of the way.

A few miles west of Cheat river, among sundry other places of high embankments, deep cuts, passages along and high up steep mountain sides, subterraneous tunnels, and other points where the passage could be easily obstructed, and where fifty brave and well armed men could stop, and for a time repel, thousands, there is one place of especial importance and marked features. It is a narrow and deep gorge, forming a chasm, (or "gulf,") with very precipitous sides. The depth is nearly 200 feet, and the width of the gorge at top is not much more than its depth. This is in the passage of the Briery mountain, an out-lying and parallel ridge of the main Alleghany range. The railroad crosses the gorge at right-angles to its direction and over an iron bridge, which, strong as it was, could easily be removed in part, in separate sections, and in a very short time, by applying proper skill and tools. The gorge extends to and empties into Cheat river, which flows in sight from, and deep below the road, though much farther off then appeared to the eye.

It was not until well advanced on the route, that the subordinate officers and privates were informed of the character of the adventure in prospect, and the duties required of them. They were found to be ready, and zealous, for the service, as had been confidently expected by the commander. As soon as arriving near to the bridge, the train was stopped, and the preparations commenced and urged on. First, a section of twenty feet of the bridge (all of open iron-work,) and the rails for the same, were unscrewed, and loosed, so that they could be quickly lifted, but were still left in place, for passing on foot. About two hundred yards eastward of the bridge, the general side embankment of the deep cut in which the road was laid, for the purpose of carting earth away during the excavation, had been levelled, so that for a small space the roadway was level with the outside surface of the ground. At this place, the rails were taken up from their straight and connected course, and re-laid in a gentle curved direction, making a "turn out," which would necessarily conduct off the track any cars coming from the eastward. The loose earth forming the artificial surface outside of the new "turn-out," was levelled, and cleared of stones, so as to make as safe a place as possible for the perhaps necessary overturning and wrecking of a train. This being done, the working party returned to aid the operations on the other side of the gorge, after removing the twenty feet of the passage-way of the bridge. The passage was still preserved, for present use, by long and thick planks, doubled for greater stiffness, being extended across the breach, serving for a narrow and fearful footway.

The approach of the railway to the bridge from the east, for some six hundred yards was in a straight line with the direction of the bridge, and through an excavation, (or "cut") of about eight feet of average depth. The earth removed from this cut had been mostly heaped on the margins, making irregular embankments higher than the natural surface a little farther on, where the ascending level of the roadway rose to the natural surface. There the track curved very slightly, so as to prevent its being seen from the bridge. A little farther, the roadway began to rise along the steep and naked mountain side, and was for more than two miles farther generally exposed to view from the roadway west of and near the bridge. To a distant spectator, especially, the passage of a train along this part of the road, clinging as it seemed to the mountain side, appeared awfully perilous. But the careful and excellent structure of the railroad rendered its use here perfectly safe, under any ordinary circumstances; but if, at certain steepest places the track were obstructed by design, and a train in full progress and speed were turned off, and over the precipitous lower side, scarcely a passenger could escape being crushed in the terrific fall.

On the western side of the gorge, and within fifty yards distance, the track of the railroad began a curve, made by slight excavation, the earth and stone removed from which made an embankment between the road and the gorge, and served well for a military breast-work. Behind this bank, and in the curved direction of the track, two of the pieces of artillery were placed, where best protected by the intervening embankment, and where they could fire upon the long stretch of the more distant part of the road. The other two pieces, on their separate platform cars, were brought nearer, and where they could fire on the bridge, and along the straight cut beyond. One of these two cars was placed at the commencement of the curve, and was thus afforded a different line for its firing, and also some protection by the embankment. The foremost car was placed in the straight cut, and in the direct line of the passage over the bridge, and the straight stretch of road-way beyond. Immediately in front of this exposed car and its piece of artillery, and across the deep cut in which it there stood, a low but strong barricade was made, of large stones and earth, easily provided from the high banks alongside. The trunk of a large tree was placed along the ridge of the barricade, making a suitable parapet, of level just lower than the cannon behind. To guard against small arms, the thick planks, doubled, were used to make a wall raised on the floor of the car, and in front of the cannon, leaving a port-hole of sufficient size for convenient and accurate firing. The artillery men all had carbines; and besides there were one hundred muskets, and plenty of buck-shot cartridges for them, ready for use, at the battery nearest to the bridge.

The ground adjacent to the station of the forward batteries, and rising steeply above the road-way, and the western end of the bridge, was extremely rough, covered with large rocks, both fixed and loose, and by large forest trees. Here, at a later time, and after previous examination and approval of the ground, the three companies of riflemen were stationed, in open and irregular array, or, more correctly, without any order of position, but directed that each man should select and occupy a spot on which he could be as safe as possible, and yet have in the range of his balls the nearest straight stretch of road.

Col. M. had chosen the ground for his different designed operations with perfect acquaintance with the topographical features of the whole route. In his arrangements, he had been as solicitous to guard against the unnecessary destruction of both life and property, if his demands should be complied with, as, in the opposite contingency, he desired to be most effective in destruction, by all available modes of military action. Also, he desired to avoid resorting to any other than legitimate military means, for destroying even declared foes. His great difficulty, in prospect, was not the simple and easy operation of obstructing the advance and passage of the federal army, and to render its present movements futile—but to do this after giving sufficient warning, and without a terrible destruction of life, to be caused by surprise, and in advance of any possible negociation, and of the refusal of the commander to draw back his army, in obedience to the governor's order. It would be absolutely necessary, and also very easy, to turn the first advancing cars off the track—and that without much previous warning. But the stoppage of these, by suddenly checking the full speed of the remainder of the train, and even if on a level surface, would, by the momentum and concussion, crush some of the cars, and probably cause a deplorable destruction of both the cars and their living freight. To prevent such an undesigned result, a lamp affording a bright light, and covered by a red glass globe, so as to give a red light, was elevated above the front of the foremost car, but concealed by a covering cloth, which could be made to fall at any moment. The exhibition of such a red light is the established night signal for danger on the track, and which requires every advancing engine to stop. But this would not be early enough warning to prevent all danger in this place, and for a long train advanceing at full speed. It was however the best means that Col. M. could devise, not to weaken too much the desired means for military coercion and destruction, should he be compelled to resort to them.

All the preparations and arrangements were completed by ten o'clock at night—when the men were ordered to eat, of food previously cooked, and then, except a sufficient guard, all were permitted to sleep, if they could—but every man on his assigned post, and with his arms at hand. The commander took care to keep awake. His post and his particular command and assumed duties, were at the forward battery. He knew when to expect the head of the main train, at from one to two hours before daybreak. But he inferred that there would still be an earlier arrival—of a light engine sent ahead of the foremost train, so as to make the latest possible examination and trial of the safety of the track. For this, he watched with intense anxiety, and ready to uncover the red light as soon as it should be needed.

I will now leave the defensive party, and return to the advancing army trains, of which the setting out was stated some pages back.

LETTER XXXIV.

War Actively Commenced—A Rail-road Battle.

WASHINGTON, May 23, 1868.

Several civil engineers, and some of the most intelligent train conductors, all well acquainted with the route, and some among them also with the neighboring country, were sent by the rail-road authorities to attend the commanding general, and to inform him as to every locality and possible source of danger, before it was reached. And (as Col. M. had supposed,) a light engine car, with its tender, was sent ahead of the foremost train, to examine and test the safety of the track. On the tender was hoisted a lamp, of which the light could be made red, in a moment, if needed to give warning of danger.

A gentle wind from the east, and the perfect stillness of the morning, more than an hour before daybreak, enabled

M., to hear, at an usual long distance, the sound of an approaching locomotive engine. The men were aroused, and ordered to be ready. As the locomotive reached the part of the track on the bare mountain side, its light permitted M., to be sure that no train was attached—and therefore he deemed no other preparation was needed. As the engine rapidly approached, it soon was out of sight in the deep cut of the curve. When it emerged on the straight track and had approached within one hundred and fifty yards of the "turn-out," the red light was fully exposed. The careful engineer immediately, and to the utmost, checked the speed, but could not prevent the car reaching the "turn out," and running off the track, before it stopped, without damage to the three only passengers. These were commanded, under pointed rifles, to deliver themselves as prisoners at the battery, which they reached by crossing the breach upon planks, and which temporary pass-way was then removed by the planks being thrown down the chasm. The captured conductor was the intimate acquaintance, as well as subordinate, of M. They had scarcely time to exchange their main points of information, before the lights of the foremost trains came in sight on the distant mountain side. The advice of the conductor was heard as to the most proper moment to show the red light, (which had been again concealed,) so as to render the first cars unfit for immediate use, but with as little superfluous damage as might be. The lamp was taken below, on the level of the roadway in front of the barricade, so as not to be seen from the still far distant cars, but was exposed to the view of the foremost engineer nearly as soon as he emerged from the deep curve into the straight deep-cut. Instantly the signal, by the whistle, was sounded and repeated through the whole line of trains, to slacken speed and to stop. A short train would have been stopped before reaching the obstruction. But this was so long, and heavily laden, that the momentum of the rear cars pushed on the more forward, and four or five had successively run off the track at the newly made turn-out, before they were stopped by the soft earth into which the wheels sank. The different trains, each drawn by a separate engine, had kept at suitable short distances apart from each other on the route, which, with the signals of danger sounded by the steam-whistles, enabled all to avoid any very violent concussion with the preceding trains. The engine and cars turned off were somewhat damaged, and the engine was upset. The cars were filled with soldiers, who suffered no more than some heavy thumps and bruises from the concussion. As soon as the train was nearly stationary, the laborers and workmen leaped off, and went to learn the cause and character of the accident, and to remedy the disaster. This, as a matter of course, M. expected, and did not desire to hinder the re-uniting of the rails, which could now do no harm to his designs. At the same time a trumpet was sounded for a parley, and a white flag displayed, and a loud voice from the forward battery required that an officer should be sent to the bridge. As soon as an order could be had, an officer bearing aloft a white handkerchief on a ram-rod, as an extemporaneous flag of truce, advanced towards the bridge. On reaching the edge of the gorge, and being stopped by command, as well as by the breach, he demanded to know by what authority the United States troops were stopped, and their safety endangered. Col. M. answered, "They are stopped by troops in the service of Virginia, commanded by Col. J. M., and by order of the governor—by which no other than state troops, or others having the written authority of the governor, will be permitted to cross the the territory of Virginia. I need not ask, for I know already, that these federal troops have no such permission. So far, I have aimed to stop and turn back, but not to damage the troops, or the trains. I could much more easily have precipitated half of these trains into this deep gulf, crushing every car and passenger, than to have turned off the track these foremost cars only, without destruction of life. And at fifty other places, which have been passed over safely, the trains could have been as effectually stopped. But such forbearance will no longer be used, unless my demands are strictly complied with. I require that the trains, except the cars and engine thrown off the track, and all the troops, shall immediately return as they came, on the rail-road, until it enters Maryland; and that afterwards, the troops shall not anywhere enter upon the territory of Virginia, either along this rail-road or elsewhere. I allow to Gen. W. half an hour for the required movement to be begun—and as long for it to be completed from this present stopping place, and to be in progress, as fast as the new circumstances will permit. If these demands are not complied with, within the times offered, or if any other hostile movement is earlier made, I shall fire, and to as much effect as is in my power. My position commands yours, and is impregnable." In addition, a written note, previously prepared, containing the like statement to the commanding general, was delivered, by being tied to a stone, and thrown across the gorge, within reach of the officer, who returned to make his report, and deliver the written communication.

Galling as would have been the defeat of his scheme to Gen. W. in any mode, this was made doubly painful by his being thus braved and defied by a small number (as he rightly conjectured,) of raw militia, and commanded by one who had been his victim, and who also now was, as Gen. W. deemed, doubly a traitor—to his employers and to the general government. However imperative the reasons for his drawing back, and however desperate any chance for forcing his passage, he could not submit without an effort to put to flight, and to punish the insolent enemy, if nothing more effectual could be done. In a hurried conference with the officer who had been at the bridge, he learned that the breach was certainly not more than twenty feet across. On inquiry of the accompanying engineers he was informed that it was barely possible that such an opening might be spanned and crossed over. Upon this information, and with directions for the mode, he hastily resolved to act.

By this time, the functionaries and laborers of the trains had separated the links which connected the cars which were still on the rails from those thrown off, and had replaced and fastened the rails in their former straight course. The cars off the track were ordered to be left, and the soldiers who, with their arms, had made their sole freight, were, by command, sent to the other trains. Gen. W. disdained to return any answer in words, to the offensive demands of his (so-esteemed) ignoble adversary, but was willing to have the answer implied, and to be understood as indicating compliance with the demand. Signals by the steam-whistles were quickly made for all engines and trains to reverse their previous course. The cars of the first train, left now without an engine, were linked to the engine of the next train. Many of the cars were emptied of their passengers, to lessen the draught, and slowly, and in reverse order, the trains moved backward until the one nearest to the battery was concealed by the curve of the cut, and its side heaps of removed earth. A little farther on, the level of the track and of the ground alongside, became even with the track for a space, which was out of sight and protected by the higher bank, from the guns across the gorge. Still farther on, the course of the track began, in gentle and varying curves, to ascend along the bare side of the mountain, and in view, (if the darkness had not forbidden,) from some one or all of the pieces of artillery for the length of two miles.

As soon as all the cars had passed out of the straight cut, and those in the curve were protected from the fire of the battery, two heavy pieces of field artillery were removed from the cars, to the adjacent level ground, and drawn to a position to fire on the hillside where the riflemen were stationed, though the intervening rise of the ground prevented the lower-lying batteries being struck from this place. Both of the pieces were fired quickly, and as fast as they could be reloaded. Luckily, round shot was the only kind then to be readily obtained, which could do little damage at such short distance, compared to grape or cannister shot. At the same time, the then rearmost locomotive engine was detached from the train, and connected, in proper manner for propelling, to the only three cars left westward of the engine. These were platform cars, which are merely floors, made of thick planks held together by a strong frame of timber, and are designed for the conveyance of heavy and rough freights, and had been then used as passenger platforms for soldiers. Their living freight had been removed, and there was no one left, except the engineer on the locomotive behind. The plan was to run some of these connected and empty platform cars, with all the rapidity and force that steam and the engine could give, across the breach in the bridge. And if this could be effected, twenty companies of infantry, now arranged for the purpose, on both sides of the road, and in it in the rear of the light train, were to rush as quickly as possible to the assault. When all preparations had been made, and in a few minutes, for both movements, the engineer jumped off as the engine was started, and the train went on without control, but with the sufficient guidance of the rails directing the wheels, and with all the force that steam could apply to the machinery. As the train started, the soldiers ran after, in the rear, and on both sides of the road, in such disorder as the irregular surface only permitted for their rapid advance.

Col. M. had anxiously and exultingly seen the first success of his stratagem—though still he regretted that Gen. W. had not afforded to him a justifiable occasion by attacking his position, to try the skill of his riflemen, and his cannoneers. He had heard the sound, but could not see (for the darkness,) even through the near straight cut, the first retreating movement of the trains. But the cessation of their noise soon assured him that the motion was stopped. Suspecting that mischief was designed, he called to warn his men, and to order renewed vigilance. Scarcely were his words uttered, before Gen. W's field-pieces were discharged, and not without effect. Two of the riflemen, high up on the hillside, were killed by the first ball, and some others wounded by the flying fragments of the rocks which were shivered by the heavy round shot.

Before the second discharge of the field pieces could be made, the moving portion of the empty train was heard rushing onward at the greatest possible rate of speed. In a moment an awful crash was heard, appalling in sound, and causing the strong bridge to quiver to its farthest abutment. From the near battery, an enormous mass was seen on the bridge and over the breach. The foremost car had shot across the whole breach, but, in passing over the vacancy, it had sunk too low for the wheels to rise upon the floor of the bridge. But the end of the platform floor of the car, and its strong frame, had struck above the surface of the bridge, and was so attached, and thus the car would have been held suspended, and making a firm passage, if it had remained whole. The next car, by the shock of the sudden stoppage of its rapid progress, broke the links connecting it with the foremost, and the wheels rose over the first, and crossed far enough to carry the platform still farther than the first car. The third car, and the attached locomotive engine followed—and though crushed, they still more increased the height and breadth of the mass of ruins. Some burning coals, spilt from the furnace of the overturned engine, gave the first faint light to the scene—and falling through the broken timbers, the fire reached fuel that produced a flame, which slowly and gradually increased. As many soldiers as could find room now rushed upon the bridge, and, with loud shouts, began to clamber over the heaped-up ruins which formed their rough passage-way. All others of the assailants, on the right and left, who could not at first find vacant space on the bridge, were firing across the gorge on the batteries, and wherever they supposed that men were concealed. Those on the bridge had not seen the place before, and did not know half the peril of the adventure; and this ignorance increased their boldness and rashness, beyond the measure of their courage, and obedience to discipline. Not a sound was

8

heard from the battery; nor from the hillside above, except the striking of the balls from the enemy's cannon. The officers of the attacking party began to hope that the position had been evacuated, and that its defenders had retreated. The ruins which made the substituted bridge were covered by the crowd clambering over, and had not yielded in the least to the weight. More than two hundred men had passed over the recent breach, and had reached the solid iron frame and floor of the bridge. As fast as possible for safe footing, they rushed on in close order, and followed by an unbroken stream of men behind. Then Col. M. loudly gave the order to fire. The two foremost pieces of artillery (which only were in range,) were immediately discharged along the line of the bridge and through the living mass that covered it. The pieces had been doubly loaded with cartridges of rifle balls, and the first discharges mowed down half of all the soldiers who had passed over the summit of the rubbish. Now the order was given for the rifles to fire—and first there came from them a general, and afterwards a dropping and sustained fire from hundreds of different places of concealment, on the rocky and wooded and steep slope descending on the western side to the precipice of the gorge. The marks for the riflemen were mostly the soldiers far beyond the gorge, and who in turn fired on the positions of the riflemen, which were indicated only by the flashes of the rifles, but with little effect. Even the cannon shot did but little injury after the accidental effects of their first discharges, as the men there exposed quickly moved to lower and protected places to fire from.

All the soldiers on the bridge, who had not been disabled by the first discharges of cannon, had continued to press on, with fixed bayonets, to the assault. But while enough artillery men were loading for a second discharge sixty others, (most of whom were attached to the two rear guns not then in use,) were ready with muskets loaded with cartridges of buck-shot, to finish the foremost of the assailants. One volley from these most destructive arms, at short distance, left alive and unhurt not one-tenth of all the men who had crossed the breach. To these quarter was offered as prisoners, which they gladly accepted—laying down their arms, and moving, as commanded, to a protected spot, where they were guarded by a few musketeers.

Daylight now began to show, and every minute the riflemen could aim better at their objects across the gorge. The attacking troops had hesitated, and slightly recoiled, after receiving the first murderous discharges. But the urging and the example of their brave officers, and the habits of discipline and obedience to authority, had brought the followers of the first storming party, in increased numbers to attempt the repetition of the desperate service. As the foremost of the assailants were seen passing over the pile of rubbish, a trumpet call was sounded from the battery, and immediately the firing of all the volunteers ceased, and not a sound of any kind was heard on their side. The signal had directed the firing to cease, and it had been made to encourage the enemy again to advance. The officer now commanding and leading the assailants (succeeding to three predecessors, and superiors in rank, who had been killed,) again indulged the flattering hope that the Virginians had retreated. The advanced portion of the storming party was hastened over, and the crowd still in the rear urged onward. The bridge was soon covered with as many soldiers as could obtain footing on its skeleton frame-work and other and more safe but scant flooring. Col. M. having had sufficient trial of his means, was now sure of success in defence, and wished to draw within his fire as many of the enemy as possible, before stopping the living stream then pouring over the rubbish to and on the iron bridge. When the foremost of the dense crowd were within a few yards of reaching the end of the bridge, and the solid road-way, the command to fire was loudly uttered, and was obeyed by both the opposing parties, or by as many of the assailants as were not too much crowded to use their muskets. Their fire, as previously, had but little effect, as it was mostly wasted on the covering barricade and other defences. But the case-shot from the cannon, and the succeeding musketry with buck-shot, opened passages through the crowd on the bridge, and the more distant rifles poured their balls on the survivors, in the short intervals of the nearer firings from the artillery. The killed, and also most of the severely wounded and helpless of the assailants, fell through the open frame of the bridge into the dark abyss below. The survivors on the bridge were again summoned to surrender as prisoners, with the offer of safety, and all who had crossed the breach hastened to accept the offer—and were ordered to come in, and lay down their arms, and join the prisoners previously captured. The firing was suspended for and during this surrender. The bridge, so far as exposed to the fire of the battery, was then clear. But behind the pile of ruins, the soldiers were still crowded, and they were also spread over the track in the rear, and over the elevated ground on both sides. As many as could conveniently handle their arms, kept firing on the places where their foes were covered—and especially on every volunteer whose head was seen exposed above the parapet, or from behind any other defensive cover, for the short time required for his taking aim and firing. But the volunteers were but rarely seen thus exposed, and the balls of their assailants were nearly all wasted.

In the short suspension of firing from the battery when the last prisoners were coming in, the field-pieces were reloaded, but this time with grape-shot. They were discharged repeatedly through the pile of broken cars, and the heavier metal thrown, served, not only to crush them the more, but to kill many of the soldiers beyond, and where previously protected from the smaller cannister shot. But a surer destroyer of the temporary bridge was in progress. The fire, which had increased slowly before, had reached more inflammable and abundant fuel, supplied by the shivered timbers of the cars, and was growing rapidly. The flames soon enveloped the whole mass, and rose so high and became so violent, that the falling sparks and coals were sprinkled over the car of the near battery, and the ammunition cases, threatening every moment the taking fire of the battery, or the explosion of the powder. By great diligence and coolness, as well as prudence and courage of the commander and his men, the burning coals were swept off as fast as they fell, and the imminent peril was passed through without damage, or any loss, except in the firing from the guns being suspended for the time. As the burning weakened the supporting timbers, they began to sink, and very soon the whole flaming mass fell to the bottom of the abyss, with a loud crashing noise, and brightly illuminating, for a short time, the scene of horror which was then presented in the heap of crushed and distorted human bodies. Probably none of these had remained alive after their tremendous fall, to die under later and worse sufferings.

As soon as the substituted bridge was on fire, and its destruction inevitable, nothing more could be done by the assailants, and they were instantly ordered to fall back to the main body of the army.

In the meantime the rifles of the volunteers were continuing their deadly work on the distant regulars, and with much improved effect, as the increasing day-light enabled better aiming at the objects. The danger to the riflemen from the cannon firing, which seemed so great from the destructive effects of the first discharges, was limited to the higher positions. Because of the swell of intervening ground, the enemy's cannon could not be aimed low enough to strike the lower places of cover for the riflemen, which thus were quite safe from this danger, though less favorable for the use of the rifles. A speedy change to lower places of cover for firing, had enabled the riflemen to be subsequently entirely safe from the cannon, which continued harmlessly to throw their balls over their heads.

LETTER XXXV.

Retreat of the Invading Army—and New Preparations.

WASHINGTON, May 24, 1868.

Gen. W. had again consulted with the attendant engineers and others, as to any other means for reaching or assailing the position of the opposing troops; and he had been compelled to abandon the idea, upon the information received. He learned that the only mode for any troops to cross the gorge and reach the battery would be by making a circuit of nearly three miles, extending to, and partly along, the rocky bed of the neighboring part of Cheat river. Of course, the volunteers would know of such a movement, and could retreat in safety, and on the rail-road, before their present position could be thus reached. And as neither the artillery nor wagons could traverse this very difficult circuit, that would render it impossible for the expedition to proceed on its first designed route, even if its continuation would not be obstructed, as it well might and certainly would be, and in many places, by the retreating volunteers. The heavy field-pieces were still being fired, as fast as they could be re-loaded. But the light now permitted to be seen, from the position of the cannon, that they struck too high to do much damage. To move forward far enough to gain a good position for effect, would expose the artillery men to the rifles of the covered volunteers, and to certain destruction. Therefore the General had to submit to the disagreeable resort of ordering the train and army to fall back for present safety, as well as for future operations. The artillery pieces were hastily re-mounted on a car—and the line of trains, lessened by the loss of sundry cars, and lightened by the absence of the hundreds of passengers who had fallen, began its retrograde movement. There was necessity for the speediest retreat, as the trains for two miles would be fully exposed to the cannon of the batteries—and these were already firing upon the most distant trains, which then only were exposed. Still, the circumstances of the trains now moving backward, and pushed on by reversed action, instead of being drawn by the locomotive engines, together with the deficiency of the power of the two engines lost, all compelled slower motion of the trains. There was another and still stronger reason for slow motion, dangerous as was any delay. The balls (now single) from the batteries had already struck several of the distant cars, and had disabled one so much that it had to be detached, and rolled off, to clear the track. If a like mishap, and stoppage of a car should occur with the train moving at the usual rapid speed, the obstruction thus suddenly produced might throw the next following cars off the track, and down the steep mountain side, producing the certain destruction of all the lives of the passengers. Therefore the passage of the trains was necessarily very slow, even when not stopped in part, by cars being disabled, and the necessity for detaching them, and rolling them off the track, which occurred in several cases. In this slow passage, Col. M. and his best gunners, directing the four cannon, and firing round shot, had half an hour of firing at the trains, before they were all out of range—and killed more than thirty soldiers, besides disabling and stopping five cars. One of these was the last in the long line, and on which had been placed, for conveyance, the two pieces of cannon which had been used in the previous action. A lucky ball broke two wheels on one side, and the too-heavily burdened car necessarily stopped. As this and the immediately preceding cars then became the object for all M's. cannon, and the round shot were thrown with improving accuracy at a fixed mark, the position was too dangerous to permit the train to wait for the removal of the cannon from the broken rear car to another. The train-conductor, there in charge, assumed the responsibility of letting loose the links which held attached the disabled car, and sounding the signal to proceed, the train was soon out of sight, leaving on the track the last broken car, and its important freight.

In this engagement, the volunteers had ten men killed,

and eighteen wounded. Of the killed, most were shot through their heads, when firing small arms over the barricade, on other defences of the batteries. The enemy had more than seven hundred killed, and lost nearly one hundred prisoners. The wounded were few in proportion, not exceeding five hundred—and of these there was not one who had passed the breach, unless he was also made a prisoner.

Not much time was required for Col. M. to be assured, by the decreasing sound of the moving trains that the army had retreated, or certainly had removed to some miles distance, at least. He then proceeded to restore his cars to travelling condition, and to prepare the engine for immediate use. At the same time, other long planks were placed across the breach in the iron bridge, and a small party of trusty scouts were sent over to learn and report the movements of the enemy. Among these scouts were some of the neighboring residents and hunters, who had hastened to the first sound of the firing, and had eagerly joined in the latter part of the fighting. These, from their intimate acquaintance with all the neighboring country, were able to render excellent service, as scouts and spies. In a short time one of the party returned to report that the two pieces of cannon were left on a broken car, and could be secured. It was highly desirable to carry these off, not only for their great present value on the Ohio, but as trophies of victory. A sufficient force of men, with their arms, were sent across the bridge, to push one of the displaced platform cars back upon the rails, and along the track to the abandoned artillery. The pieces, by proper appliances were removed to the other car, which was then pushed back to the bridge. This was easy enough, as nearly all the way was a gentle descent. By this time the barricade had been removed, and the displaced sections of the iron bridge restored. As the superstructure of the bridge was entirely of iron, the fire had done it no harm—and the violent concussion had not so much warped the strong frame, as to prevent the safe connection with the displaced sections. The car was carefully and safely brought across with its heavy and precious freight, and then attached to the train. A single section only of the bridge was now again removed, to prevent any passage of a hostile train, but a pass-way of plank substituted for safe crossing on foot. The troops now had food and rest, while waiting for the further reports of the scouts.

This time of necessary detention for the companies was also used to inter, with such solemn testimonials of respect, and of sorrow, as the occasion permitted, the bodies of their comrades who had been killed in the action, and previously in its unwarned and treacherous commencement. The bodies were buried, side by side, on a spot in view of the passage over the bridge, and near to the places where they all died. A huge rock, perpendicular on its lower side, which had served as the breast-work, and imperfect protection, when firing, for some of the killed, was made use of as an appropriate head-stone for the graves.

LETTER XXXVI.

New route taken for the Northern Army in Virginia. Operations on the Ohio. New movement of the Northern Detachment.

WASHINGTON, May 27, 1868.

The commander of the federal army had to choose between three routes. One was northward, to the Pennsylvania line, and thence to the Pennsylvania railroad from Harrisburg to Pittsburg, and by that, when obtaining facilities for transportation, to follow after the northern detachment, which had passed over that route the preceding day. The first and marching portion of this route would be very rough and difficult. The only road to set out upon was on the western side of Cheat river, and a considerable distance off. This road, (from which also the army was now shut out by intervening pathless wilderness,) if reached, would be bad for artillery—and there was no other road practicable for wheel-carriages. Of course, this route could not be attempted.

The next movement considered was to return by the railroad conveyance, as the army had come. But shame forbade this course, amounting as it would be to a confession of utter defeat of the objects of the expedition. In addition, and still stronger objection, the commander inferred that some of the many tunnels, and other difficult and dangerous and easily obstructed passes, through Virginia, and especially in the Alleghany range of mountains, had been already blocked up, or rendered impassible, by like orders and operations as had here produced such disastrous results.

The third route, or general plan, was adopted. This was, to proceed, as at first designed, to the Ohio river—but by way of the North-Western turnpike road, which was within two miles south of the railroad, where both cross Cheat river, with a practicable cross-road connecting them. This route offered a broad and excellent road for the march of an army all the way to Parkersburg, on the Ohio—or, if enabled to use it, the North-Western Railroad for the last one hundred and four miles of the journey, from Grafton, the point where that road diverges from the main Baltimore and Ohio Railroad. The inhabitants of the whole country to be passed over Gen. W. supposed to be loyal to the federal government, opposed to negro slavery, and friendly to the northern and anti-slavery party—or certainly that they would not be hostile to the passage of the army. As to any attacks, on open ground, from the few volunteers who could be assembled from a distance in time to oppose his march, Gen. W. held them in too much contempt to count their opposition as anything. By this route, the army would reach the Ohio more than eighty miles lower than at Benwood, where the termination of the first designed passage would have been. As had been learned, and counted upon, before the armies moved, the Ohio was now swollen by a slight fresh, and sufficient depth of water, which would last long enough for Gen. W. to reach the river, and embark on the numerous steamers and other boats which had been prepared, and ordered to await the arrival of his army. The objection to taking this route which might be raised because of the prohibition of the state of Virginia, had no weight with Gen. W. After the events of the last few hours, no peaceable terms could be supposed to continue between that state and the federal government.

Having slowly moved on to Cheat river, the army left the train. The infantry and riflemen encamped on ground easily secured from attack, and remained until the artillery, wagons, and draught horses, and those for the use of the superior officers, could be removed from the cars. The whole army then marched to the turnpike road, and on it proceeded towards the Ohio.

As soon as this purpose of the federal army was evident to the scouts, some of them returned to report the facts to Col. M. He was delighted with the course of things. The necessary new dispositions were immediately made, with the hearty concurrence of his followers. He gave up the present command of the three companies of riflemen to Major C., an excellent officer for the service required—and who, like M., had been long ago an experienced hunter in this wild region. Major C. was advised by his superior to follow the march of the enemy, but not to let the presence of his, or any hostile force be known, if possible, to Gen. W., until he should have moved at least twenty miles on his route, for fear that he might find out his error, and retrace his steps towards Pennsylvania or Maryland. It was further recommended to Major C. that, after enough delay, he should take every effective mode for harassing the army, without much exposing his own men—and in the course of his operations, to endeavor to raise the neighboring people, and to induce them to increase his force, and also to concur in the plan of procedure.

Col. M. placed on his train the company of artillery and their field pieces, his wounded men, and the prisoners, and attached the car with the captured cannon. The cars that could be dispensed with were left behind. With the others he proceeded as rapidly as could be, westward, and at the junction, took the North-Western Railroad to Parkersburg. There having properly disposed of his train, and its other freight, and also formally vacated his railroad employment, he proceeded to select the most suitable spot for the purpose, and there to construct an intrenched battery, to command the river, and to prevent the passage of United States troops in steamers and boats. For the required labor, he had plenty of aid from the neighboring population, including all the prisoners who were not wounded. He had summoned to his aid another disbanded officer of artillery, and his friend and former comrade, Capt. L., whom he employed as his assistant engineer, for constructing the works, and also assistant instructor of his artillery men, and especially of the later recruits, who were coming in fast.

The recent military events, produced a great sensation, wherever made known, and especially on the rude and hardy people of this region. The treacherous and bloody attack, and in violation of an apparent and implied agreement, on the Virginia volunteers by Gen. W., after his army had been spared, and saved from all damage by Col. M., aroused the hostility and excited the patriotic zeal of many who were before quiet and indifferent. Still more, the circumstances and results of the battle, its signal success and the valuable trophies of victory, incited hundreds to take an active part in the contest. The captured pieces of artillery, at Parkersburg, and soon after when placed in the new battery, served as most attractive exhibitions, and as eloquent incitements to patriotic and gallant efforts. Many of the young men of the surrounding country who came merely to see and hear about these guns, were thereby induced to remain to fight with them. And many more of the hardy mountaineers and hunters, with their better understood and good rifles, hastened to join the ranks of the volunteers who were hanging about the invading army.

In a few days, the condition of the new battery was so strengthened, in both men and artillery, and its defences made so secure, that the commander felt sure that no vessel or flotilla, of the only kind to be used, of slight built steamers, could pass without suffering greatly.

Gen. B., of Wheeling, had taken a like course. On the most suitable point on the river, and below Benwood, (and ten or twelve miles below Wheeling,) he had constructed a strong battery for its purpose, and manned it with the second company of Wheeling artillery, which garrison was speedily and largely reinforced by new recruits.

The northern detachment of the army had reached Pittsburg safely, and encamped near the Ohio, awaiting the numerous vessels of all descriptions of the ordinary river craft, which were being assembled to transport the army down the river. This required some days delay—and before this time had passed, Gen. N., the commander, had been informed that the southern detachment had been stopped, and forced to change its route—that the passage over either land or water in Virginia, would be resolutely resisted by military force—and that batteries were already constructed along the Ohio, and manned and armed, to prevent the passage of any United States troops. Under these circumstances, Gen. N. deemed it necessary to change the previously intended plan of transportation. He accordingly, crossed with his army into the state of Ohio, and by railway, and at leisure, proceeded through that and the other friendly and loyal states, Indiana and Illinois, to the designated camp near the mouth of the Ohio river, there to await the reinforcements of regulars from the far western posts.

As soon as Col. M. heard of this diversion of the route of the northern army, he inferred that there would be but small chance for any enemy to attempt to pass his fort, or for him to find therein any fighting duty. Therefore he left the command to Capt. L., with a garrison of new recruits entirely, except one skillful gunner to command and to point each cannon. Capt. L. was sure of soon teaching raw men to perform the other duties of artillery service, behind ramparts. Col. M. pushed on, with the remainder of his men, and many recruits, by the railroad passage, to the (supposed) nearest point to the federal army, and fell in with his other detachment after only eight days absence. He had brought with him two companies of riflemen, one of them just formed, and the other made, by change of arms, of his own first company of artillery. M. knew that artillery would be an incumbrance for this service. And he, and most of his men, were as well fitted for the rifle service, and for irregular guerilla service, as for the artillery.

LETTER XXXVII.

Progress of the Federal Army. Beginning of Extensive Guerilla Operations.

RICHMOND, May 29, 1868.

For the first two days of Gen. W's march from Cheat river, no enemy was seen, or even heard of. No obstacle was met with, except the delays and difficulties of obtaining provisions and forage, which it was necessary should be provided from the outset, and well in advance of the actual exhaustion of the scant supplies brought in the wagons. There was plenty of grass to be found along the road, for the horses' daily consumption. But the stocks of hay had been nearly consumed before the beginning of warm weather. There is but little grain raised, and there was none then exceeding the wants of the owners. Almost the only meat to be obtained was of the numerous lean cattle ranging at large on the mountains. It was the designed policy of the government, and was carried out with especial care here by the commanding general, to permit as little as possible of military licence, or coercion, either to injure or offend the inhabitants. The payments made for their property taken for the army, they received with silent and sullen acquiescence. None who were met with exhibited any certain indications of feelings either friendly or hostile to the army and its objects. The foraging parties were not opposed, but they found but little provisions, and brought in supplies very slowly.

On the third day of the march, (May 13th,) when the army had advanced only twenty-five miles, altogether, enemies began to be felt, though they were rarely seen.

The reports of rifles were heard, as if of single marksmen, from every place of concealment within the most distant rifle range of the line of march. Unless of the very distant shots, but few missed, and many were of deadly effect. Most of the balls so sent were evidently from the rifles in ordinary use by the hunters of this country, and were most probably then used by private individuals and practised hunters, who were shooting at soldiers for excitement and pleasure, as they were accustomed to shoot deer, or bears and wolves. To the influence of this excitement, and love of dangerous adventure, were added the promptings of patriotism, and, to some extent also, the love of gain. The improved military rifles of the best kind, which can be aimed to good purpose at a man half a mile distant, and can kill at more than a mile, were highly prized and greatly coveted by all the hunters of this country. There was no toil or service they would not go through to obtain one of these much valued weapons. And among the most ready means, one was to shoot the straggling federal soldier who carried a rifle; and another, to join a volunteer company, and so to be armed with such a rifle. The arms which had fallen with the dead or wounded soldiers through the iron bridge into the gorge of the Briery mountain, had soon and eagerly been sought for and appropriated by the neighboring hunters; and all not too much damaged for use, or for speedy repair, were soon again in war service, in opposition to that for which these arms had been designed.

The number of these concealed marksmen, and the injuries inflicted by them, increased from day to day. It became necessary that foraging parties should avoid the neighborhood of all covers for concealed marksmen, and that the encamping ground for every night should be far from suspicious places, or otherwise be intrenched. Every care was used for safety, but without being able to obtain it. It was in vain, on the march, to extend the front, flank, and rear guards, or patroles—or at night to increase the number, and extend the circuit of the surrounding sentinels, far beyond usage in ordinary warfare. The outer patroles or sentinels were often shot. In covered ground in the day, or anywhere in the dark, these volunteer or individual riflemen, from their knowledge of the ground, could come within the outer guards, and choose their object on either side. The remarkable character of the country greatly aided these bold adventurers. The road was excellent, having been constructed by the state, at great cost. But it passed through a route naturally as rugged as is general in this region. Broad and level as is the road, it is, in many places, bordered by steep mountain sides, often sheer precipices, and it crosses, on bridges, deep channelled and rapid rivers, and deep and steep-sided gorges, and along narrow defiles between high and steep mountain sides—while rugged rocks, and tall and thick forests, and "laurel thickets," (impenetrable excepting by bears and other wild beasts, or by men following, by crouching and crawling, through their long-used paths,) cover as much of the bordering ground as there is in cleared and open fields. Under all these difficulties, with the necessity of obtaining grain and meat, and of carrying along the baggage wagons and the two remaining pièces of heavy field artillery, it is not strange that, though over a good road, the daily march, one day with another, did not exceed ten miles.

LETTER XXXVIII.

Military Movements in Virginia. Hasty Preparations for Defence, and for Offensive War in the North-west.

RICHMOND, June 6, 1868.

The governor of Virginia had received from his agents the earliest information, by telegraph and mail, of the movements of the two federal armies. The manner of their first movements left no doubt of their destination being different points on the Ohio river. The governor immediately issued the military orders deemed necessary, which were added to on the next day, after hearing of the invasion of north-western Virginia. The orders were, in general, to all commanders of regiments, that in the immediate localities where troops were needed, to obstruct or oppose the march of federal troops, to call out volunteers of the neighborhood, without limit. As no such need had been expected west of the Blue Ridge, there had not been there previously called into service a single company—nor was it known that there was a volunteer under arms, until a telegraphic dispatch from Col. M. (the latest sent on the line before its connection had been broken temporarily,) informed the governor of his first movement, and design to stop the federal army. The 3000 men previously encamped near Alexandria were sent on westward as quickly as possible, by the Alexandria and Loudoun Railroad, which took them by a connecting link to the Baltimore and Ohio Railroad, at Harper's Ferry. On this railroad they proceeded westward. At two different points, of the railroad, where in Virginia, and crossing the Alleghany mountains, the track had been blocked up, by orders, as soon as the report had been received of the stopping and retrograde movement of the federal army. But though the obstructions were sufficient to stop any army, and could be maintained by a few men, still they could easily be cleared away when no longer needed. Thus, the track had already been cleared, and now there was no impediment to the most rapid movement of this body of troops, to Cheat river, whence they proceeded by the North-western turnpike in pursuit of Gen. W's army, then three days of its slow march ahead.

Other bodies of volunteers and "minute men," amounting to 9000 more, were specially called out for immediate service. The selection of the companies called into service was determined by one or both of the considerations of better training and military preparation, (which was to be found mostly in volunteer companies of towns,) and the more ready access to the scene for service, which applied to the infantry and artillery nearest to suitable railroad routes. As to cavalry, the most effective troops were in country localities. And because the necessary accommodations for transporting the horses on railroads could not be prepared soon enough, the cavalry would have to march the whole distance, without any aid of rapid railroad transportation. Therefore, the troops of cavalry nearest to the expected place for action, were chosen, and these were mostly eastward of the Blue Ridge—and very few cavalry companies had been organized west of the Alleghanies. As fast as the foot companies could be assembled, they were sent on, by the most convenient line of railroad, to the north-west, whether the Alexandria or the Manassas Gap, which conveyed the troops only as far west as Strasburg, or by Harper's Ferry to Cheat river—or on the Central Railroad to Covington.

The companies of cavalry took their several best routes over the shortest ordinary or private roads. This is a description of military force peculiar to these southern states; and considering that it must be composed of both raw men and horses, it is a most effective and admirable force. All southerners of country rearing and residence are accustomed to riding, and are mostly good riders—and every man in even moderate circumstances owns a good and serviceable riding horse. Also, every country boy learns, for his amusement, the ready use of fire-arms, and every man is, or has been, a practiced gunner, and most are good marksmen. In every county where there is a troop of volunteer cavalry, it is made up of men of these kinds, and also possessing from moderate to large properties, and who are as respectable as any class whatever, gentlemen in character and in conduct, and mostly companions and friends to each other throughout each troop. Such men are the best possible material of which to make efficient soldiers in the shortest time—able, from their previous habits of life, and of employment, to bear any hardship, and with principle and pride to induce every effort required by duty and patriotism. They, and also their horses, need only the training of actual service—and most of the early duties in actual service may be well and efficiently performed in advance of any martinet drilling, or even of all soldierly accomplishments, and proficiency, save the readiness to obey orders and to stand fire. Such companies can be ready to march, well equipped for war, at a day's notice—and, if not previously provided by the government, or if having no commissariat at first, each trooper can carry his food, and grain for his horse, for three days, and supply his own money to buy provisions and forage for a month's service.

As an example of such service, I will cite the facts of a single county, of which the two troops were among the best of this description, and both of which were of old establishment, under good command, and as well trained as can be at home and during peace. The Black Hussars and the Mountain Rangers of Fauquier county, were among the first troops of volunteer cavalry called out. Both had served in the short Harper's Ferry campaign in 1859—and now, as then, were severally commanded by Captains S. and A.—Each of these officers, years ago, had been offered the command of a militia regiment. But both had declined the promotion, preferring the special command of their own troops, composed of old comrades and friends. These two troops were of the best qualities, physical and moral, of citizen soldiers. The men were capable of great bodily exertion, were all good and habitual riders, and, on their own good and well tried horses, could make long and rapid marches, in which they would have far outstripped any regular cavalry. The final call to immediate service, sent to their colonel by telegraph, reached the captains of these two troops on the afternoon of the 11th of May. General arrangements had been previously made for the speediest distribution of the orders. By 11 o'clock, the next forenoon, the two troops were assembled on their respective muster grounds, ready for marching. Half a day's march was made before night—and for every day afterwards, to the scene of action, these troops accomplished, on an average, five miles more for each day, than is deemed sufficient for good marching of well trained regular cavalry. But little later than these, and the earliest on the march, other cavalry, and also infantry and rifle companies of uniformed volunteers and minute men, specially summoned, were pouring across the mountains towards the north-west. Those nearest to suitable rail-road routes, and on that account selected for this service, even though remote from the scene of action, were placed far in advance of nearly all others, and even of cavalry marching from the nearest homes. The 3000 men from the previous camp near Alexandria had early orders, and the earliest start, and also the longest rail-road transportation—and therefore were soonest near the enemy of all that came from a distance. The other summoned troops followed in daily and rapid succession; and the various companies, according to their routes, proceeded to one or the other of the two points, west of the Alleghany mountains, designated for the first concentration. One of these was in Taylor county, at the crossing of the Baltimore and Ohio Railroad over Tygant's Valley river, (the main head stream of the Monongahela,) and which is also the point of junction with the North-Western Railroad—and where the passage of both these roads, and of the bridge and only passage there over the river, were then commanded by the army—and later by a single company, left for that purpose. These railroads were now open, and used, as previous to the late interruption, for private transportation of passengers and freights. But secure, (though easily moveable) barriers were placed here, and at some other suitable places, to compel every train to stop, and be examined by the military guard, before being permitted to proceed. Of course no troops or arms, or supplies, except those of the state, or by order of the Governor, could pass. Such barriers, each under guard of a company of militia, were maintained, near Harper's Ferry, and in the Alleghany mountains, where the railroad crosses from the Maryland side of the Potomac, and passes (at the latter place for a few miles only,) over the territory of Virginia, and through formidable natural obstacles. These measures placed the command and use of the Baltimore and Ohio Railroad, from Harper's Ferry westward, completely under the control, and at the service, of the forces and the authorities of Virginia, and withheld them from the federal or any other hostile troops. The other place, for rendezvous, was much farther south, but also westward and clear of the main Alleghany range. This was for the smaller number of volunteers called from Augusta and the neighboring counties between the Alleghany and Blue Ridge mountains, and of the more eastern and southern counties whose troops could go by the Central Railroad as far as Buffalo Gap, and thence, by a long march, could easiest reach the scene of expected service.

Under these circumstances, and various difficulties, the different companies were arriving at the two places for rendezvous at from three to fifteen days after the battle at the Deep Gorge. But from both places, troops were marched off, to their designed guerilla service, as speedily as they could be organized, and properly provided for duty. At first, they thus moved onward in separate bodies, and, even in some cases, as small as single companies, but as designated parts of organized regiments and brigades, of which the detached portions would come together on the march.

Major General S., who had been the earliest and continued superintendent of the Virginia Military School, (at Lexington,) was commander of the whole army. Among the best disciplined and most efficient of all the troops, there came in one company eighty of the best trained youthful cadets of that admirable institution, commanded by officers of their own corps. Gen. S. had the gratification of recognizing in many of the best officers of volunteers, from various parts of the state, his former pupils, and graduates of the Military Institute. To this long established system of military instruction, South Carolina and Virginia, more especially, and also, later, other southern states, were indebted for hundreds of good officers of volunteers, who, in a few weeks of camp service, could sooner bring their perfectly raw men into fitness for all military duties, than would have been done by any length of ordinary militia training, under ordinary officers. To this source of instruction, and supply of officers fitted for command, has been due much of the military strength recently displayed by these southern states, when almost destitute of any legal military organization, or general military system.

The first ordered service of all these various bodies of troops was of the same general character with that begun some time before, and well maintained by the Wheeling and Parkersburg rifle companies, (recently all reunited under Col. M's immediate command,) and still more efficiently by the numerous riflemen and hunters of the neighboring country, who had already come in as auxiliaries, either with or without organization, to the number of 1500, and were still added to daily by new recruits from more distant localities. These men were gradually, and at their own choice, formed into companies, and rated as if under regular organization and command. But whether as thus organized, or, as at first, when each man acted for himself and according to his own will, their service was mostly separate, and independent, and not the less of great value. For all these men were accustomed to all the hardships and toils of a mountain hunter's life, were strong and brave, excellent marksmen with their universal weapon, the rifle, and well acquainted with the natural features and topography of this region—the most difficult that can be well conceived for the passage of an army, if opposed by any determined force under competent command.

LETTER XXXIX.

Continuation and close of the guerilla campaign in the mountains of Virginia. Events on the coast.

RICHMOND, June 9, 1868.

Leaving the hastily summoned volunteers and raw levies of Virginia hurrying, along their various routes, to the places for concentration or for action, I will now return to report the further progress of the federal army in Virginia.

On the fifth day of the march of Gen. W's army, and after entering Harrison county, as it approached a deep gorge, report was brought from the advance guard that the bridge across the gorge had been burnt, and that the passage of the wagons and artillery farther on that road was rendered impracticable. Examination confirmed the truth of the report. From the best information of the country afforded by the still attendant engineers, and from what could be extracted from the few people of the country who could be seen and questioned, the General learned that another passage of the gorge, the nearest and best, for horses and wheel carriages, was a difficult path-way some miles farther south. This diverging route was taken—and the ruggedness of the ground and of the narrow road presented the only difficulties, as not an enemy had lately been seen, nor the firing of a gun heard. This branch road led to the central and more southern part of Harrison county, through which the bold and rapid river (the West Fork of Monongahela,) passes with a course so exceedingly crooked, caused by the many interlocking and high spurs of steep hills, that to get over eight or ten miles of distance in a straight direction, the river meanders, in many abrupt curves, from thirty to thirty-five miles. The road reaches this river about midway of the most tortuous portion of its course. Here there is a fording place, which is not only very difficult to pass, owing to the depth of the water and rough bottom, and the steepness of the banks, but also is a most suitable place for the concealment of an enemy. Still there was no indication of any enemy being near. The army had passed the river some miles westward, when another deep and narrow gorge was reached by the advanced guard, and of which the indispensable bridge had been so lately burnt, that the flames were in full progress, though beyond any possibility of control. To pass infantry down and up the steep and rocky sides of the gorge seemed impracticable, (and certainly was so to strangers,) and for the conveyance across of horses and wheel carriages there was no possibility here, nor probability within any near or available distance. During the pause at this place, rifle shots, which had been suspended, began again to drop in irregularly from distant covers beyond the gorge, and soon increased in number and in deadly effects, beyond any previous experience, of the like invisible foes. There was no choice left for the General but to order the army to fall back. On returning to the river where it had been lately crossed, for the first time there was seen a body of men of military appearance and array, and posted as if to oppose the passage of the retreating army. A few volleys were exchanged, and the Virginians fell back, and seemed to retreat, but in reality sought covered positions from which to fire most safely, and with best effect.

Here commenced the operations of the volunteers as one army, under regular command, and upon a general plan. But the manner of the military operations continued to be as irregular as they had been at first, and differing only in the greatly increased numbers engaged, and the increase of effect. By this time, Gen. S. had under his command, and near the enemy, 5000 men, in regularly organized bodies—besides an unknown and daily varying number, perhaps from 1000 to 2500 riflemen of the neighboring country, who served and fought at such times and in such manner as suited their convenience and pleasure—and who were known as soldiers only by their drawing rations, arms and ammunition. Nevertheless, these were most valuable auxiliaries, and who even alone, if using their full power for annoyance and destruction, would be enough to prevent an army of thrice their numbers from marching through their mountainous and wild country.

And now having dwelt so long on facts which are severally of very small importance, but which serve to illustrate the kind of warfare, I will pass hastily over the consequences which must be anticipated from the causes stated. To continue to describe all the guerilla operations in like detail would be useless and wearisome. For however various were the different operations of every day, and whether of offensive or defensive measures, and numerous as were the incidents of intense interest to the actors, and to their countrymen, the general operations and results may be sketched in a small space.

The late temporary cessation of firing, and of all annoyance of the invading army had been made by order of the commander of the militia army, and which order it was very difficult to persuade the hunter-riflemen of the neighboring country to obey. The destruction of bridges, and the show of offering battle, had been used to draw the regular army into the most difficult ground, where its superiority in discipline, and its artillery, would be of no value. And as soon as these ends were reached, the whole power of the irregular opposing force was put in action. No regular battle, on open ground, was to be offered, or accepted, by any party of the Virginians, whether large or small. But, on their march, every cover or place of concealment was to be made use of, for ambush, or to make advantage of for firing on the enemy. The riflemen occupied every such place along the line of the march of the regular army; and those of the organized companies, who were armed with the improved rifles, could make deadly shots at distances of more than half a mile. The rifles of the regulars were all of this best kind, and could strike as far. But these were usually fired from open and exposed positions, and directed against adversaries rarely visible, and generally sheltered by rocks or trees. Such generally was the kind of warfare carried on through every succeeding day, if on the march; and but few places could be chosen for encamping for a night, which, unless protected by intrenchments, were not in some degree exposed to fatal rifle shots from some distant place of safe concealment. The cavalry of the militia were much restricted by the rough surface of the country, which made it very unsuitable for the full use of such troops. Nevertheless, the volunteer cavalry, untrained as were both horses and horsemen, performed excellent service in obtaining and conveying intelligence, restraining and sometimes cutting off foraging parties, and in surprising and cutting down patroles, or straggling parties of the hostile army. Not only was this general course of procedure used by Gen. S., at first, when his force was inferior in numbers as well as in training, but he continued it after his daily accessions of reinforcements had given to his army such superiority of numbers, that that advantage might well have compensated for inferiority in discipline and equipment, and enabled it to cope with the regular army in battle. For the Virginian General judged it proper to avail himself of all his advantages; and if ever so sure of success in open and regular conflict, he would not have so made the necessary sacrifice of the valuable lives of his citizen soldiers, in a contest on equal terms against the regulars, who, however useful as soldiers, were men of the lowest and most worthless conditions. There seemed to be no need of such risk and sacrifice, as Gen. S. was sure that his cautious warfare, with time, would certainly serve to conquer, and as effectually as the best fought and most successful open battle. On some occasions, during the sundry days of hostilities thus conducted, the Virginian army, or some large portion of it, seemed to offer battle, on ground accessible to the invaders. But when there assailed, the militia would soon retreat, or change position to some adjacent and protecting cover, from which to fire without danger. There were but few places where the enemy's artillery could be used to good purpose, to prevent annoyance to its march; and the possession of artillery, with the care necessary to secure it, was more an incumbrance than an aid. The commander of the militia army had preferred to dispense altogether with artillery, for this service.

Besides these general and daily means for annoyance and damage, by which the enemy lost many men daily by death or disabling wounds, there was one extraordinary occasion of disaster. After a succession of sundry days of such operations, over obstructed roads, and with changes of direction, frustrated marches, and continual loss of men from the distant shots of mostly concealed marksmen hovering around, the harassed, but still pursuing regular army overtook the Virginians embodied, and apparently in full retreat. The pursuit was urged, and volleys of musketry were sometimes exchanged, when the front ranks of the pursurers approached near enough to the rear of the retreating army. At last the infantry of the Virginian army entered a diverging branch road, passing along the bottom of a narrow valley. The whole body of cavalry had gone on by the broader and direct road. This seemed to Gen. W. to indicate that the route taken by the retreating infantry was impracticable for cavalry—and that, deprived of that support, the infantry might be overtaken, and compelled to fight—and an open fair conflict was all that Gen. W. thought was required for his perfect success. The artillery, wagons, officers' horses, all the wounded, and 500 good soldiers for a guard, were hastily separated, and ordered to encamp on the nearest safe position—and no danger was expected, when the whole opposing army was fast retreating ahead. The remainder of the regular army, now unincumbered, pushed on as rapidly as possible in pursuit of the retreating infantry—which, when approached more nearly, seemed to the pursurers to be in utter disorder—and it was inferred that they were panic stricken, and that they were pressing forward to reach some known place of safe refuge. Some old flint muskets thrown down by the retreating volunteers, by command, served to increase the confidence in their supposed panic and disorder, and also induced the belief that the muskets generally were of this inefficient description. The eagerness of the pursuit prevented Gen. W's duly noticing that at some points the valley was reduced in width to a very narrow defile, with precipitous and rocky sides. At last, the volunteers reached the designed termination of their retreating movement, which was a secure barricade, which had been previously and carefully constructed across a broader part of the bottom. Behind and facing this rampart the musketry were disposed, and the riflemen spread over the adjacent rugged and wooded and steep mountain ascents, on both sides of the valley. There the attack of the approaching enemy was awaited, and soon arrived. Repeated and desperate assaults were made in vain. The whole attacking force, in close and dense order, was exposed to every musket and rifle of defenders who themselves were but little exposed. Every successive assault was repulsed with great slaughter—and when it was manifest that success was hopeless, the assailants were ordered to retreat, retracing their steps through the bottom towards the designated encampment—necessarily leaving on the ground many of the wounded with the dead. This retrograde march within two miles distance brought the advance guard to the narrowest defile, and to find that across it a strong barricade had been erected since the previous passage of the army, and that it was defended by as numerous a party behind the barricade as could have room there. The mountain sides here also were occupied by scattered and concealed riflemen. As soon as this new obstruction was seen, the regulars rushed on to scale and storm the barricade. The hasty but strong defences had been prepared, and were commanded by Col. M., who was at the barricade, with as many men as could act in so narrow a place, armed with muskets and buck-shot cartridges. He waited until the front rank of the storming force was within fifty yards of the barricade, when his muskets were discharged, and immediately replaced by others loaded in like manner. The rushing living torrent was checked for a while, and with great slaughter. The deadly firing was kept up from behind the barricade and from the scattered riflemen. The assailants again advanced, and were again driven back. Just then, the larger body of the militia, which had been left behind the first barricade, and which had again formed and in their turn made pursuit, appeared in the rear of the regulars, and poured a volley into their disordered and crowded ranks. Gen. W. again urged the assault upon the much smaller force defending the last erected barricade—and now despair of safety in any other manner was added to all that courage and discipline had been able to attempt before. The rear ranks of the regulars fired upon the newly arrived and main body of the volunteers, and checked their advance, while a general rush was made towards and over the barricade. The loss of the assailants was very great. But whenever a man fell, his place was immediately occupied by another. By physical weight and pressure, as much as by courage and the use of arms, the surrounded army succeeded in forcing a passage over the barricade, and also over the bodies of most of its brave defenders. The remnant of the federal troops, still pursued and fired upon by the volunteers with deadly effect, continued its retreat to the camp, which had, in the mean time, been prepared by the detachment left for that purpose.

The camp was soon invested, and its garrison, though composed of all that remained of the federal army, was barely strong enough, with the aid of its artillery, and under the protection of hastily constructed intrenchments, to maintain its position. The commander of the Virginians, with all his present and still increasing superiority of numbers, still would not risk attempting an assault, and was content to wait a short time for the now inevitable result. His troops were posted so as to be as little exposed to the enemy's fire as was consistent with maintaining a strict blockade of the invested camp, from which there was no possibility of egress by the garrison, or any portion of it to serve as foraging parties, or of any supplies being received from without. And if the beseiged army could have forced its passage out, there would have been no benefit from the change of position, but, on the contrary, the loss of the present secure defences. But though protected for the present, the delay offered no hope of relief, except in the possible arrival of strong reinforcements. This hope, Gen. S. had taken effectual care should be fallacious. From the beginning of his command, he had kept the greater number of his cavalry acting as patroles, or as larger detachments, and had placed sufficient guards of infantry at every important passage through which reinforcements could be sent. To guard, and, if needed, to obstruct suitable points on the railroad, and to destroy bridges on common roads, was enough to prevent the entrance of any reinforcement of federal troops from the east, which was the only direction from which they could be brought. Under these circumstances, Gen. W. could only maintain his position, and protect his men, until his small stock of provisions should be exhausted; and for that, but a few more days of the seige or blockade were required. The then inevitable result would be the capitulation of Gen. W., and the surrender, as prisoners of war, of all his forces. This occurred on May 26th. His army was then reduced to one-fourth of its original number, and of this remnant, many were wounded. The officers were immediately liberated on parole—and the privates as soon as the proper arrangements were consented to by the northern federal government. Thus, of this lately well equipped and provided, and well disciplined army of 7000 regulars, there remained alive, and as prisoners, scarcely 2500 men, (including all previously captured)—and all the arms and munitions of war, which had not been destroyed in service, were the spoils of the victorious militia. And these very striking military successes were easily effected by an undisciplined opposing force, and also much weaker in numbers at first—and would have been effected with still more speed and certainty, if the enemy's invasion had not been made so suddenly, and by surprise, when there was no military array, and scarcely any preparation, in all the great region west of the Blue Ridge mountains.

Strong garrisons or smaller out-post guards were placed at the points suitable to control the great routes of ingress, and to prevent another invasion by surprise. A few such military posts on the Baltimore and Ohio Railroad served to give the command of all that road, and its facilities for transportation, to the Virginians, and effectually to exclude all hostile invasion west of Harper's Ferry, from the north, unless by forces marching through a difficult country. A few other posts, and intrenched batteries of artillery, on different points of the Ohio river, effectually closed that channel for invasion to the enemy's armaments, and also controlled the commercial and ordinary transportation on the river, so that it could not be used for hostile purposes. Even before the latter successes of Gen. S's army, he had countermanded and turned back these advancing reinforcements. And immediately after the surrender of the remaining federal forces, he had sent home, for discharge, a large portion of his acting army. The remainder served in part to supply garrisons for the posts just mentioned, and for another destination.

Except the decisive success of the militia forces, the most gratifying result was in the very small numerical loss suffered by the victors. All the Virginians killed in the campaign did not amount to 400—and of these much the greater number fell in the conflict at and last desperate charge of the barricade.

LETTER XL.

Military operations in the East. Removal of seat of northern government. Popular feeling in Washington, and the early consequences.

WASHINGTON, June 11, 1868.

Earlier than most of the latter reported events, there had been effected some important military operations elsewhere. As soon as the governor of Virginia learned that blood had been shed in battle, he deemed that actual war had been begun, and that nothing was then to be hoped except from vigorous measures. He deemed that any further forbearance towards the federal power should be dictated solely by policy. He thought that Virginia ought still to refrain from any measures of aggression outside of her territory. But he did not so consider any of the former soil of the state of which the property and occupancy had formerly been ceded to the general government for forts, &c., for the better common defence, and which would now be used to endanger and damage the state. With these views, among the earliest war measures of the governor, were authority and orders issued to seize upon the Dock Yard at Portsmouth, and Fortress Monroe. By a strong attacking force of neighboring volunteers, and by bold as well as artful procedure, the Dock Yard was taken, with all the valuable naval arms, munitions and materials, and other public property, including several vessels of war in progress of repair or of construction. The very spacious and strong Fortress Monroe, to be fully garrisoned would require not less than 4000 men, and it had only 200 regular soldiers. An entrance was effected by surprise, and by an overwhelming force, including companies of volunteers from Norfolk and Hampton—and the possession, thus acquired, was secured by a state garrison of 1000 militia, under the instruction and command of good artillery officers, some of whom had formerly served in the United States army.

* * * * * * * * *

On account of the political difficulties of the country, and the increasing complications of the northern government, there had been no adjournment or recess of the Congress at Washington, since the beginning of the year. Since the recent outbreak of actual war in Virginia, and the practical revolt and expected formal secession of that state, Washington, on the very border of a hostile state, had become an inconvenient and unsafe place for the seat of the federal government. However galling to the pride of the President and the Congress, and of the northern section, the necessity of the case demanded a speedy removal. The necessary enactments to authorize this measure were hastily adopted by the Congress, and Albany was fixed upon as the temporary new seat of government. Within two days after the passage of the law, the President and the chief officers of government, and the members of Congress, were on their way to Albany. The most important of the archives of the government, and other moveable property, were sent off as soon. What necessarily was left, for the present, was placed in the charge of a few of the clerks and other subordinate civil officers, and under the authority of the mayor of the city. The military garrison then of 3000 men still remained, to defend the city and navy yard, and protect the public buildings. The mayor, under the previous advice of the President appealed to the public spirit and patriotism of the residents of the city and district to form volunteer military companies, for the better maintenance of order and security. This call was promptly responded to, and a regiment of volunteer infantry was speedily organized, armed, and was diligently drilled. But the public spirit which inspired these volunteers was very different in its source and aim from what had been supposed and expected to operate.

The wealth and support of the people who, either as permanent inhabitants or temporary sojourners, made up the population of Washington and the adjacent small rural portion of the District of Columbia, were derived from and dependent upon the vast expenditures there made, because of the residence of the federal government. There were but few persons whose incomes were not either made up or increased by direct receipts, in some way or other, from the government expenditures. And there were none, whose gains and incomes were not greatly increased indirectly from that source. Great wealth, in lots and houses, and profitable rents, had been thus created. And it was recognized by all, that the removal of the seat of government, at any time, would have taken away full two-thirds of the value of all private landed property, and reduced all incomes of remaining residents full as much. This complete and permanent condition of dependence on the general government had naturally made the population of Washington especially loyal, and, though southern in locality, and also generally by birth, the people had throughout submitted silently, if not always approvingly, to all the measures and policy of the northern section, directing the federal government. The like considerations of self-interest had originally silenced all objections of the residents to being separated from Maryland and the District being made the domain of the United States—and had induced acquiescence of the people in their being deprived of any share of political power. But at last, the dreaded and fatal and doubtless also final act of removal of the seat of government had been consummated, notwithstanding all the foregone submission of the inhabitants to, and support of, the federal government, and its oppressive measures—and their having been compelled to bear the virtual extinction of slavery in the District, and all the increased evils of a large population of emancipated and other free negroes. All the political and domestic evils of the condition of the people remained in full force, and yet all the previous compensating benefits of gain were ended. These various considerations served to bring about a general and sudden change of opinion, and of views of political affairs and prospects. The former merely mercenary supporters of the northern power had no longer any thing to gain from that kind of loyalty; and to them, as to the more patriotic, the existing connection with, and exclusive subjection to the general, or now northern, government, appeared now fraught with evil. To all classes, it became desirable that their District, and their political condition, should be united with the original parent state, Maryland, whose territory still nearly surrounded the district—the circuit being completed by a few miles of the water of the Potomac. This re-annexation was the more earnestly desired by the more patriotic inhabitants, because the secession of Maryland was then expected, and which soon after was formally announced. Under the influence of these opinions and feelings, the ranks of the new regiment of volunteers were filled, and the officers elected. Of course, the members were the most ardent of secessionists in opinion, and southerners in sentiments and preferences. The ordinary militia companies, embracing all other persons of military age, and merely organized, amounted to about 7000, were but partially armed, and were without military practice or instruction.

Before the removal of the seat of the northern government from Washington, and after open hostilities with Virginia had been commenced, it would have been very easy for an expedition of a few thousand brave men to surprise and capture the President and every important officer of the administration, and perhaps most of the members of both houses of Congress, and to take them as prisoners into Virginia. But, besides the desiring to avoid any act of offensive war, or of assault to be made outside of Virginia, or of southern territory, the authorities of that state did not desire the fruition of the object referred to, at even moderate risk and cost, or at any sacrifice of designed policy. No substantial gain would have been made by the capture, and confinement as prisoners, of every officer and member of the civil government. As soon as the President, or any other officer of the government, should be a prisoner in a hostile country, he would, *ipso facto*, cease to be a political functionary—and a substitute, previously designated by the constitution, or to be designated by executive appointment or popular election, would be either instantly or speedily supplied, and be ready to assume the place vacated. The country whose functionaries or representatives should thus be removed, would not be the worse for the loss, and might well be bettered in the substitution. The most ardent southern patriots and seceders, (to which party all the people of the south have now substantially acceded,) would much regret to have Seward and his supporters in the northern Congress substituted by men less devoted to and blinded by northern fanaticism—which fanaticism alone has enabled the South to become independent.

LETTER XLI.

New legislature of Virginia. Important political events.

RICHMOND, June 13, 1868.

While the events which have been narrated or commented on in the latter letters, were in progress in the South, the North, and the West, there were also still more important political occurrences elsewhere, which have not yet been mentioned. I will now return to take up these affairs, more than a month after the dates of the earliest of them. Of course, the most important or impressive incidents have been communicated to your readers much earlier than this letter will appear in your columns. But I do not seek, nor even desire, to report very early news—but only such statements of facts, and comments thereon, as the lapse of time, and the comparison of all conflicting reports, may permit to be considered as correct. Also, by avoiding very early communication of particular occurrences, I am enabled to treat more regularly, connectedly, and also concisely, each separate series of connected yet separate affairs, and to pursue each particular subject to a proper time for its suspension. In this way, my remarks are now some six weeks in arrears of the political affairs of Virginia, which will now be resumed, and brought up.

The last legislature of this state, elected two years before the termination of its service, and without any reference to latter events, did not correctly represent recent public sentiment and opinion, which had been heated and exasperated by the political events of later occurrence. And, under the corrupting and stultifying influence of the present state constitution, and its system of universal suffrage, and caucus nominations for all public offices, that legislature, like its near predecessors, was low in intellect, patriotism, and the standard of character in general. Yet, while, even after the latest and worst acts of the northern section, (controlling the federal government,) that legislature would do nothing to resist past wrongs, it resolved and threatened loudly (as has been the time-honored custom of Virginia,) against any *such future* assaults and injuries. And, taking advantage of this always prospective fervor and patriotism, the governor and the minority of true southerners in the legislature were enabled to obtain the enactment of every measure desired for preparation, and as authority necessary for future military defence. The voting for such enactments of postponed and prospective measures, and for the fiery and wordy resolutions which preceded them, were generally concurred in by even the most submissive members, and who were very willing then, as before, to utter "brave words" as a substitute and full compensation for the omitted brave acts for defence, which they would never have been ready for. However, with whatever views and mental reservations, the threatening enactments of this poor and contemptible body were voted, they were sufficient to provide for the better organization, and for the full authority for the employment, of the militia, which the then unexpected action of the federal government soon required to be put in practice—as has been described in my preceding letters.

The present legislature is very different in composition and character from any of those of latter times. The time of the elections had been (some years ago) changed from May to the last week of April. The general ferment then and previously excited in the public mind, by the continued and increasing encroachments of the North, the last evident movement for absolute domination, and for the complete subversion of slavery, and consequent destruction of the South, and the brave stand in opposition thereto made by some of the more southern states, all concurred to create an interest and excitement in the public mind, that served, for once at least, to over-rule and supersede the usual influence of unprincipled and low demagogues, working, through caucus machinery and political fraud, for their own personal advancement and gain, or that of their leaders and patrons. The honest mass of the people had been generally awakened to a sense of the existing dangers, and would no longer be deceived and misled by the knaves and the party names and phrases which had heretofore served as words of absolute command to party followers, long after they had ceased to apply to current events, and to requirements for political action. Under this new influence, the people generally threw aside the long worn bonds of caucus nominations, and the direction and rule of base demagogues and mercenary office-holders, and their subordinate and servile tools. The best and ablest men, as representatives, were called for by the public will; and the most intelligent, patriotic, zealous and worthy were generally designated, and elected. Many of the wisest and best citizens, who, by the previous course of things had long been kept in the obscurity of private life, were now recalled to the political service which they had formerly honored and dignified; and others, among the most highly qualified for public trusts, were for the first time brought into the public service of the state. Among the former class, two of the most distinguished by their former and long suspended public services, are the venerable J... R......., who may deservedly be esteemed, for his stern integrity and his political wisdom, as the Phocion of the latter degenerate times, and W. N. not less distinguished for his ability, for patriotism always disdaining party shackles, and for his private worth. Among the much larger number of new legislators, yet able men, and distinguished in other though private stations, was J. P. H. whose statemanship, profound knowledge of the philosophy of government, and rare powers of eloquence and of reasoning, all would serve to designate him as eminently fitted to serve admirably in the public councils of his country in this time of difficulty and peril. Many other men of good talents, and high character and worth, are elected. And perhaps it is not less an advantage that mere party names have been ignored, and corrupt party politicians have very generally been excluded from the legislature. It would seem as if the country generally had adopted and acted upon such opinion as was set forth in a sentiment offered as a toast at a public and political dinner in Richmond, some six months ago, and which was then concurred in and applauded with enthusiasm. It was in these words: "May the existing party names and divisions and enmities, throughout the southern states, be extinguished and forgotten; and henceforth, may we recognize as the only political parties, the one including all persons who will maintain the rights of the South, and the other, all who oppose, neglect, or would betray them."

On the next day after that of the elections, the governor issued (as was previously promised and expected,) a call for an extra session of the new legislature, on the 2d of May. On that day, the body met; and as soon as organized, both houses went into private session, (with closed doors,) and so continued for seven days, and (as since made known, with the proceedings, so far as yet made public,) secrecy was enjoined by the oath of every member, until the prohibition should be withdrawn. Private communications were received from the governor, the subjects of which, with the general state of political affairs, it may be presumed occupied the deliberations and guided the decisions of the assembly. The principle measures (as since made known,) were all acted upon, and put in operation, or progress, before the actual breaking out of war in Virginia, (on the 11th,) was known or anticipated in supposition. That event, and its immediate and stirring consequences of course produced new and strong excitement and determination everywhere. But the political position of the legislature had been fully assumed previously—and was not directed or altered by these sudden and unlooked for incidents of war, which operated so powerfully as the first sufficient impulse to many other slower minds in Virginia, and upon other southern states. One of the measures adopted, and which but lately has been permitted to be made public, was a course like that proposed by South Carolina and Mississippi, in 1860, to Virginia, and which this state, under the prevailing influence of "conservatism" and the fear of disunion, then rejected. This is a proposal from Virginia for a conference of the authorities of all the slaveholding states which have not seceded from the union with the northern section. The request for, and recommendation of this conference, accompanied by an elaborate exposition and argument in favor of these states' concurrent secession, was immediately sent to the several governors of all these states, and with an invitation for the meeting of the representative commissioners, for the conference, in Raleigh, on June 1st. But, while thus deferring to the other states, and wishing to act in concert, and simultaneously with them, if they should concur, the legislature of Virginia still proceeded to prepare, and to act in reference to present and pressing contingencies, as if resolved to persevere alone, if unsupported by the aid of any of her neighboring sister states thus sought. Every necessary aid and support to the then open war was given. One of the first measures of the session had been to approve unanimously of the governor's previous vigorous military preparations and general orders, and to confer on him, and require the exercise of, the previously implied, but somewhat indefinite authority, to prevent the passage of troops through Virginia, without the permission of the state authorities. This was some days before the actual exercise of that authority and service, which, however, would have occurred as well without as with the latest and formal authorization by the legislature.

The recent secret deliberations of the Virginia assembly, the argumentative and eloquent appeal from that body to the other like endangered states, and every surrounding manifestation and political indication, all concur in presenting to these states, in a voice no longer to be disregarded, the questions, "Shall we remain in the federal union with the northern states, by whom we have been deprived of all political power, and all means for redress—when the fast approaching measures for the destruction of the institution of negro slavery, and of the only foundation of the security and prosperity of the South, are no longer disguised, and are nearly ready to be enforced—when after having lost all equality of political power, we have now lost, in the secession of six southern states, nearly half of our previous feeble political support, and means for resistance or defence? Shall we still remain in political bondage to the North, and at its mercy—or shall we re-unite our political destiny with our southern brethren, who are already independent, and are now bravely defending and maintaining their rights, and determine, with them, to live free, or perish in the attempt?" Such questions, in different modes and aspects, had been considered by every thoughtful and patriotic citizen of Virginia, in advance of their being presented by this legislature. And the like anxious and feverish interest had been fast spreading through all the other slave-holding states similarly situated—unless the western shore and larger portion of Maryland formed an exception. The close neighborhood of the seat of the federal government, the much dreaded consequences of practical emancipation in the District of Columbia, (if intestine war should take place,) the still abiding love and veneration for the Union, (especially cherished by all the weaker states,) and the fears of what were deemed the certain consequences of disunion, in bloody border war, and successful servile insurrection, all had served to render the State of Maryland, especially loyal to the federal government, and entirely submissive heretofore to every wrong and outrage which had been perpetrated under cover of the federal Union and the federal constitution. In addition to these influences, the great city of Baltimore has long been northern and anti-slavery in the character of the dominant portion of its population, and therefore a source of weakness, and of terror, to the whole eastern and pro-slavery portion of the state. Further, Baltimore had long been the most disorderly and lawless city of the United States. For years together, its elections were effected contrary to the known will of the people, by the irresistible violence and control of armed mobs, composed of individuals of the worst habits and character. The favorite representative of this mob of lawless desperadoes, was H. D., who of all the members of Congress from the slaveholding states, was the only one who voted with the northern section, through the latter and worse acts of that party. As his influence and vote (as a southern member,) could now render no more useful service to the administration, he had lately been rewarded by a seat in the Cabinet.

A large minority of the rural and village population of Maryland, and the much larger portion of all east of the Chesapeake bay, are true and zealous southerners in sentiment, and are for maintaining their rights and vital interests in the institution of slavery. But all these, being a minority of the state, are scarcely heard in the state counsels and government. Their danger, as slaveholders, on account of their position near the border lines, and for the other general conditions of Maryland, are more grave, and more calculated to cause alarm for the future, than those of any other state in the original federal union.

The sudden breaking out of hostilities, and the manner, in western Virginia, served to quicken and strengthen the disposition for resistance wherever it had existed before, and to awaken it wherever dormant.

LETTER XLII.

Political movements of border states. More acts of secession.

RICHMOND, June 26, 1868.

At the appointed time for the conference, June 1st, commissioners from North Carolina, Virginia and Arkansas met at Raleigh. There were none sent from Texas, and could not have been for want of time. Also, for different reasons, none had been sent from Maryland, Kentucky, Tennessee and Missouri. The commissioners of Virginia as instructed by the legislature, and for reasons stated at length, urged the secession of all the remaining slaveholding states, and their joining the southern confederacy. They added to their general argument, that since the recent invasion of their state, and the actual war carried on between it and the northern section and federal government, the secession and independence of Virginia might be deemed accomplished. But that, in deference to her sister states similarly exposed, she proposed that all of them, or as many as would now concur in the policy, should secede together and under one declaration. These three states, by their commissioners, soon agreed in such a declaration of secession, and of accession to the southern confederacy—which was immediately communicated to their several legislatures, all in session, and the acts were speedily ratified and made complete by all the several necessary authorities.

The legislatures of the states of Maryland, Kentucky, Tennessee and Missouri had still hesitated, and therefore, failing to send commissioners to the conference, had so far indirectly opposed the recourse to secession. But after

Virginia, North Carolina and Arkansas had actually taken the preliminary steps for secession, and with the certain assurance that Texas will follow immediately, the question became very different to the other four and only remaining states. These four states, if still remaining attached to the nominal general government, and really to the northern section, would certainly be powerless, and at the mercy of the northern states—and could not expect to have their property in and rights to slaves respected even for a year. Further—if the war continued, the loss to the agriculture and commerce of these four border states would be incalculable, if they continued attached to the northern section. Kentucky, Tennessee and Missouri would have no southern (and scarcely any) outlet for their productions, and must share fully in the sufferings from all the restrictions imposed by the south on their northern enemies. Maryland depends for her commercial existence on the trade with Virginia and the foreign commerce carried on almost exclusively through the broad waters and strait of Virginia. To lose these advantages, or to have their use made very hazardous, would be ruinous to Maryland. These views left no choice to these states—and, compelled by the necessity of the circumstances, they also qnickly followed in the declaration of secession. Texas is now the only exception, and will not be so longer than her authorities can act. And with that temporary exception, it may be considered that, in effect, the fourteen slaveholding states have now all seceded from the northern section, and are re-united in the southern confederacy.

LETTER XLIV.*

Occupation of Harpers' Ferry. Re-annexation of the District of Columbia to Maryland.

RICHMOND, June 30, 1868.

Everything being again quiet in the north-western part of Virginia, and the political and military condition of things elsewhere indicating that no new invasion, or assault, could be soon attempted there by the northern power, weakened as it was by recent events, the governor of Virginia had ordered Gen. S. to withdraw all the remaining troops, except the necessary frontier garrisons. The discharged volunteers were sent to their homes by the most convenient routes. All the others, and including all who had come by the way of Harper's Ferry, returned, embodied, by that route, and for other required service.

In passing, the United States arsenal and manufactory of arms at Harper's Ferry, were occupied, and a sufficient garrison left in charge. The ground used for these purposes had long ago been ceded by Virginia to the federal government, and had since been retained. The arms in the arsenal (formerly 200,000 stands or more,) had been mostly removed northward some months ago; and since the war began in Virginia, the removal of the remainder had been hurried, and the manufacturing operations stopped. The military guard (a company of United States infantry,) had been withdrawn, as the place is incapable of being defended

*The Letter No. XLIII is missing—for reasons which will be stated hereafter—with explanations of the contents.—EDITOR.

against any superior numbers, having possession of the higher surrounding eminences. There still remained 50,000 stands of small arms, which there had not been the means for conveying away in time to secure them. These, and all the moveable implements and facilities for manufacturing arms, were deemed proper prizes of war, and ordered to be removed from this exposed frontier, to the armory and arsenal at Richmond. This service, at Harper's Ferry, required but the temporary detention of a few hundred men. The main body, of 5000, moved on with all speed, by the Alexandria and Loudoun Railroad, to the camp near Alexandria, there uniting with the 4000 troops sent by the southern confederacy, which (as stated in my last letter,) had lately occupied that position. Consultations had been previously held with the governor of Maryland, who was ready to act in advance of the (now certain and) fast approaching formal secession of that state—and consequent secret arrangements had been made with the commanding officer of the militia and volunteers, and a few other leading persons in Washington. Within two hours of the same time, in the latter part of the night of June 29th, all the troops from the Alexandria camp and 2000 volunteers from Maryland, reached Washington, and attacked the several posts of the federal army. The regiment of Washington volunteers was under arms almost as soon as the first signal was sounded. As soon as the alarm had aroused all the inhabitants, and they had learned the cause, and the object of the assailants, nearly 2000 men more of the militia, very irregularly armed, and mostly with private arms, severally hastened to join the volunteers and the southern army. The garrison of the city though regulars, 3000 in number, were mostly new recruits; and even if they had not been taken by surprise, would have been unable to resist with any chance for success. As soon as the first onslaught had been made, and the advantage of a surprise gained, a parley was sounded, and the garrison summoned to surrender. This was promptly agreed to, the arms and munitions of war to be surrendered, but the troops to be permitted to withdraw, and to be forthwith marched, under an armed escort, to the border of Pennsylvania, and there left to proceed northward.

At the same time, a strong separate force, having howitzers and shells, had assaulted Fort Washington on the land side, sixteen miles lower on the Maryland bank of the Potomac, where its defences were weakest, and the fort is commanded by higher neighboring ground. Its small garrison of 200 men soon capitulated.

The capture of these places, and especially of the Navy Yard and Fort Washington, placed in the possession of the southern army a large quantity of cannon, and material for land and naval war, and several small vessels of war in a more or less advanced state of construction, or of repair. The possession of the District and city was forthwith offered to and assumed by the commander of the Maryland contingent, for his state government. The 4000 troops sent by the southern confederacy, strengthened by 2000 of Maryland volunteers, (all now in the service of the southern confederacy,) were left as a garrison for the city. The public buildings and all other property of the former federal government are ordered to be carefully guarded from all damage or depredation.

In addition to these successes of the South, a report has just been received of the capture of Pensacola, with its two forts and its important dock yard, by an expedition ordered by President M., and composed of troops that had served and been instructed, and had gained military experience, at Charleston. Pensacola being of but little importance as a place of trade, and being strongly defended, had been heretofore left unassailed. But it is the only southern harbor admitting vessels of twenty-one feet draft, (at high tide,) and therefore, with its dock yard, was an important possession for the northern power, and for the repair of vessels blockading the southern harbors, The gallant conquest of this place, lately effected, has restored to the southern confederacy every acre of its whole territory, and removed every armed enemy from its soil—with the exception of that occupied by the northern army in Mississippi—which by the latest accounts, was in slow, but almost sure progress to a deplorable exhaustion of its strength, by disease, if not by still worse inflictions.

LETTER XLV.

The progress of the federal army in the South-west. Negroes and Negrophilism.

RICHMOND, July 1, 1868.

It has already been stated that the northern division of the federal army, which moved from Philadelphia through Pittsburg, finding the passage by the river Ohio opposed by hastily constructed batteries, had proceeded by railroad conveyance to the site and designed camp for concentrating the different corps, in Illinois, on the Ohio river, and near its junction with the Mississippi. There, Gen. N. had rapidly assembled under his command, in addition to the force brought from Pennsylvania of 9000 regulars, (including artillery and cavalry,) 6000 regulars, infantry and riflemen from the western posts, and 10,000 drafted militia from Ohio, Indiana and Illinois—making 25,000 in all. There were still expected to follow speedily the 7000 men under Gen. W., whose progress was merely known to be delayed, in Virginia, but whose impediments were not then suspected to be serious. Later and large reinforcements were expected of recently recruited regulars, from the northern cities. But, as so much time had already been lost, speed was of the utmost importance, when summer and the sickly season were so near; and Gen. N. determined to proceed down the river with his then assembled strength, leaving the expected reinforcements for later embarkation and passage. A numerous flotilla had been collected, and was hourly augmenting, for transporting the army, and its munitions and provision—composed of every kind of vessel used for freight on the western rivers, from the largest sized steamers down to flat boats for towing, and row-boats. None of these vessels were suited for purposes of war, and all were of the slight and light construction best adapted for speed and for carrying freight, on narrow and sheltered rivers, and for cheap service. Of course such vessels are altogether unfitted to serve for fighting, being too weak to bear the concussion of firing heavy artillery from their decks, and every one was liable to be disabled by a single well-directed cannon ball from an enemy. But no opposition was expected, before reaching Mississippi, the first hostile state—and none was supposed possible to be offered by either of the more northern slaveholding states, Kentucky, Tennessee and Arkansas, whose entire devotion to the Union, and to the federal government, was then undoubted.

The fleet of steamers, and the various other vessels towed by the steamers, reached the northern extremity of the state of Mississippi on the 25th of May. A strong fortification of earth-work, called Fort Calhoun, had been hastily constructed on the most northern site suitable for defence, and having exposed to its guns two long stretches (one above and the other below the fort,) of the great but narrow river. But hasty and rough as was the construction, the fortification had been planned by the best skill and science of engineering. It was also ably commanded, and its guns were well served and directed. The guns were but few, and still fewer of these were of large calibre, and of long range. If there had been no deficiency in these respects, at this and sundry other favorable positions on the Mississippi river, a good battery at any one such place could sink or disable, if not entirely stop, one-half of any fleet of ordinary river vessels that could attempt to force a passage.

Col. D., the brave and experienced artillery officer in command, had a superfluity (2000) of raw and newly arrived volunteers, armed with muskets and rifles—but had but few cannon, and barely enough good gunners and artillerymen to serve them well. And these made up nearly all his fighting force, except for the short time when the vessels were nearest, when the rifles, and especially those of new construction and longest range, could operate with effect. Gen. N. had not known, until when descending the river, that such fortifications had been constructed, anywhere on the river—and even if knowing the general fact, would have supposed the defence that could be made would be so contemptible, as scarcely to delay his progress, unless requiring him to land and capture the fort, and disperse its raw garrison. Neither he nor the federal administration seemed to have counted upon any but raw and incapable officers serving the seceded states, and commanding the new levies of militia. The abundant supplies of excellent officers, which had been furnished by the former unjust sectional policy of the federal government, was not thought of, until after sundry trials, and most disastrous proofs.

With such limited means for offence, Col. D. could do but little compared to what might have been done by proper means. But still, his operations were as disastrous to the enemy, as they were unexpected and surprising. The fleet came down the river towards the fort, and when within range of its guns, with all possible speed. The cannon from the fort were well directed, and whenever a ball struck the frail hull of a steamer, it rarely failed to pass through, and in most cases disabled either the machinery or the vessel. The light pieces of field artillery, on the decks of some of the stoutest steamers, only could be fired in return, and the rifles, when at nearest distance—and neither with any effect. The fleet passed on, the uninjured vessels leaving to their fate such as were either stopped or retarded by shots from the fort. To have stopped often enough and long enough to succor or relieve all the crippled vessels, would have too much endangered all the others. At the first suitable landing place on the left bank of the river, (and which was some miles below the fort,) the fleet was stopped, to repair damages. The forces were here landed—which would have been required because of the injuries to the vessels, but which was also deemed necessary to capture the fort, and so prevent its destructive fire upon the next passing expedition, whether of the returning empty vessels, or the succeeding fleets coming with reinforcements and supplies for the army. The trial made had clearly shown that no such fleet could pass such a fort, if fully armed and well manned and commanded. The serious damages now sustained amounted to the sinking, or disabling and stopping, of four large steamers, and one of small size, laden either with troops, cavalry horses, cannon or provisions—and twelve large flats or smaller boats similarly laden. The loss to the enemy, were more than 500 men, killed or drowned, 150 cavalry and artillery horses, ten pieces of heavy field artillery, and a quantity of provisions. Some of the disabled vessels either ran on shore or sank in shallow water near the fort, so that afterwards all the cannon, and much of the other dead freight, were saved by the captors.

The results of this encounter produced other unexpected difficulties and prospective heavy pecuniary costs. Besides paying (as usual in all such contracts of governments,) most extravagant charges for the use of all these chartered vessels, the government had to insure their safe return. The safe return up the stream, by the fort, of steam vessels of hostile character and ownership, was almost impossible, and certainly too hazardous to be ventured—and whether detained uselessly below, and also guarded to prevent surprise and capture, or destroyed in attempting to return up the river, in either case, the whole estimated or charged value of the vessels would be a dead loss to the government. The same would be the case as to every succeeding fleet, or vessel, with the dangers increasing with every day's delay serving to allow better preparation for this fort, and the construction of others. The taking of Fort Calhoun thus became a necessity. Therefore, if it had not otherwise been required, the army was disembarked, and as soon as possible proceeded to invest and besiege Fort Calhoun on the land side. Some efforts had been made by Col. D. with his garrison, and other volunteers, amounting in all then to 4000 men, to oppose the landing, and harass the subsequent advance of the invaders. But though his riflemen, without suffering much in return, killed or wounded more than 400 of the enemy, he was obliged to retreat, while fighting, to the fort, and there to stand a siege. The works were too strong, and the defence too resolute for Gen. N. to attempt to take the fort by storm, and his cannonading had but little effect. He could not prevent supplies of men and provisions being received on the river side—and within a few days, the guns were increased by the recovery and placing of the ten pieces of artillery from the sunken vessel. But though unable to take the fort, at first, and the prospect of its capture seeming daily to grow less, as the place was reinforced, still half of the invading army was enough to maintain the siege, leaving the remainder disposable for the present, for any other purpose. Portions of these, principally of cavalry, were used as foraging parties, to scour the neighboring country, and visit all the plantations, and to collect as much of provisions and forage as could be obtained. These supplies were taken wherever found, and nominally on purchase. But the only mode of payment was in certificates of the debts, signed by the officers, and which obligations, it was promised to the unwilling creditors, would be subsequently redeemed by the United States government. But there was so little credence given to these promises, that every man for whose property such certificates were held, deemed them almost worthless, and supposed that he had been robbed of their full amount. Of course, every effort was used by the proprietors to prevent their provisions or other moveables falling into the hands of the enemy. And owing to some circumstances peculiar to this country, these efforts could be more successful than would be supposed in advance of knowledge of the facts.

Rich and productive as is the soil of this region, there has been but little of grain or provisions raised. It has been the general and bad practice of the planters, in their effort to make as much as possible for market of their great and profitable crop, cotton, to rely upon buying more or less, and often the larger proportion, of the grain and other provisions needed for the plantations. These supplies had heretofore been furnished abundantly, and cheaply enough, from the upper states, (and formerly mostly from the north-western states,) by steamers. Thus the planters had usually provided themselves with the needed grain and meat from time to time, barely in advance of their wants, and did not often, from April to October, have a supply on hand of provisions for three months' use. But this ordinary scarcity of surplus provisions had been made much greater by the late interruption of trade and navigation on the river, and the shutting out supplies from all the hostile or north-western states. The only recently permitted navigation, or trade, had been of the vessels and products of the slaveholding states of Virginia, Kentucky, Tennessee, Arkansas and Missouri, with which there had been no interruption of intercourse, or friendly relations. These different circumstances had caused a general absence of superfluous provisions throughout the cotton country near the rivers—though everywhere there would have been an abundance for the usual wants of the inhabitants. But it followed, that even when the foraging parties of the enemy swept off all the grain and provisions which they found, they obtained barely sufficient supplies for the temporary consumption of the army. A large proportion of all the surplus grain, &c., of the neighboring planters had been transported to the fort, before the invasion, and so was protected from the enemy. Much of the small quantities remaining on the plantations the proprietors concealed, or moved off in advance of the expected visits of foraging parties. And many planters who could not thus save their grain, destroyed it, to prevent its being taken for the use of the enemy. In addition to the difficulty of obtaining supplies of provisions, owing to their absolute scarcity on the plantations, and especially near to the fort, within a few days after the landing of the invading army, the foraging parties met with other obstructions. Troops of cavalry, and other volunteer forces had been assembling rapidly. And though neither their numbers, at first, nor their condition of preparation and discipline, of these new levies permitted them to face the invading army in open battle, they cut off and restrained the foraging parties, and soon rendered such operations very difficult and dangerous, unless conducted by a force able to face and repel the whole body of the new troops that could be brought together to oppose the invaders. Gen. F., who commanded the new and rapidly increasing force of raw Mississippi volunteers pursued the proper policy for the circumstances of avoiding all fighting on open ground, or otherwise unless when with some advantage of position which would more than compensate for the want of discipline and experience on his side. His tactics and operations consisted mainly of a succession of retreats from the serious attempts to attack his main body, and of frequent changes of place of every detachment of his army, so as to mislead and frustrate every exertion of the superior military strength of the invading army. As soon as the southern army, (increased by the superfluous portion of the garrison of the fort,) had been increased to some 5000 in number, Gen. N., leaving enough of the northern army to maintain the siege, moved rapidly with the larger portion to attack the main camp of the southerners. But rapid as was the movement to assail, the arrangements for information had served to fore-warn Gen. F. and to enable him to retreat, in good time and in good order, and without any loss, to another temporary position. No open resistance was offered to sundry other like attempted attacks. The invading army marched wherever it was ordered, with scarcely any opposition. But still it commanded obedience, or submission, only on the ground held for the time in military occupation. Though this country offers no mountain steeps or defiles, and is generally well adapted for the operations of an invading army, still there are many swamps impassable by armies, and miry-bottomed rivers and *bayous*, and ground covered by woods and thickets of cane and dense shubbery, to afford excellent cover to a defensive force, acquainted with the localities, and, thus to enable a skillful commander to foil and to damage a superior attacking force. Such movements were made, by Gen. F's orders, as to draw the invaders into difficult localities, and where the rifles of the concealed volunteers could have effect. In this manner, day after day passed, with small but continual losses of men. and still more of cavalry horses, of the invaders, and almost with impunity on the part of the defenders. In the progress of these operations, Gen. N's army, which included the greater number of the whole invading force, was drawn to a considerable distance from the portion left to carry on the siege, and another smaller encampment of troops at the landing place, which was required there to protect the vessels, and also the landing of the daily expected and large reinforcements of men and provisions and other supplies. Under all these circumstances, the invading forces were daily weakened, and still more discouraged, while the southerners were as regularly increasing in numbers, and in their readiness and fitness for military duties.

The small steamer which had been disabled and captured by the fort in the passage of the fleet, was but slightly damaged, and was soon repaired and put to good use. It was of shallow draught, and was a swift runner. Col. D. armed this steamer with a twelve pound cannon, and twenty riflemen, having rifles of the longest range. The aid of this vessel and its armament, to the guns of the fort, was sufficient to stop, or capture, every passing unarmed vessel belonging to, or in the service of the enemy, and to prevent the possibility of the passage of any flotilla, except by force, and with great loss. Previously, some of the invaders' steamers had attempted, at night to return up the river, by the fort, and a few had succeeded in so escaping, by favor of the darkness, and the distance of the firing from the guns of the fort. But after having the use of the little armed steamer, no steam or other vessel could possibly pass, unless sufficiently armed to force its passage, which was not the case with one on the river, unless when armed for conveying troops. The same measures served to prevent completely all supplies of provisions being brought by unarmed boats from the upper or north-western states. Those from all the upper slaveholding states, continued to be freely admitted, but only to furnish their supplies to southerners. Thus the fort, and the outside southern army, and also the population of the invaded country, were well supplied with provisions from Tennessee, Kentucky and Missouri mostly, while the invading army was already beginning to suffer from the privation of sufficient and wholesome food, and the consequences in sickness and discontent.

There was one means of offence, other than military, which had been much relied on in advance, by northerners at home, and also greatly feared by many southerners, as the most dangerous and injurious incident or consequence of secession of slaveholding states, and their invasion by northern troops. This was the seduction and incitement of the slaves to desert their masters and seek freedom in the camp or country of the invaders—if not also to make extended insurrection, under such encouragement and aid, and to convert the whole slaveholding country to another St. Domingo. This invasion served as the first occasion to test the correctness of these opinions of northern abolitionists. From the beginning, and with every visit of a foraging party to every plantation, or wherever a military detachment of the invaders was encamped within a few miles distance, every slave had it completely in his power to desert his master's plantation, and join the invaders, and be protected by them from any immediate punishment or damage from his former rulers. In addition to these wide-spread opportunities for escape, known to all, the many fanatical abolitionists of the invading militia, and those from Ohio especially, exerted themselves to invite and persuade the slaves to use the present means offered, and in their power, to assume their freedom, by desertion or insurrection. These seductions and inducements had effect on a few slaves, and especially in the beginning. But, in general, and with few exceptions, the failure of such attempts was signal and complete. The ignorant negroes in general were more alarmed at, and more fearful of the invading forces than were their masters; and the better informed among the slaves had learned enough to make them altogether distrustful of such offers of freedom, even if desirous at heart to attain the promised condition. They had heard of the sufferings, in their new condition of freedom at the north, of many slaves who formerly had been seduced by the false statements of abolition agents to flee—of the inhuman neglect of these their victims by the abolitionists at the north—of the base treachery of other northerners, who induced and aided the escape of slaves, merely afterwards to arrest and carry them back to their masters, for the offered rewards. Further, all of them had heard the traditionary accounts of the like invitations and encouragements for the desertion or insurrection of slaves having been offered by the British forces and commanders in the invasions of the southern states during both the wars of 1776 and 1812, and of the disastrous results to the victims, who, whether of their choice, or by compulsion, were changed to the so-called condition of freedom. These old stories, with all their exaggerations, of the falsehood and cruelty of the invaders, and the sufferings of their victims, the fugitive slaves in the war of 1776, had doubtless been generally communicated to the succeeding generation of slaves, and had produced on them such a distrust and fear of any like offers, that, in the war of 1812, with every facility at command, the remarkable fact was universal that not one slave in Virginia (or elsewhere, so far as known,) voluntarily deserted to the invading enemy, or went off with any of the numerous foraging and plundering parties which at various times had complete control of hundreds of different plantations, on which the slaves then only remained at home to receive the invaders. It is true, that at a later time, and after any voluntary desertion of slaves was hopeless, many hundreds of them were carried off to the British ships. But it was in every case by force, and not by consent of the abducted slaves. These facts are well established. By the treaty of peace, England agreed to pay, and did pay, the full value of these slaves, some thousands, I believe, in number, on the admitted ground that they had been carried off by force. These later and more noted occurrences in Virginia and Maryland, added to the older traditions of the war of 1776, had probably been regular fire-side narrations of the older to the younger slaves, and had impressed them with horror for any such attempts. Many of the negroes of Mississippi, and of the other south-western states, had been brought from the tide-water counties of Virginia and Maryland, and were acquainted, by report, with all the circumstances referred to, and were respected as authorities for the most exaggerated incidents. Some additional and stronger influences for discontent were now operating, in the personal persuasions of fanatical abolitionists, having or professing religious affiliations with some of the slaves, which influences prevented as complete failure, at this time, of the attempts at inveigling of slaves from their service, as occurred to my philanthropic countrymen in the war of 1812. Still, up to this time, it is understood that all the slaves who have so absconded to the enemy's army in Mississippi, were less than forty in number, and that no cases had occurred later than the first week of the invasion.

I do not mean to intimate that this slowness or reluctance of negro slaves to accept of the offers and to trust to the promises of freedom, as in this recent case, and in still more marked manner, and universally, in the war of 1812, is evidence of their preferring their present condition of bondage, or of unwillingness to be free from the control of a master. I fully believe that that control, and bondage, are necessary for the well-being and greatest possible usefulness and happiness of the negro race. But negro slaves, as well as all other persons in bondage of any kind, even of loving children to loving parents—would prefer to be free from constraint, and of obedience to any but their own will. A negro especially hates labor—and his idea of liberty is the licence to be idle. Of course a negro slave would generally desire to be relieved, by emancipation, from the obligation to labor at a master's command—and his ignorance would generally prevent his knowing, or duly appreciating, that the necessary alternative would be, if free, to labor under the compulsion of want. But even when influenced in feeling by these considerations, and by the false as well as the true, there are other counteracting influences operating to deter any attempted action, besides those referred to above of suspicion and distrust of his pretended friends and patrons, the abolitionists. The negro is naturally timid, unenterprising, fearful of and averse to change to any new and untried condition. Also, he is especially in awe of his master's authority, even though it should be absent or suspended for a time, and of the power of the superior race and dominant class to which his master belongs. Therefore, even if the southern slaves were as willing to achieve their freedom by flight, or by insurrection and bloody general massacre, as the northern abolitionists are to incite them to such acts—if they had not the existing love for their master's family, which is general, and feeling of compunction or horror for the murderous acts enjoined upon them by such advisers—still, before negro slaves could be so moved, it would be further necessary to quiet their fears of future punishment, by the perfect assurance that no suffering, or reverse of circumstances, would ever follow their assumption of freedom. And such assurance can never be given by any hostile power or invading army, that is at the same time struggling to maintain its temporary supremacy, or which has not already completely subdued the invaded country and people, and suppressed all appearance of opposition. Should the northern section, and its armed forces, ever be thus supreme in the southern states, then, the offer of freedom to the slaves, if made by the conquering and impregnable ruling power, will doubtless be generally accepted. But until then, the offer of freedom to the slaves, even though accompanied by the promise (from the abolitionists) of seizing and possessing their masters' property, as the reward for general and successful insurrection and massacre, will have but little effect. By such efforts, in time of war, or in political separation, a few slaves may be persuaded and enabled to desert their southern service, and flee to the north. But, with the restraints that either war or political separation will enable to be enforced, these losses will be less in number than have heretofore been suffered by the southern slaveholders, when under the same general government with the abolition emissaries—who, as fellow-citizens then had free access to every slaveholding state, and almost to every slave.

The admission that negro slaves probably would generally rebel, and free themselves and seize on their masters' property, if perfectly assured of success, has no more of special application to negro slaves than to the most destitute and suffering white and (so called) free citizens or subjects of the most refined and philanthropic countries of Europe, or even of these northern states, where negrophilism is most rife and rampant, and where the anti-slavery fanatics rely with most confidence on negro insurrection both as a condemnation and a remedy for slavery. Suppose that England or France or either of these oldest northern states, was subdued, and powerless in the military occupancy of an overwhelming hostile power—and that that power offered and proclaimed to all the destitute classes relief and freedom from want, and invited them, under the secure protection of the conquering power, to take possession, at will, of the property and wealth of any or all who possessed any. Does any one believe that the destitute classes of England and France, thus encouraged, and assured of entire success and safety, would not eagerly accept the offered benefits? And if the owners of property should dare to resist its peaceable seizure, would the new claimants hesitate to assert their new rights by force? Or, if necessary for their successful assertion, to use fire and sword, and every other means of terror and destruction, to enforce their new privileges? Even in this comparatively plentiful country, where so few as yet suffer from hunger, would the most destitute and suffering classes in the great cities of the north-eastern states decline to accept such offered privileges and bounties, at the expense of the property, and even of the lives also, of their fellow-citizens, the present property holders? For one, I verily believe that, if the most unbounded privileges of these kinds—of licence of every kind, and with the assurance of undoubted impunity in the exercise—were offered both to the people of Massachusetts and to the slaves of any southern states, that the latter would be slower to use these offered benefits, than that every wealthy abolitionist in Boston would be shot or hung, and his property seized by his near neighbors, and present disciples and followers.

The latest accounts from the seat of war in Mississippi leave the contending parties in the positions and conditions above stated. The northern army, though unresisted in field operations, and able to move, and to command, at will, (except to conquer Fort Calhoun,) gained nothing, of value to its cause and objects, by its superior strength, and undisputed sway. The commander dared not attempt to proceed farther down the river, with the hostile fort still commanding the passage of the river in his rear, and able to stop all reinforcements and supplies—nor to march far into the interior—nor to leave his fleet without a strong guard. He was daily losing men slain by unseen or retreating enemies, and his sick list was increasing alarmingly, by wounds, privation, and diseases, the consequences of privation and hardships of his raw troops. But large reinforcements of men, and arms, and all needed supplies were expected daily; and by aid of which all opposing difficulties were expected to be speedily and effectually removed. The last reports from the army were up to June 20th, to which time, Gen. N. had not learned the previous occurences, military and political, which, if known, would have served to show the utter fallacy of all his plans, and all hopes for reinforcements of troops, or supplies of provisions being sent to him. The latest of all the events referred to, the states of Arkansas, Missouri, and Tennessee, and Kentucky, having joined the southern confederacy, will render the navigation of both the Ohio and Mississippi rivers, and even the lower Missouri, utterly impracticable to all northern and hostile vessels. These new circumstances, must place the situation of the northern army in Mississippi in great peril, from which I cannot conceive any possible mode of escape. If the army shall merely remain as it is, until late in July, even if abundantly supplied with provisions, and without danger from any opposing forces, the diseases of the climate and season alone will be enough to prostrate and destroy the army. To this end, the invading army may be left, if the means of Gen. F. should not enable him earlier to attack and fight the invading army with certainty of success. In the meantime, his army is daily increasing in numbers, and improving in discipline and efficiency.

But even if reinforcements and provisions could be supplied to the army—and supposing that it had met with no check or disaster—it still would be a grave question for consideration, whether any benefit or gain can accrue to the invading power or to its objects. Putting aside the aid and success of negro insurrection, (which so far has been entirely a failure, and seems utterly hopeless in this case,) the conquest, and enforced submission of even this one state, Mississippi, alone—to say nothing of the whole southern confederacy—and if with the aid of quadrupled military forces, must be impossible. With such greater force, or even with his present force, Gen. N. may march whenever he may choose, and put down any opposition that may be presented. He too may ravage and destroy the country, while so unopposed. But still he would command no more territory then the ground enclosed within his surrounding line of out-posts—and as the army would move, so would be changed and shifted its limited territorial supremacy. If the northern government shall pay for all its supplies, obtained by compulsion from the inhabitants of the country, as engaged and promised in the certificates, it will be an enormous expense, for no important or abiding benefit. If the debts shall be disavowed, for which certificates are given, then there will have been committed a stupendous system of cheating and robbery, which will draw on the government the scorn and contempt of the civilized world.

LETTER XLVI.

Negro insurrection incited by Northern fanatics. Events in Maryland.

RICHMOND, July 8, 1868.

The events of this war, short as it has been, ought to have shown to all reasoning abolitionists of the northern states that there is little aid to their cause to be expected from negro deserters and allies, and still less from negro insurrections. But fanatics are incapable of correct reasoning, or of learning truth—or of seeing anything otherwise than through the distorting and deceptious medium of their one engrossing idea, and the resulting false dogmas of the peculiar wretched condition of negro slaves in these southern states, and of their readiness and fitness to attempt, with the offer of aid from abroad, to achieve their enfranchisement, through insurrection, rapine, and general massacre of the whites. The sanctimonious philanthropists, who ardently sought the result of the general emancipation of the negroes, were not repelled or discouraged by the use of any means for that end, however destructive, bloody, and even if more horrible than one general massacre of all the whites. Notwithstanding their previous disappointments, and especially of the most notable former attempt under John Brown, these fanatics still fully believed that the only reason why their cherished means for general emancipation—wide-spread and successful insurrection of the slaves—had not already occurred in the South, as a consequence of this war, was the want of sufficient encouragement and support to insurgents, and of evidence of sympathy and zeal for the negroes, and of power to sustain their efforts, in an acting and efficient force of competent and resolute white leaders and co-operators, and directed by abolition counsels and policy. From the beginning of hostilities, the associated and organized abolitionists, especially of the New England states, and in western New York, and Ohio, and Delaware, had been preparing means, and forming plans, to excite insurrection on a large scale of operations. In their expanded philanthropic views, the movers of these measures were not limited in their designed action to the then seceded states. Though the actual war of the northern government was then confined to the six early seceding states, the fanatical conspirators were at war with negro slavery in general, (in these southern states,) and held all the slaveholding states equally as foes. And as the previous secret communications and plots, and various operations of northern abolition agents, on slaves, had been mostly set on foot in Maryland, Virginia, and Kentucky, it was much easier to renew and extend communications with slaves in these localities than to begin new ones in the more remote southern states. Through various organs and channels of communication, which northerners had maintained, in ostensible business or religious pursuits, in the southern states, hundreds of slaves in these border states had been tampered with, and more or less indoctrinated with the northern ethics of emancipation and insurrection, with their incidents and aids of robbery, arson, and murder. And these then dormant connexions could easily be revived, and extended as far as would be safe, or would not bring about disclosure, before the designed time for the actual out-break. Before the final secession of the border states, and while as yet there was no new or effective obstacle to the entrance and sojourn and machinations of northern agents, the plan and means for extended insurrections were cautiously made known to many negro preachers, and others of the most suitable among the slaves in the particular localities designed for the early operations. It was not deemed safe to trust many with knowledge of the designs, for fear of their being disclosed. But, as the northern conspirators proceeded upon the established abolition belief that every slave will be anxious and ready to assert his freedom as soon as he is offered arms and support, it was deemed of but little importance that the numbers of the first initiated and chosen leaders should, in the beginning, be very few. The lights and views of the fanatical abolitionists and prime movers of these attempts were in no respect altered from the time and incidents of John Brown's raid in 1859; and the present plans were but copies, or continuations, of that earlier effort. It was believed by them that the sole cause of the total failure of the attempt under Brown's leading, and why not even one slave joined him, was that he did not have at least a few hundred whites to begin the work, and encourage the slaves by their support, instead of only the two dozen northern desperadoes whom he was so sanguine as to believe were sufficient for the supposed easy work.

To make the now designed out-breaks more terrible and effective, it was determined that they should be made at the same time, or as nearly together as could be, in two remote places, in Maryland and Kentucky, which states, by previous facilities and operations, had especially been exposed to the machinations of the abolitionists. In Maryland the great number of free negroes, and the close vicinity of the numerous recently freed negroes in Washington and Delaware, had offered every facility for secret communication, and for making arrangements with the slaves. In Kentucky, in the counties near the Ohio river, there was a still more dangerous influence operating on the slaves, from abolition emissaries, both black and white, of the state of Ohio. In addition, there was a considerable tendency to abolition in Kentucky, which had been nursed and strengthed by the tolerated presence and teachings of such preachers as the Rev. Mr. Fee, and the speeches and publications of the noted Cassius M. Clay. It had been intended to invade the two localities chosen for the out-break, with as strong a force as could be brought from the North, of both whites and negroes, and with plenty of pikes and muskets to arm immediately some thousands of the insurgents expected as the earliest auxiliaries. It was at first designed to let these operations appear as merely private enterprises, having no encouragement from or connexion with the government. But the subsequent secession of the border states, and their being thus placed in the position of hostility to the northern section, enabled the abolition invasions to have the much stronger support of the countenance and pay of government, and its organized military aid. The requisite funds for the early arrangements, for both expeditions, had been provided by the associated abolitionists of the northern and western states.

As arranged for the operations in Maryland, five of the ordinary coasting vessels of New England, at Boston, received on board secretly, and at night, (to prevent information abroad,) nearly 700 whites and negroes, who had been enlisted for the expedition, and commanded by a noted white abolitionist and rescuer or abductor of slaves. The negroes were mostly unemployed sailors—and the whites were all fanatical abolitionists, and many of them desperadoes, well experienced in civil broils, or military service in foreign countries. Besides the arms for these men, there were carried 10,000 muskets and 5,000 pikes, for arming the first levies of insurgent slaves. The vessels also carried some pieces of field artillery, plenty of ammunition, and a sufficient stock of provisions.

The vessels sailed together, and kept in sight of each other generally throughout the voyage; but not so near as to seem as if acting in concert, and so to attract observation. They drew together when near the place designed for landing. This was that peninsula on the Chesapeake bay nearly surrounded by the broad and deep lower waters of the Potomac and Patuxent rivers. The vessels lingered until night-fall, and then approached the shore, and landed all the troops, with a sufficient supply of provisions, and a portion of the pikes. The very narrow "neck" of the peninsula, a few miles up the two rivers, was speedily occupied and strongly guarded. The vessels, retaining only their necessary crews, and some non-combatant passengers, were anchored together, not very far from the shore, where deemed safe from attack. Communication through the mail, and directed to white emissaries, had been made a few days earlier with a few only of the neighboring slaves who had been entrusted with knowledge of the plan. Thus, the vessels were looked for, and recognized by a preconcerted signal flag borne by one of them. Thus the engaged slaves were notified to come into the camp of the invaders, or, more generally, to begin and spread insurrection and massacre in every direction, and to arouse the uninitiated slaves to join the work. The locality was well chosen for the designed operations—and the plan was well devised for success, if the existing conditions of the slaves, and their sentiments, had been what the fanatics foolishly but firmly believed. But putting aside all other, and sufficient, causes for failure, if the plotters had known anything of *negro* human nature, they might have been sure that any such conspiracy, if confided to as many as fifty negroes, would necessarily be discovered or betrayed. This result had been produced in two different cases, and from very different causes. Three days before the arrival of the vessels, (on June 20th,) the whole plan and designs had been communicated to the commander of the southern troops then occupying Washington, from two different sources. One was a free negro resident of Washington, and a preacher, who was one of the early initiated, and among the most confided in, and who, under the combined operation of the fear of failure and the mercenary hope of reward, voluntarily betrayed his fellow conspirators and their instigators. Another like communication was received from a wealthy planter on the lower Potomac, who had been informed by one of his slaves who had enlisted in the scheme. He had at first thought only of the pleasure of becoming free—perhaps also rich, by the general division of property, as promised by abolition emissaries. But when he came to learn that the probable means for these ends would be the general massacre of the whites, to whom he bore no ill-will—and including the members of his master's family, and who were also his best friends, and to whom he was strongly attached—and, if not the butchery of his master's wife and daughters, always his kind benefactresses, their far more horrible fate—his feelings and conscience revolted from what he had thoughtlessly undertaken. He used the earliest safe opportunity for such dangerous confidence to inform his master, who, enjoining on him silence, hastened to give the information to Gen. S. only. This officer deemed it the best policy to let the plan proceed until all the agents now concerned could show themselves. He therefore enjoined, and took means to secure the silence of the only three other persons who knew of the disclosure—and he hastened, though very quietly, to make all the military and naval arrangements necessary for crushing the plot, and for securing as many as possible of the participators in it. Luckily for his object, he was able to induce silence and secrecy on three persons, and for three days, on a subject which the conspirators had entrusted to nearly fifty negroes, and to some of them three months before.

As the numbers, the arms, and the first designed operations of the northerners, and nearly the time for the beginning, were all known to the General, he was not required to employ more means, and nor at an earlier time, than would be amply sufficient for securing his objects. By judicious applications of these means, the five northern vessels and their crews were all captured, and without even an alarm gun being fired, before daybreak after the night of their being anchored. As soon as this was effected, and made known by a rocket from the vessels, the land forces which had been placed without the peninsula, armed with rifles, and bringing two field pieces, marched into the peninsula, first scattering and driving in the advanced guards at the neck, and soon after reaching the main body, and pouring upon them a murderous fire from long range rifles, and of cannister shot from the cannon. Most of the whites and some of the negroes fought bravely. But the northern preachers and abolition lecturers, and most of the negro soldiers, after receiving the first few volleys, fled, and endeavored to hide themselves. But there was no place for concealment, and no means for escape. The fighting men were shot down, and at first from distances too great for them to do much damage to the assailants. They fell back, continuing to fire, until driven to the waters' edge, where, pressed upon more and more by the advance of the assailants, the last of the resisting northerners died under sword cuts and bayonet thrusts. No quarter was asked for, or would have been given. The fugitives did not long enjoy their temporary escape. The peninsula was too small to permit long concealment. During the day, nearly all who had at first escaped were either shot in the pursuit, or brought in as prisoners. A few had resorted to swimming. But the water was then rough as well as very broad —so that probably not one of these escaped drowning. The prisoners were all hung, as soon as a gallows could be erected. Among those hanged was the notorious abolition leader, and apostle of insurrection and massacre, Wm. L. Garrison, who came to witness the expected certain success and triumph of his long and zealous labors in the cause of negrophilism. With him were hanged seven negro and nine white preachers or public lecturers on slavery and abolition. Gen. S. had not had time, (with due regard to secrecy,) to receive instructions from the President. But he had communicated with the Governors of Maryland and Virginia, and found their opinions to concur with his own, that, in such a case, there should be no prisoners made, and no delay of death to any who participated in the attempted execution of the designed atrocities. The common sailors of the crews of the vessels were allowed the benefit of future trial, to decide whether they should be hung as murderers, or held as prisoners of war. But the masters of the vessels, whose entire complicity in the general plan could not be doubted, were all hung, in company with Garrison, and the other lecturers and preachers. Two of these captains were noted characters, who had deserved hanging long before. They were Drayton and Sayers, who, as abolition agents, had carried off seventy-three slaves stolen from Washington, and had been captured, tried, and condemned for one of the felonies only. Before this first punishment, of confinement in the penitentiary had near expired, the then President, Fillmore, had pardoned these villains, secretly, and permitted their escape from the still remaining seventy-two prosecutions impending. The vessels, with their freight of arms and munitions of war, and the crews as prisoners, were sent to Washington, to which station also Gen. S. and his troops speedily returned.

In this affair there were killed in the fight and pursuit, or afterwards hung, 685 of the northern invaders, and 27 negro slaves of the neighborhood, who only had joined. Subsequently, there was seen the bodies of 12 of those who attempted to escape by swimming, and were drowned. There were, doubtless, many other slaves who had engaged their service, and had designed to join the enterprise, if it had not been so speedily crushed. But as there was no attempt of insurrection, nor even any indication of insubordination, outside of the camp of the northerners, nor any evidence against any slaves who were not there put to death, there was no further investigation, or acts of punishment or vengeance. What has been done is deemed a sufficient security against such future attempts of northern abolition in the South, or of negro insurrection—and much more to be relied on than all the legal and constitutional obligations and guarantees that could be devised, and which might be entered into, and sworn to be obeyed, by all the functionaries and people of the northern states.

LETTER XLVII.

Invasion of Kentucky by an abolitionist and negro army.

RICHMOND, July 9, 1868.

As nearly as could be at the same time with the events stated in my last letter, the abolitionist army, coming from Ohio, had invaded Kentucky, in strong force, and with awful effects.

Owen Brown, a son of John Brown who led the Harper's Ferry raid in 1859, had been one of the actors in that outrage. He, with a few others, then escaped from the deserved punishment of death, suffered by his comrades in guilt—and subsequently, when demanded for trial by the governor of Virginia, had been protected from arrest and trial by Gov. Dennison of Ohio, who thus violated his official duty and oath, to protect an atrocious criminal, because his crime had been committed to forward abolition. The associated northern abolitionists, having abiding and strong faith in the name and blood of the martyr John Brown, had sought out his son to command the strong force designed to excite the work of insurrection in Kentucky. By aid of the influence of men in high position in New England, New York, and Ohio, this Owen Brown had been authorized to raise a corps of volunteers, to serve as an independent command, and wherever Brown deemed he could best operate against the revolted states, and also where he could support, recruit, and increase his forces, from the enemy's country. According to the number of men that he might enlist, he was to receive a suitable military commission—whether as captain, if for a single company, colonel, for a regiment, or general, for numbers requisite for a brigade or a division. His troops would be armed, equipped, and provided with every needful supply, in the outset, at the expense of the federal government. But, after invading the territory of the seceded states, it was understood that the army must be self-supporting, in every thing except in the stated monthly pay of officers and soldiers. There was no restriction as to the kind of recruits. With all the organized aid and influence of the associated abolitionists of the North, Brown had enlisted 3500 men, of whom 2700 were northern negroes, and mostly drawn recently from Canada. The larger number had been fugitive slaves from the South—and, when enlisting with him, had long been suffering the ordinary evils of hunger and cold, to which are generally subjected these ignorant and improvident and deluded victims of northern philanthropy. To escape from these sufferings, much more than to obtain the promised future rewards and benefits, induced the ready enlistment of nearly all of these negroes. Brown received the commission of brigadier general—and on his nomination, the subordinate officers were appointed and commissioned. Most of these he selected from his white recruits. But some of the commissioned company officers, and many of the non-commissioned were mulattoes or negroes. But of whatever color, all the officers were violent abolitionists, and ready tools for any work in aid of abolition. As soon as mustered in the United States service, armed, equipped and provisioned, (all of which was done as hastily and secretly as possible,) the corps proceeded, mostly by railroad conveyance, through Ohio, to cross the river into Kentucky. At that time, (which was very soon after the secession of Kentucky,) there was not a single company in service in all the state, except 1000 men, who had been called early into service under the former government, and who then, as before, were guarding different points on the Ohio river, and all of them remote from the scene of this invasion. The expedition crossed the Ohio into a part of Kentucky where there is no great distance to reach a numerous slave population. With resident abolition agents, (Fee, and other preachers from the North,) and through them, with slaves near the river, communications had been established and maintained. Gen. Brown immediately, by proclamation, offered freedom and protection to all slaves who would join his standard, or otherwise assert their freedom by insurrection. Fire-arms or pikes were promised to all who would thus use them. Enough pikes and spare muskets had been brought to arm 10,000 men. And these, with a good supply of ammunition, made up nearly all of his baggage. For provisions, and every other supply, the General expected to draw abundant contributions from the neighborhood of his march or encampment.

The General moved on slowly towards the interior of the state, to afford the better opportunity for the operation of his proclamation. His scouting and foraging parties were spread out widely—and these, and also many others of the army, without command or discipline, sought for plunder as far from the main body of the army as they could venture. Whether by order or consent of the commander, or because he could not restrain the offenders, every thing near the line of march was doomed to destruction. The approach of so large a force could not be kept secret, and most of the inhabitants, both whites and blacks, had fled before the invaders. About 300 slaves, who had been previously engaged, came in and joined the invading army in the first twenty-four hours (and nearly all in the night time,) after the leaving of the river. But few white families remained in their homes long enough to be captured, or even seen, by the negro troops. But in some few cases, where the extreme illness of some member of a family compelled others to stay, and to trust to the mercy of the invaders, the consequences were too horrible to be described in detail. All the men, women and children so captured were butchered—after the infliction of still greater horrors. Whatever property was deemed of enough value for transportation, for the supplies of the army or for the individual plunderers, was so used. Everything else that was easily destructible, was destroyed. Every house, stack of forage or straw, and fence, was burnt—the horses and cattle killed, and as many as could be of all other domestic animals. The route of the army, for miles in width was left a waste, and a scene of devastation, in which scarcely a living being remained, and in which no movement was seen, unless of the smoke, or still raging flames, rising from the ashes of numerous homesteads, which, but a few hours before, had been the abodes of peace, industry and happiness.

The second night, the army encamped about twenty miles from the Ohio river. The next morning, the commander was surprised to learn that no more than forty-eight fugive slaves had come in to join him, and accept of freedom, during the previous night. But a still more remarkable thing was that one of the negro sentinels, a recruit from Canada, had absconded, with his arms; and that twenty-three others, of the same class, had also deserted the encampment. The cause and manner of these desertions were not known until later. But as they continued, and increased, through every subsequent day's march, or night's encampment, they will be explained here. Hundreds of these refugees in Canada had enlisted only to escape from their miserable condition—and in the hope of being thus enabled to get to the southern state whence they had formerly absconded, to flee to the North—and when there, to return if possible to their former respective homes and servitude. Or, if not, then to slavery to any southern master, rather than to continue free and starving with cold and hunger at the North. The sentinel who deserted had formerly escaped from a kind master, whose residence was within ten miles of the camp. As soon as placed on his post, he ran off, and pursuing his course through unfrequented routes, which he well knew, he arrived at his old home, and through one of the slaves was enabled to see his master, and to surrender himself to his mercy, without conditions. His master was then hurriedly preparing to flee, with his family and slaves, farther from the enemy. He received his repentant slave with forgiveness, and his reports with trust. He thus learned that hundreds of other fugitive slaves, in like manner, had joined the expedition merely to get back to their former condition—and that nothing was wanting but a safe mode for their desertion, security from ill-treatment by any person to whom they might surrender, to induce all these to escape as he had done, even at the risk of being transferred to a new and unknown master. This information was soon conveyed to the nearest civil and military authorities—and orders were issued, and made known, that every negro thus surrendering himself, and submitting to any white man, should be kindly treated, and transferred to the nearest authorities for subsequent arrangements. By these regulations, which were soon made known to the negroes of the army, every one who escaped, and made a signal of surrender and submission to the first white person he could see, was sure of protection from his late companions and rulers.

The third and the fourth days' marches of the army were made, as the preceding, without meeting with any military resistance—though on the last of these days, glimpses were caught of patrols of irregular cavalry. When the sudden irruption of this army of negroes, commanded by murderers and abolitionists, was first heard of, the neighboring inhabitants were horror-stricken—and all who were within eighteen or twenty miles of the army thought of nothing at first but to convey the helpless members of their families to more distant and secure places. The next thing was to order the conveyance to places of security, of the most valuable moveables, and lastly, to be followed by the slaves, after the adults had performed their duties in forwarding the other property. Of course, the last order was obeyed or disregarded at the choice of each slave, as there could be no compulsion or control. Some few deserted to the negro army. But nearly all hastened to follow the previous flight of their master to his then place of refuge. Indeed, in the general, the slaves seemed to be as much alarmed as their masters, and fully as anxious to get out of the way of the invaders. Until the men of the neighboring country had removed and taken the necessary care of their families, they could not attempt any military service. But as soon as these first duties had been attended to, every man who had been a temporary fugitive hastened to join in some military organization, and all were eager to be enabled to oppose the hated enemy.

On the fifth morning of the march, Gen. Brown found that his new recruits from absconding slaves of the neighboring country, for the preceding twenty-four hours, were no more than thirteen, and the desertion of negroes from his army, in the same time, amounted to fifty-seven. He had counted with certainty upon inciting the great body of the slaves to insurrection, and thereby subduing the white population by their own slaves; and that the mere presence of his army would be enough to spread the wave of insurrection, and negro supremacy far in advance of his own march. On the contrary, so far there was no symptom of insurrection, or insubordination, except in the desertions of slaves to his camp. And the small number of these, and their rapid decrease, showed plainly enough, that however willing to flee from their bondage, negro slaves were too fearful of consequences to desert to and join any hostile army, of whose superior power and entire success the least doubt was entertained. If Gen. Brown could have maintained, from the beginning of his invasion to this time, the firm confidence of the negroes in his power and success, the effects on them might have been very different—though, even then, not as great as he had anticipated. But they will rarely incur risk of personal danger to join new and doubtful allies—and never to sustain a weak and losing cause. Like all other northerners, Brown was entirely ignorant of the peculiarities of negro nature, disposition, and character —of the particular good and praise-worthy qualities, as well as of bad and despicable, in both of which the negro race differs from and far exceeds the white. If he had been as well-informed as he was ignorant on these points, Brown would now have inferred that he had already lost the little confidence which his first bold and successful movements had produced—and that there was no longer a prospect of any important co-operation or aid from the slaves.

Owing to the consternation of the neighboring residents, and the pressing first necessity for conveying away their families, the earliest military companies that reached the neighborhood of the invading army were from localities not less in any case than thirty miles distant—and mostly from much more remote residences. Some of these companies from the more remote localities, were of uniformed town volunteers, previously organized and drilled, and well armed, either as cavalry, infantry or riflemen. But even these had to lose one or two days, while waiting to be supplied with ammunition. Other companies, and much the greater number at first, were hastily raised and organized for this occasion and special service, irregularly and very insufficiently armed with such private and various weapons as men could supply themselves, or obtain from their neighbors. There had been scarcely any state organization of the militia—or preparation for actual service before the then very recent secession of the state of Kentucky, and none of the subsequent arrangements for military defence had yet been completed, or made effective for immediate use. Under such circumstances, more or less delay was incurred in making indispensable preparations for the first movements of troops so entirely unprepared. Thus it was not until the fifth day of the slow and devastating progress of the invading army, that it met with even a show of military resistance. Early on that day some troops of cavalry hovered around the army on its march, and began and continued to harass the flank and rear guards, and even repeatedly threatened the rear of the main army at favorable points. Much more damage was done by shots from distant and usually concealed riflemen, who selected their marks with deadly effect. Brown's cavalry force had been barely organized, with horses seized on his march, and therefore, was especially inefficient. He could do nothing except to use every care and safeguard against sudden attacks, and to repel them vigorously. He and his white followers were all men of tried courage, and as daring and fearless as their desperate undertaking required. They had to stand foremost in every post of danger, and to bear the brunt of every assault, not only for the most efficient service, but to encourage and stimulate the negroes, who, even if they had been naturally as brave as they are timid, were entirely without military training, and that artificial military force derived from discipline. Thus the whites were especially exposed, and even more than for their greater exposure, were the chosen marks of the concealed riflemen. And this continued to be the case throughout. Even when standing intermingled in the same ranks, the very few whites, if distinguishable by their foes, were made to supply much the greater number of the dead and wounded.

Before night, it was obvious to Brown that his enemies had much increased in numbers and in the boldness of their demonstrations. Late in the night, after some hours of quiet, a sudden and vigorous attack was made on his encampment, but which was soon withdrawn. It however cost some 150 killed and wounded to the invaders, with but little loss to the assailants in this hasty skirmish. The distant rifle-firing, through the previous day, had either killed or disabled nearly 100 of Brown's army, most of whom were whites. Of those who suffered in the night skirmish, nearly all were negroes.

The next morning, Gen. Brown found that in addition to the 250 of his men killed or disabled by wounds, nearly 200 more of his negro troops were missing—and whose course, as he rightly conjectured, had been to desert, and offer their submission, to the opposing troops. During the last preceding day and night not one fugitive slave had come in to join his forces. With the knowledge of these facts, all hope of efficient aid from that source was abandoned even by his sanguine mind. Still, to the eyes of others, he had lost nothing of his confident assurance of success. And he continued to advance, because a movement in retreat would have been an implied acknowledgment of failure, and the certain and speedy forerunner and cause of defeat.

The slow and guarded march of the invading army continued this day as before, and also the skirmishing, and distant firing of the Kentuckians, and with much increased effect. In this manner about 300 more of the invaders were either killed or disabled this day, and nearly all of them whites. To these so violent was the hatred of the Kentuckians, and their thirst for vengeance, that it was obvious that they reserved their shots for the whites, and deemed them thrown away on the negro soldiers, whom they had learned to hold in contempt. Gen. A. who now commanded the Kentuckians, also had ordered this course to be pursued, under the conviction that the whites constituted the strength and the life of the negro army. Further, it was jocularly argued by the Kentuckians that it was too wasteful to shoot a negro, who was worth $1500, and who would be certainly captured, and secured as a slave, as soon as his white leaders were all killed.

Reinforcements were hourly arriving, and before night, Gen. A. found that his force amounted to 1500 men. With these, he determined to delay no longer than to the next morning giving battle to the invaders, though they still were double his numbers. If this had been before any fighting had occurred, it would have been a rash, if not a fatal resolution. For the 1500 hastily levied Kentuckians, badly armed, untrained and scarcely organized, brave and patriotic as they were, could not have successfully fought with Brown's 700 hardy white desperadoes, trained to arms and to deeds of blood in the civil wars of Kansas, and on foreign soils, as mercenary allies. But this main strength of the invading army had so suffered that less than half their original number then remained capable of performing duty.

To this time, the main body of the Kentucky army had been slowly retreating before the advancing march of the enemy. During the night, a suitable place on the route was selected for the battle ground, on which, when reached early the next morning, Gen. A. halted, and arranged his troops, to receive the attack. When the invaders had advanced within musket range, they began to fire, and it was returned by a general volley. The firing was continued, and the superior skill of the Kentuckians, as marksmen, compensated for the inferiority of their numbers. General Brown's white followers, and a few of the negroes, fought bravely and desperately. But the negroes generally showed no ardor or disposition for fighting. When engaged, their ranks soon showed wavering and confusion. The Kentuckians were then ordered to advance, and continue firing. The natural timidity of the negro race, and the acquired sense of inferiority to the white race, were now getting the ascendancy over their previous arrogance and assurance of security and success. The fire of the Kentucky riflemen and infantry, as advancing nearer and nearer, was delivered rapidly and accurately upon the now disordered black mass. Soon the ranks were completely broken, and the negro army began to retreat hastily. A few more volleys from the Kentuckians converted the retreat to a preciptate flight. The volunteer cavalry then charged upon the fugitives, and cut them down when overtaken. The negroes threw away their arms, which nearly all had ceased to use, and which impeded their flight. As far as they were seen in flight they were pursued, and killed, if not surrendering. But early in the flight nearly a thousand together had thrown down their arms, prostrated themselves on the ground, and in the most abject manner begged for mercy. These, and all others who subsequently surrendered, if negroes, were secured as prisoners. But the whites, whether surrendering or continuing to resist, were put to death, either instantly, or later, when it was known that they were whites, and the leaders and deceivers of the misguided negroes. And this was not always known at first. For because of the manifest selection of the whites as marks for the Kentucky rifles, and their consequent peculiar suffering of wounds and death, Gen. Brown had commanded, the previous night, that every white should blacken his face, or disguise himself as a negro, and himself set the example.

The pursuit, and the killing or capturing of the fugitives, were continued until dark. When the victors were recalled, and collected, it was found that they had lost nearly 100 of their number, who were supposed to be killed or disabled, besides many more slightly wounded, but not disabled or absent. The losses of the defeated army could not then be estimated, except as to 1200 negro prisoners then secured. Gen. Brown, and most of his officers had so far continued to escape.

The next morning there was commenced a general hunt for the fugitives. The dead and wounded, of both sides, were collected—and the scattered arms, and other property, (the fruits of previous pillage,) were secured. Messengers were sent off with orders to have all the passages of the Ohio river, guarded, and all the boats secured, so as to prevent any chance for the escape of fugitives. Newly arrived reinforcements this day increased the Kentucky army to 2500—and in addition, every man and boy of the neighboring country were united with the military force, and all spread over a breadth of twenty miles, hunting for the fugitives. Of these there were about 800 scattered about the previous night, of which 500 were killed or captured in this day's hunt. Among the captured, were Brown, whose thigh bone had previously been shattered by a musket ball —and two of his principal officers, also disabled by wounds.

These, with all the other captives were conducted to the encampment, and the whites received speedy sentence of death by hanging. Brown loudly and boldly protested against this sentence, and demanded that all should be regarded and treated as prisoners of war, and with due respect to rank. For himself, he exhibited his commission, signed by President Seward, of Brigadier General of the United States army, and demanded to be respected accordingly. He was answered by Gen. A. that his rank would be taken into consideration, by hanging him higher than all his inferiors, and with his general's commission attached to his breast. And if President Seward was also in his power, Gen. A. assured Gen. Brown that he would hang them together. Ropes suitable for halters, and in sufficient quantity for the occasion, could not be immediately obtained. But the surrounding woods supplied plenty of flexible grapevines, which were substituted. With these rude and slovenly appliances, and from the different spreading branches of one gigantic oak, were hung Gen. Brown, with twenty-seven of his subordinate white officers, who had been brought in alive, and the bodies were left there, to be devoured by carrion vultures. The executioners, acting under orders, were a number of the negro prisoners, who, when invited, readily volunteered to perform the required duty, and appeared to enjoy much pleasure in the performance. Indeed they had already come to regard Brown and the abolitionists as their most hateful enemies.

The hunt was continued, from day to day, as long as any fugitives could be found. It was thought that not one escaped death in the field, or capture, of the 3500 men who entered Kentucky, or of the 400 slaves who soon afterwards joined them. Of the 800 whites, every one was either killed, or, if captured, was afterwards hung. Of the negroes, nearly 300 had voluntarily deserted, and had surrendered themselves, separately, or in small parties, before the battle—and 1200 had been made prisoners. All these were divided, by strict scrutiny, into three classes, viz: 1st. All former fugitive slaves who had voluntarily surrendered, and who, as supposed, had before joined the invaders for that purpose, were delivered to their former owners, with a recommendation for their forgiveness of the former desertion. The slaves of this class, whose former masters were unknown, or not accessible, were sold to the highest bidder. 2d. All who were guilty of any of the acts of murder, rape, or arson, during the march of the invading army, and were convicted thereof by a court-martial, and also all slaves who had deserted to the invaders, were to be hung. 3d. All negroes who belonged to neither of these classes, and who had been made prisoners, whether previously fugitive slaves or born free, were to be sold as slaves, in the more remote southern states, to prevent their future communication with the northern states, or abolition agents. The money obtained from the sales will be made a fund from which to indemnify the losses incurred by citizens whose families or property were wasted in the route of the invaders, while their progress was yet unchecked.

Nearly 1900 negroes were either restored to their former owners or sold. Most of the valuables which had been plundered from the residents, or their abandoned homes, were recovered. Most of the arms of the combatants were saved for the state, besides the extra supply of 10,000 muskets and pikes, for which there had been no demand for the expected new recruits or insurgents.

LETTER XLVIII.

War operations on the southern coast.

RICHMOND, July 15, 1868.

By the unfortunate steamship Australia, which was wrecked, and its freight and mails totally lost, I had sent a long letter, narrating some interesting and important events which had occurred on the southern coast not long before. The first and most important of these events, (in its consequences,) was the assault and conquest of Castle Pinckney, effected by land forces, aided by the armed flotilla prepared and commanded by Capt. S., a South Carolinian, and an experienced and able naval officer. Important as was this gallant exploit in itself, and more so for its early consequences, it is unnecessary for me to repeat the details stated in my lost letter, and of which the principal facts have been published in the newspapers long ago. Among these incidents were the details of the capture of Pensacola, with the dock yard and two protecting forts. Other later consequences, important as causes, but less prominent as effects, or incidents of war, will require more extended notice.

As soon as Castle Pinckney had been taken, it was forthwith well manned, and put under the command of Col. R., another son of the state, and an excellent artillery officer. This, added to the previous possession of Forts Sumter and Moultrie, insured Charleston from all possibility of attack, under the then exisiting circumstances, and permitted all the other land troops, before serving as a garrison of the city, or to blockade the forts, when held by the enemy, to be dispensed with. Soon after this time, the speedy formal secession of Virginia was in certain prospect, and indeed had been virtually consummated. On this ground, the authorities of the southern confederacy offered to the governor of Virginia the service of 4000 southern volunteers no longer needed to defend Charleston. When this offer was received, all the ready and best of the state volunteers of Virginia had been sent to meet the unexpected necessity in the north-west—including the previous frontier encampment of 3000 men near Alexandria. On this account, the offered aid was opportune, and was readily accepted. The southern regiments came on as soon as the acceptance of their aid was made known. They at first re-occupied the previous encampment near Alexandria—and were soon engaged in the capture of Washington, as has been stated before. From the dates of the later secession of the border states, and their adhesion to the southern confederacy, their troops then in service were made parts of the whole general armament, and put at the charge and under the command and direction of the southern federal government. As by the later acts of secession, the northern frontier had become identical with that of the border slaveholding states, it was now needless to guard the former frontier, or any interior line of defence. Therefore garrisons were kept only at suitable posts along the southside of Mason and Dixon's line, and on the left bank of the Ohio, for general frontier defence. Forts, or earth-work batteries, were also constructed, and kept garrisoned, on sundry points of the lower Mississippi river, as well as on the Ohio, where the cannon of the forts could best command the channels and navigation of these rivers. Besides, there were garrisons left in the city of Washington, (for a time,) and permanently in Fortress Monroe, and all other of the most important forts which protect the blockaded harbors and cities.

LETTER XLIX.

Naval preparations South and North. A naval encounter.

RICHMOND, July 17, 1868.

The greatly increased recent strength of the southern confederacy has forwarded naval preparations for harbor defence, which had been commenced some months ago, with inferior means. Especially has a new and great impulse to these objects been afforded by the capture and possession of the dock yards of Portsmouth, Pensacola and Washington, with all their supplies of materials, and facilities for ship-building, and with the means for employing hundreds of workmen, who were quite ready to transfer their service. Several small war vessels, nearly fitted for service, were also captured, and large quantities of cannon and munitions of naval war. At Charleston and Portsmouth, and at other dock yards along the Mississippi river and some of its great tributaries, many small steamers are now being constructed, of peculiar form and strength, and designed for shallow waters, and to annoy the blockading vessels. Former officers of the United States navy, and southerners, will command most of these vessels. Flotillas of other armed vessels have been prepared, or are fitting out, in Charleston and Portsmouth, for harbor defence and other connected services. The steamers are very strongly constructed, are long but low, and require but little depth of water. Their only armament (except of small arms,) consists of two long guns of large calibre, and long range, one pointed over the head, and the other over the stern of the vessel. These guns will carry a ball as far, and with as much accuracy as any used in the navy of the North.

The recent naval preparations by the northern government have served to increase the number, and still more the efficiency of the war vessels employed in blockading the southern ports. The ordinary ships of war, designed mainly for service on the ocean, or in deep water, could not cross the bar of any important southern port. The water on the bar of Pensacola, though some feet deeper than of any other harbor, only could admit the entrance of a frigate drawing twenty-one feet, under the most favorable circumstances of wind and high tide, and without any hostile opposition. The later constructions for the navy of the North, made with reference to this blockade service, have recently added to the several squadrons fifteen new war steamers of small sizes, and drawing from twelve to as little as nine feet of water. These can pass over the bars of any of the southern blockaded ports. But the greater annoyance which might be caused by these smaller war steamers has been to some extent prevented by some preparations for naval defence, and by use of steamers of still shallower draught, in every important southern harbor. The new screw steamers for this service have already been described generally. The two belonging to the flotilla in Charleston, were of the general model—long, low, and of but six feet draught—very strongly framed, and of great speed. In addition, Capt. S. had caused to be arranged some additional means for the efficiency of these particular vessels, which he supposed would be especially useful for the service required. One of these was a complete equipment for rowing these vessels by many oars, when silence and secrecy were necessary. Thus, the vessels could be rowed by their numerous crews with considerable speed without using their steam power—and, by muffling the oars, without noise to notify their presence, or close neighborhood. In addition to the ordinary defences of gun-boats, or other small vessels of war, Capt. S. had fitted these vessels so as to be surrounded (when needed,) by a barrier of connected cotton bales, in close contact with each other, and low enough to cover and protect the vessel's sides, above the water, and high enough to serve as a wall of defence for the men on the deck. This wall of closely compressed cotton was completely impenetrable to musket balls or grape shot, and even a cannon ball could not do more than displace a bale, when striking it. By a particular action of the steam engine, these bales could be easily kept wet, and thus be made incombustible. And if, by neglect, one should take fire, the cutting of its rope attachment would let it fall off into the water. This arrangement of cotton bales formed the best possible barrier of defence, both for the hull of the vessel and the men. It would have been a very cumbersome appendage, if permanent, and especially for rough water. But it was easily detached and removed, or replaced, and was used only when suitable.

The capture of Castle Pinckney released the Charleston flotilla from its previous confined position above the city. The benefit was immediately made use of by Capt. S. to exercise his crews, and very soon after to annoy the enemy. Under cover of the forts, Moultrie and Sumter, on the opposite sides of the lower harbor, Capt. S. soon made trial of his long guns on the blockading squadron—which now consisted of a ship of the line, a sloop of war, and one of the new war steamers. Taking advantage of the times (of night) and weather most favorable for the purpose, Capt. S. frequently had approached by rowing with his two small steamers within range of the ships, and fired as many shots as he could before there was necessity for retreating. These assaults were rarely without damage, especially on the seventy-four, which presented so large a mark for the long guns. These attacks, by the harbor steamers, were made in the night, or during foggy weather, and either in calms, or with such winds as would prevent the steamers being pursued by the sailing vessels of war. Under the most favorable of these circumstances, the assailants, before being discovered, would approach within half the distance of the range of their guns. Then their balls were especially effective; and though within reach of the larger guns of the enemy, the low and small steamers offered such small and such variable marks, that they were rarely struck. When pursued by the more powerful steamers of the enemy, as was usual, or (wind permitting) by the sailing ships, Capt. S. easily escaped by steaming over some one of the sundry shoals which form the bar, and of which some lie in the middle as well as on the land sides of the outer harbor. The blockading squadron had been frequently thus annoyed, and sometimes considerably damaged; and, as subsequent events showed, arrangements were made with the design to retaliate so severely, as to put an end to these assaults.

On a calm and moderately dark night, Capt. S. with the two steamers dropped down with the beginning of the ebb-tide from the previous anchorage of the flotilla above Fort Sumter. He kept up a head of steam, discharging the excess regularly and silently, but used the oars only, to advance. The oars were muffled, and every care used to prevent any noise, before the first firing of the guns. The two steamers came within the closest distance deemed not too much in danger from the numerous guns of the enemy's squadron, and dropped anchor, near to each other, on a shoal, where the vessels would have barely enough water at low tide. The three ships of the blockading squadron were plainly seen against the sky, while to them the low steam boats were invisible, except by the fire of their guns. The seventy-four especially offered an excellent mark for the long guns. The steamers soon began to fire, and both of them at the largest ship—and it was not long before it was made manifest, by the falling of the ship's main-mast, that the firing had been well directed. The fire was immediately returned by all the guns of long range, but without true aim, with no effect. After some time, the two sailing ships weighed anchor, and, favored by the ebb-tide, dropped below, until out of danger. It was soon seen that the cessation of the previous cannonading from the ships was rendered necessary for the purpose of permitting another mode of conducting hostilities. The enemy's steam vessel was seen advancing towards the assailants' position, and as advancing its large bow gun was continually discharged upon the position of the steam boats, but luckily, without much accuracy, or damage. Next, while firing the smaller side guns, the steamer coming incautiously upon the edge of the shoal, struck on the sand bottom, with such force as to be careened too much to aim the cannon. The now useless steamer was a fixed mark for the long guns of the boats, and was repeatedly struck by their balls. The crew with their small arms, took to their boats, and soon joined and returned with all the other boats of the squadron, which were before coming on as rapidly as their oars could effect, designing to carry the steamboats by boarding. The approach of the boats was heard before they could be seen in the very dim star-light. This contingency had always been expected, and was prepared for. As soon as the approaching boats were heard, the round shot then in the cannon were fired on the supposed position of the fleet of row-boats, and the next and all the subsequent charges were of cannister shot, made up of either musket balls, for the longer distances, or of buck-shot for the nearer. When within two hundred yards, the boats became visible, and were fired upon with terrible effect. Four of the boats were so riddled by the balls, as to be disabled, and put in a sinking condition—and most of the crews of these wrecked boats, who had escaped the shot, were drowned. Many men of the other boats were killed—and the advance was retarded by the killing or disabling many of the rowers and the filling their places by other men. The remaining boats, with all the force of their many oars continued to advance rapidly, and in open order, the better to avoid the destructive discharges from the cannon. As they came very near, the prospect of success was better. There was a cessation of the firing of the cannon, necessary to prepare for using other weapons, then of more utility. The advancing boats closed in to each other, preparatory for boarding the steamers. The two cannon of the steam boats, previously trained to suit this closer distance, and double-charged with buck-shot cartridges, were fired for the last time when the boats were within one hundred yards distance. Several more of the boats were stopped, and disabled, but the living portion of their crews could not be waited for by the other boats. While the rowers pushed these on with all their might, the musketeers in the boats had been firing on the steam boats from the time they came within range. And when the row-boats were near enough, the crews of the steam boats, began to fire with muskets and buck-shot. The muskets were barely reloaded in time to give another still more destructive volley, at close distance. And now as the designed boarders were reaching the steamers and beginning to attempt to board them, another previously arranged and novel mode of defence was put in use. Metal pipes had been connected with the boilers, so that by turning a cock eight of such pipes discharge boiling water, which, through flexible tubes, could be aimed with the accuracy, and thrown with all the force of the most powerful fire engine. These streams of boiling water were directed upon the boarders. Many, in rapid succession, and as fast as the spout could be changed in direction, received the full volume for a moment. Others were but slightly sprinkled on their faces and other naked parts of their limbs or bodies. But even the smallest quantity was enough to stop the progress of any assailant. These brave fellows would have faced any danger from cannon and musket balls, cutlasses and boarding pikes, and would have continued to rush on, despite of any but disabling wounds. But they could not stand up against a stream, or even a sprinkling of boiling water—and I think that Napoleon's old guard, or the three hundred Spartans of Leonidas, would have fallen back under a like discharge. When the scalding water touched them, the men dropped their oars or their weapons, and many threw themselves overboard, to relieve their horrible torment. All who were not disabled, either by severe injury, or by the severity of pain, hastened to row off and escape. Six boats only, out of eighteen, the original number, and these with crews reduced below the number they had brought, and with scarcely any men without some hurt, returned to the remaining ships of the squadron. A few only of the men of the shattered boats were able to swim long enough to be taken up, and saved on board of the steam boats.

Some of the shattered or deserted boats, still floating, were brought back into the harbor by the returning flood tide, and were secured by the victors. The abandoned steamer could not then be floated, except by throwing over the greater number of the cannon; and as the water is there shallow, and the bottom hard, they may be recovered hereafter. The steamer, thus lightened, was towed to the city, on the next high tide, and sent to the dock yard to be repaired.

This was not the end, nor the greatest of the disasters. The seventy-four had not only lost its main-mast, but had been so damaged in the hull, that it was necessary to go into a dock-yard for repairs. There was none to be made use of south of the Delaware. The ship sailed northward for this purpose; and encountering a violent storm, off Cape Hatteras, and being too much disabled to be navigated safely, it foundered, and the whole ship and armament with nearly all the crew were lost. Some twenty of the men only, floating on part of the wreck, were afterwards saved by a passing vessel.

The cotton-bale ramparts of the steam gunboats were struck by many harmless musket balls, discharged from the approaching boats—and several of the bales were knocked out of place by cannon balls, which, but for this interposed defence, might have disabled the vessels. But there was but little damage to either the steamboats or the men. Only five men were killed, and seven wounded.

LETTER L.

Close of the compaign in Mississippi.

RICHMOND, July 18, 1868.

The condition of things, in the conduct of the war in Mississippi, was not much changed for some weeks after the 20th of June to which date my latest notice reached. The war operations lingered, so as to cause surprise, and even to draw censure upon the authorities of the southern confederacy. There had been no want of vigor elsewhere, as the previous events had shown. But it really seemed that so little had been done by military action, by the general government, that it had been designed to prove to the northern power that its armies, even if unopposed in the field, cannot conquer the south. Whether the result of design, or necessity, or of chance, (which last has so often the chief direction of affairs of government and of war,) it is certain that the absence of military enterprise, and apparent inability for prompt, vigorous and efficient defensive measures, which seemed to have marked the conduct of this campaign, have served to show in the clearest point of view the natural defensive strength of the country, against invaders coming from the north.

Col. D. continued to maintain and to strengthen his position in Fort Calhoun, and to command perfectly the navigation of the river by his post. Other batteries, as effective for this purpose, though with small garrisons, had been established at several of the other commanding points on the Mississippi river both below and above Fort Calhoun, and also on the Ohio. It was made perfectly impossible for any hostile army, or supplies for one, to be brought on either river.

The northern army under Gen. N., notwithstanding all its losses by death and sickness, was still more numerous than all the militia (and these all raw levies,) that had yet been brought to oppose the invaders. The northern general continued to try to force his opponents to join in battle, and this design was cautiously and successfully avoided. All that the southern troops aimed at, and executed, was to hover around the main body and the two smaller detachments of the invading army, to cut off out-posts and foraging parties, to fire on the larger or smaller bodies from covered positions and ambuscades, and to prevent the obtaining of supplies. This procedure continued, the invaders being continually harassed and daily weakened, and the defenders being daily strengthened. Gen N. was sustained by the daily expectation of large reinforcements and abundant supplies, until he at last received information of all the important events, military and political, preceding the 20th of June. At the same time that he thus learned that all his hopes of reinforcements were vain, he was also informed of the then beginning invasion of Kentucky by the negro army under Gen. Brown, and the expected results of that movement. Thus the only chance left for getting his army out of its otherwise desperate situation, was the speedy and general spreading of servile insurrection, through Mississippi in common with all the South. For this Gen. N. continued to wait—making, as before, daily aggressive movements, and sustaining continual and fast increasing losses—until the middle of July. Then he received dispatches from which he learned the utter failure of Brown's expedition, and of the attempts to excite insurrection. By this time, besides all the many losses of men killed, 2,000 more had recently died of diseases of the camp and of the climate, 5,000 were then sick, and the remainder of the troops were suffering greatly for want of sufficient and regular supplies of food, and entirely discouraged. His guard left to protect the remaining river fleet, had been just attacked by a much more numerous detachment from the Mississippi army, and all killed or made prisoners. The vessels moored near the shore had at the same time been attacked both from the land and the water, (the latter force including Col. D's little armed steamer,) and had been captured. The horses of the main body of northern troops had nearly all perished for want of food, and the artillery could not be used or moved except by hand force. Under such circumstances, which would necessarily and continually grow worse, Gen. N. proposed negotiations. He could obtain no better terms than that the army should be surrendered as prisoners of war, and the arms and remaining other public property be given up to the victors.

Thus, with scarcely any fighting, and no maintained resistance, (except of the fort,) and not a blow being struck in the open field, or arranged battle, this numerous and well equipped army was beaten, and when reduced to less then half its former military strength, had to surrender at discretion to raw militia.

LETTER LI.

Effects of the separation of the states on both the northern and southern sections.

RICHMOND, July, 27, 1868.

The condition of the later seceding states (to which Texas is now added,) in the southern confederacy, is just what it would have been if they had seceded with the first, with the important exception (to their politicians) that these states, by their delay, have waived their right, and lost the opportunity, of having any voice in shaping the federal constitution, or in the earliest consequent congressional enactments, and the appointments to office. By their postponed secession, and becoming members of the southern confederacy, they simply ratify, and concur in, all the measures that had previously been adopted by the other earlier moving states, and their representative statesmen.

The relations of the now border states of the opposed sections are somewhat peculiar. There is no hostile action, or attempt, of either population along the separating line on the other—though there is no general friendly feeling. Even the abductions of slaves, from the slaveholding states, formerly so frequent across the line, have almost ceased. These inoffensive relations are mainly produced by the military patroles and guards on the southern side of Mason and Dixon's line, and on the left bank of the Ohio river. There is also maintained in the border states, and especially near their boundaries adjoining the northern section, a strict system of police, under which all persons coming from the northern section to a slaveholding state, and especially across the separating boundary line, are subjected to strict examination—and all unknown or suspicious persons are excluded, or punished, if violators of the law, or known enemies. Northern visitors, known as worthy and friendly, or strangers bringing sufficient vouchers for deserving such character, are received and permitted to pass as friendly, but must be supplied with a passport, and exhibit it in every new place of the traveller's appearance. If known former abductors or inveiglers of slaves, should be found south of the border line, they will be subjected to summary trial and speedy hanging. Some such examples were made very early. Hence the cessation of such attempts, and the already increased security of slaves, and confidence of their owners, in the border counties. Immediately after the secession of Virginia, and the enactment by that state of these stringent measures against abolition emissaries and agents, all the northern settlers or sojourners who had been suspected of being favorable to such designs, speedily departed for the North, and sundry others who had not before been suspected. Among the latter, were several preachers, connected with northern anti-slavery churches. Except this watchfulness and rigor in reference to the entrance or stay of unknown or suspicious northerners, there has been no interruption, along the border line, between the neighboring inhabitants of the two sections, of friendly intercourse, or of trade not prohibited, or subjected to payment of duties, by either section.

But there will begin, and increase in operation, a more general and stronger reason for the cessation of abolition action. Except with the fanatical abolitionists, who are comparatively few in number, the great mass of the northern abolitionists, and all the politicians, care nothing about negroes or negro slavery, and have heretofore used the slavery question merely as the best means for their own political advancement and gain. The fanatics led the fools in making this the most prominent question. Politicians readily took it up, and used it to the fullest extent. As no man could then be elected to any public station who was not an opposer of slavery, of course every man avowed himself to be such—and all vied with each other in the excess of devotion and of violence displayed against negro slavery. But as soon as there is separation of the two sections, and northern votes can have no possible effect on slavery, or on the South, this political action must die for want of support. When there is no political connection between the North and South, and no possibility of the former controlling the latter, there will be no longer any abolitionists heard of, except such fanatics as rave in Exeter Hall, in England, without damaging, or being regarded by, any slaveholder. The southern states (except in proximity along the border line,) will then, in regard to slavery, and the North, occupy the same position as heretofore Cuba and Brazil have done. In these countries the hardships and evils of slavery are certainly ten-fold worse than in these southern states. Yet never have the northern abolitionists meddled with the horrors of slavery, or troubled themselves to meliorate the condition of slaves, in these foreign countries—and for the sufficient reason that no politician could command a vote by any such direction of philanthropy. Fanatics do not reason. Therefore the northern fanatics will exhibit their anti-slavery madness as long as they are sustained in it. Therefore they will use, (as has been attempted,) to the utmost extent, the supposed great means offered by the present war against the slaveholding states. Possibly they may effect something by these means and facilities. But as soon as the political separation of the northern and southern sections is confirmed, and peace established, there will be an end to political abolitionism, and to all mischievous power of the fanatics, who only, whether in Exeter Hall or in Faneuil Hall, will continue to utter their harmless negrophilist ravings, in religious reports and resolutions, and political speeches and pamphlets. * * * * * * *

The recent secession of all the remaining slaveholding states, and their becoming parts of the southern confederacy, have produced most important changes, not only in their political condition, but in the condition of the northern section, (still claiming to be "The United States of America,") and of the commercial affairs of Europe in connection with the South. The blockade by the northern naval force has been extended to the ports of Texas, North Carolina, and the capes of Virginia, of which, the last also excludes Maryland, from the ocean. The foreign commerce of Virginia and Maryland, while thus blockaded, may partly be carried on from Norfolk, through the new canal to Albemarle sound, and thence through some of the shallow inlets and channels to the ocean. The guns of Fortress Monroe prevent the blockading squadron from coming above, or endangering the navigation of the inner waters. Much as the blockade has served to obstruct the ocean commerce of these two states, it has damaged their interests less than those of the northern states. These are already suffering for want of the supplies of grain and tobacco, and especially of cotton, which they had before received from and through Virginia, and of course in northern vessels. They must now be supplied with the indispensable products of the now united and hostile southern states indirectly through European ports or vessels, with the additional charges incurred by two trans-shipments, or perhaps by two voyages across the Atlantic. In addition to these difficulties and increased expenses, all the duties forcibly collected on imports to the blockaded southern ports, are of such small amount, that they scarcely serve to pay the salaries of the collecting officers. And the imports to the northern cities are now limited to articles for the supply of the northern states only, and these reduced to suit their present impoverished condition. The greater portion of the former importations to northern ports, and in northern ships, was for trans-shipment to and consumption of the southern states. A still larger proportion of the northern ships found regular employment in transporting southern exports and imports, and these also mainly, through northern cities, and northern factors or purchasers. These former great sources of profit are now either greatly reduced, or cut off entirely. Still worse, the regular commercial debt due from the merchants of the late seceding states to northern merchants and manufacturers, computed at fifty millions of dollars, (and making ninety millions for the whole confederacy,) has also been sequestrated in the hands of the debtors, or is, at their choice, to be paid into the treasury of the southern federal government. These different causes have produced great increase of general distress in the north-eastern states, and especially in the manufacturing and great commercial cities.

The people of the South, and their federal government, though straitened in their operations and their income, still are both in good condition, and with better prospects for the future. The experience of the war, so far, has confirmed the previous opinion expressed by judicious southern statesmen, that even if the North were able to send armed ships into every great port and river of the South, and to march armies wherever they choose to go, and thereby greatly to distress the invaded country, yet its subjugation or coercion would still be impossible; and that every effort to effect either of these objects would be (as they have been, so far,) much more costly and injurious to the stronger and aggressive North, than to the weaker and invaded South.

The northern government now feels a heavy pressure of financial difficulties. The war expenses have added greatly to the demands on the treasury, and exceeded those of the former general government, extravagant as they were, while the supplies, from all sources of taxation, have fallen to less than one-third of the former amount. Loans to the northern government cannot be obtained because of its bad credit—and the treasury notes, which have been issued to great amount by authority of the Congress, have already depreciated twenty per cent. below their nominal value. Added to these evils, every aggressive movement by the North since the war was begun, has been a failure.

Under these circumstances, of failure and defeat, of great losses and general discouragement, it is not strange that in the North there are already many voices now clamoring against the government, and for peace, of persons who before were among the most confident of crushing all armed opposition of the South with ease, and even with profit. Of course, the minority of discreet men, and faithful to their duties as citizens, who had always wished to do justice to the southern people, and never to attempt their coercion by arms, are now much strengthened in influence, and the number of their disciples has been latterly increased by thousands. Still the spirit of fanatical and rabid abolitionism is not in the least quelled, but rages the more fiercely because of the failure and disasters suffered in its cause, and for its attempted support.

LETTER LII.

Outbreaks of disorder and violence in the northern cities. Sack of New York.

RICHMOND, August 10, 1868.

The former riots and plunderings by the destitute and lawless residents of the great northern cities, had been promptly quelled, by military force, and by bloodshed. But though the criminal actors had been subdued, and their complaints and clamors silenced, the causes of their action remained, and were still growing in strength. The recruiting for the regular army aided by the large additional bounties for recruits, offered and paid by the cities in which they resided, and which their presence and desperation continually threatened and terrified, had served to withdraw from the streets, and from the goadings of the severest want, nearly 20,000 men of the destitutute and dangerous classes. But since, there had been still larger numbers added to these classes, by the continued and general decrease of employment for laborers, and the increased price of food, new and much more alarming riots occured in the cities of New York, Philadelphia and Boston, with indications of preconcert and arrangement. In New York, the rioters and plunderers, even in advance of seizing food or money, rushed to the shops where fire-arms and ammunition were sold, and from them, and from all the private houses subsequently entered, procured as large supplies as could be obtained. The arsenals of two of the volunteer military companies also were broken open, and all the arms carried off. Though arms and ammunition were first and most eagerly sought, every article of value was seized as booty. The actors and their operations increased rapidly with their means. Before any resistance was opposed, except of the ordinary police, the rioters had increased to thousands, who forced their admission into every shop and mansion, and plundered at their discretion. The uniformed volunteer companies, only, were first called out, as for the former riots. But these were too few to put down the rioters—and large reinforcements were ordered of the ordinary militia, and urgent requests were sent by the city authorities to the quarters of the commanding general, for the aid of the United States' regular troops in the neighboring garrisons. The plunderers did not at first assemble in a body, or in large numbers in the streets, where they might be opposed and fired on by the volunteers, and by artillery. If any considerable number happened to be collected together, by accident, they immediately dispersed to avoid being conspicuous, and so putting themselves in danger. They spread themselves, in numerous small parties, of ten to twenty, through all the residences and shops of rich owners, or wherever they expected to find the richest booty. Arms, money, plate, with food and intoxicating liquors, were demanded everywhere. Hundreds of liquor shops were entered, and left open, and their contents thus made free for the use of all who chose to partake of them. And when thus tempted, and stimulated, thousands of the lower classes who had designed merely to be inactive spectatators, became, in their subsequent drunken excitement, active rioters, plunderers, and, in many cases, murderers. The terror-stricken property owners rarely resisted the entrance of the plunderers into their houses—or any acts of plunder or outrage they might commit. The few who at first had attempted resistance, were promptly stabbed, and their bleeding bodies thrown into the streets. A few such known examples and warnings were enough to render the hundreds of thousands of peaceable inhabitants submissive to every command, and silent under every outrage of a few thousand desperadoes. Even a single rioter might rob alone, and without resistance. For those who suffered his acts knew not how near were his companions—and even if the one could be easily killed, other stronger visitations would succeed, to complete the unfinished plundering, if not to avenge the punishment of the first offender. It is believed that the horrible and extensive massacres by the "Septembrisers," in Paris, in 1793, were committed by less than one thousand assassins, who, for three days, held that great city in subjection, by terror, and in quiet submission to the most atrocious and extravagant shedding of innocent blood that the world had ever known. It is not then strange that three or four thousand bloody miscreants of the most degraded conditions of society, should have paralysed with terror the people of New York. But these few thousands were growing rapidly, and with every minute of time, to ten-fold greater numbers.

As soon as the volunteer companies appeared, they promptly quelled all riot and open opposition for that time and place—and they shot down hundreds, whether of the guilty, or of the innocent, who, in many cases, were struck by the balls designed for others. The ordinary militia companies were more slow to reach the scene of action. The more worthy of their members had either families or property which they desired to remain with, to watch and protect. Others were afraid to face the fierce and murderous rioters—and many, who had nothing to lose, sympathised too much with either the previous sufferings or the present excesses of the rioters, to heartily oppose them in arms. Many of the men of these companies, when ordered to hunt through the houses, and to shoot the plunderers, used the opportunity, of being thus scattered, and out of sight of their officers, to slink away, and return home, or otherwise to desert their duty. Others, when opposed by bands of armed rioters, and fired upon, fled in haste. And not a few joined the plunderers, bringing the still more welcome aid of their muskets and cartridges. This aid so encouraged the rioters, and their numbers were also now so much increased, that they no longer feared to face the volunteers in the streets, and to exchange some destructive volleys with them before retreating. But more generally, and to more fatal purpose, they fired on the troops through the windows of the houses, and from other places of concealment. Their success rapidly increased their numbers, and their boldness and ferocity. In a few hours from the beginning, there were more than 30,000 miscreants, mostly armed with some deadly weapon, engaged in sacking the houses and shops, not only of the rich, but of all whose moveables were supposed to be worth being plundered.

When they were masters of the city, and the only city troops remaining to oppose them, (the trained volunteers,) were reduced to the necessity of defending themselves, instead of pursuing or assailing the furious mob, the United States regular troops arrived, from their barracks, to the number of 4000. About 1000 of these, who had been longest in service, fought well, but to much disadvantage against greatly superior numbers, and their enemies also being as much concealed, as the soldiers were exposed to be fired upon. About half of this number fell before the conflict in this place was over, and without being able to unite and co-operate with the volunteers, who were merely defending their position in another quarter—and of the other half, most were killed, fighting desperately to the last. The remainder of the regular soldiers, about 3000, were all new recruits, very lately enlisted and taken from the streets and cellars of this city, and from the habits, and companionship, in misery and vice, of the present rioters, among whom they recognized their friends and relatives, and whom they saw to be now almost masters of the city and all its wealth. They had no inclination to risk and very probably to lose their lives in fighting their recent companions and friends, in whose feelings and wishes they fully and heartily shared. The usage of discipline was not yet old enough to restrain them, and they soon began to drop off, at first singly, and next in numbers, to join and aid the plunderers. This decided the success of the rioters. The previous opposition of the yet remaining defenders of the city, ceased, as hopeless. No one dared longer to resist. Every man who had a wife or children, endeavored, if possible, to flee with his family from the scene of horror, leaving his house and other property at the mercy of the plunderers. Those who had no families exposed, took no thought of their property, but only of saving their lives by escaping from the city devoted to ruin. But it was impossible for many to escape out of the almost water-surrounded city. Not many of the fugitives could obtain, at any amount of cost, conveyance by boats, or by carriages of even the humblest kinds. Carts and small wagons, to carry the feebler members of families, or their most necessary or valuable moveable property, to places a few miles out of the city, were freely hired at prices from $200 to $500 for each. One of the very wealthy merchants, who, by too long delay had been robbed of his own carriages and horses, and was too late to obtain any more comfortable vehicle, paid $1000 for a furniture wagon to take his wife and children, and as much luggage as would complete a load, into the country. The supposed great value of the contents of the trunks, inferred from the immense wealth of the owner and the circumstances of the flight, tempted the driver and his assistant to emulate the worst crimes of the other plunderers; and they first murdered the merchant and then his wife and older children, to possess themselves of the rich booty. Two children only, too young to report the crimes, were left on the street, to perish by other means. Many thousands, mostly feeble females and children, and, in numerous cases, members of the richest families, intermixed with the poor inhabitants, now all nearly alike destitute, helpless and despairing, were crowded together, and struggling on foot to reach the upper suburbs, and, if able, a still greater distance from the scene of horrors which already overspread all the richest and most populous portions of the city. Night had come on, to add still more to the horrors of this flight for life.

The rioters were now too numerous, and too well armed, to be subdued, or even restrained, by any possible force that could soon be brought against them. Their boldness and ferocity, had been stimulated to the highest degree, by intoxication, plunder, successful conflicts, and profuse blood-spilling. But few of them reasoned, or thought of consequences—but sought only present and unlimited enjoyment, in gratifying every appetite, even at the expense of any amount of crime. There was no order—no command. Every man acted for himself, and as directed only by his own infuriated or drunken will—unless he should thwart the like pursuit and object of some other desperado, when personal conflict, and the slaying of one or the other, usually and speedily settled their contested claims. More than 40,000 of such wretches were engaged in the work of waste and destruction throughout the city. And even one of them, if alone, was enough to strike terror upon, and command the complete submission and obedience of, any of the inhabitants, who had not yet fled from their homes.

As soon as it was generally known that all military opposition and defence had ceased, the only previous restraint, that of fear, was removed, and numerous and strong parties of the most criminal of the rioters, set out to spread their depredations to other localities, or to enterprises which they had not before dared to attempt. The churches were all broken open, and the plate seized. The banks, and the United States sub-treasury, were all forcibly occupied, and their vaults speedily robbed of every dollar. These last acts, if they had been committed in some former prosperous time of the city and of the federal government, might have caused the loss of from fifty to a hundred millions of dollars. But the then penury of the treasury, and the previous commercial distress, had reduced very low the hoards of coin. The federal treasury scarcely contained a million of dollars—and all the banks together had but three to four millions of coin. And when military defence could no longer be hoped for, and the robbery of the deposits, by the mob, was certain, the officials, in charge of the sub-treasury and the banks, deemed it best to begin themselves the appropriating of the treasures, nominally, for the rightful owners, but probably, to no small extent designed for themselves. This work of removing the deposits was well advanced, though no where completed, when the actors had to flee for their lives before the approach of the less adroit and more violent robbers, the raging and murderous mob. Though most of the money had been before taken off, there still remained enough to make rich, beyond his previous conception, every individual of these first gangs of robbers. But no equal or fair division was possible. The strongest hand enforced the most successful claim. The immense magnitude of the booty, instead of appeasing, served still more to inflame the rioters with insane lust of gain, and of blood. The first comers to the exposed great heaps and boxes of gold, and packages of bank-bills, attempted to exclude all others from the spoil, by armed resistance. The later comers were more numerous and equally greedy. A bloody fight took place in every case, and when any one party remained the final victor, so as to take possession of the contested spoils, they were sought for and removed from beneath a heap of the dead and dying bodies of the plunderers, and drenched with their gore.

As soon as the city was completely under the control of the rioters, and no more resistance was offered, many of the more considerate of the plunderers began to arrange for securing their booty, and their own personal safety. As the night advanced, and as more and more of them had become glutted with plunder, these efforts increased, and continued as long as there was rich booty to be removed, or ability for its removal. Thousands of those who had put their stolen valuables in a small compass, and of portable weight, and hoped to conceal it, or its true character, at first spread themselves in other quarters of the city, which, because of their poverty and meanness, had not been yet attacked by the plunderers. Many others went out of the city, designing to assume the character of plundered inhabitants, fleeing with a remnant of their wasted property. Many others, who were among the most desperate villains, and experienced robbers, and now the most successful, formed parties for combined operations, and seized steamers and sailing vessels at the wharves, and either hiring by enormous bribes, or compelling, the services of the crews, had their plunder brought by carriages and carts, and placed on board, and then started for the ocean. This procedure was facilitated by the previous unusual condition of the port. The great need for vessels of war to aid the blockade measures on the southern coast, and its being supposed by the government that no vessels could be needed for defence of northern ports, had induced the removal of every vessel of war, fit for service, from the Hudson river—so that there was no force to oppose the passage and escape of the stolen and plunder-laden vessels, and their passengers. Many of the sailors, and black as well as white, had been engaged in the sack of the city, and joined with, and enabled, others of their companions, to seize the vessels to which they were attached. One of these vessels had its rich lading of booty supplied entirely by a gang of negro sailors, who embarked under a negro captain, and set sail for Hayti. The crews of other vessels aimed to reach other places where they hoped to be sheltered long enough to divide and secure their booty.

These scenes of terror, crime, and suffering, continued through nearly all the night, unabated except by thousands of the criminals becoming gorged with plunder, or being rendered insensible by drunkenness—or by the moving away of large numbers with their booty. But the numbers of the actors were still maintained, by new accessions of recruits, who had been too remote, too cowardly, or perhaps too conscientious, at first, to join in the early operations. Every property-holder, and every honest citizen, who had anything to lose, had fled, unless physically unable to escape. Every house was left open after the visiting of the mob, and every remaining article of valuable and moveable property, was left at the disposal of any who would take possession—and with scarcely any chance of being preserved for the use of the rightful owners. Under such temptations, and ground for excuse, many persons become plunderers who had before been esteemed to be honest and law-abiding citizens. The only limit to the extent of the plundering was the utter impossibility of removing or securing even one-tenth part of the moveables.

But the unhappy city and its inhabitants had yet to go through still increased horrors. In the latter part of the night, when the plunderers could take no more booty, because unable to transport or secure any more, and when nearly all were drunk and furious, it was proposed by some, and readily acceded to by all who heard the proposal, that the city should be burnt. This might well have been the result of wanton love of mischief, of excitement, or of drunken folly and madness. But a stronger and an earlier motive was doubtless operating, in the malignant hatred, which many of the actors, who had been the greatest sufferers from want and hunger, entertained for the rich, and even for all property-owners, whom they had learned to deem their worst enemies. They desired to glut their hatred and vengeance, as well as to gratify their appetites and their cupidity. The proposal to set fire to the city was therefore received with shouts of applause; and thousands of the rioters, armed, and bearing torches, spread themselves through every quarter, putting fire, as they went, to the more inflammable buildings. A strong wind was blowing, which soon spread the flames faster than did the numerous incendiaries. In two hours, this great and rich city, containing with the adjacent suburbs and connected minor cities, 1,200,000 inhabitants, was so covered by flames, that no possible human means could have prevented the full consummation of the calamity. The fires had been kindled in so many places, nearly at one time, and so generally over the city, that the whole space was, at once, one raging sea of flame, rising in billows and breakers above the tops of the houses higher than ever sea was raised by the most violent hurricane. The roar of the conflagration was like continued rolling thunder. The fire, in showers of burning combustibles, was driven upon the ships lying at and near the wharves, and even to many lying separate in the river, and more than half of all in the port were consumed. Of the houses, not one, in the closely built portions of New York proper and Brooklyn, escaped destruction. Some of the remote and thinly-built suburbs only were spared. Scarcely any of the moveable property was saved—owing to the magnitude and suddenness of the destruction, and the want of force to remove property, as well as the state of despair of the then remaining inhabitants. Very many of these, being hemmed in by different fires around, were unable to get out, and perished in the flames. And very many more of the drunken incendiaries suffered, as they well deserved, the same horrible manner of death. Of the many thousands of charred and partly consumed skeletons, which were afterwards to be seen among the ruins, it was conjectured that the lives of as many had been destroyed by the burning, as by armed violence in the previous combats and assassinations.

This, the most terrible calamity that perhaps any great city has ever experienced in modern times, though much the worst, was not the only such result of the sufferings of the destitute and vicious classes. The reports of all the circumstances of this awful event, while it struck with fright and horror every good citizen—and even induced the commiseration of all but the most embittered of the southern foes—served merely as an encouraging example for many of the worst of the city populations, and which they speedily proceeded to follow both in Philadelphia and Boston. In Philadelphia, the rioters had complete command of the city through one night, during all which time they were glutting their appetites, and plundering, at their will, and committing every outrage to which they were invited by their vile propensities, and ferocious tempers. They were, however, subdued by military force, aided by artillery, at last, and thousands were slaughtered in the streets and houses, and other thousands are imprisoned, to be tried and punished under the criminal laws.

In Boston, the like riots, with plundering and murder, were acted, but to less extent. There a different phase was given to the out-break, inasmuch as the rioters, besides their main acts of plundering, denounced vengeance against the leading abolitionists as the authors of the existing distress, in their having caused the secession of the southern states, and the war on them, and all the consequent losses and distress of the North. These charges were made the pretence for especially seeking out the prominent and wealthy of the fanatical abolitionists, for robbery and maltreatment, and destruction of their property. Not one of these escaped being made heavy sufferers, in person or property, at the hands of the rabble who had been so long taught and trained to lawlessness, by the doctrines and example of these vile fanatics, or still worse hypocrites.

The enormous sacrifices of life which have already been suffered by actors in these criminal deeds, and the slower punishments of the law, yet to come, on all the survivors who can be convicted on trial, will, for a long time, repress such worst operations of the spirit of insubordination. But the seeds and causes still will remain, and are inherent and inevitable in the northern social and political system—provided great wealth shall still remain, with great inequality of condition of the people, great destitution of the lower classes, and yet every member of them, however poor, ignorant and vicious, being a voter, and having political privileges and power equally with the most worthy and intelligent citizens, and largest tax-payers. Moreover, the juries for the trials of these criminals, will more usually include among their numbers men of the lowest character and position in society, who will be more influenced by sympathy and fellow-feeling for the most atrocious of these offenders, than by reverence for law and good government, or the sanctity of their oaths as jurymen. But putting aside all fears for future events, the evils of the recently past are too great for estimation. In addition to all private losses and sufferings, the government is a heavy loser in various ways—and one important loss is in its *prestige* of authority and power, in consequence of the disobedience and desertion of 3000 of its regular soldiers, and the easy and unresisted plunder of its chief sub-treasury. A general clamor has already been raised against the war, and especially in regard to its alleged bad management. Under the present circumstances of the recent disasters, and of changed public opinion, it does not seem probable that any more regular troops can soon be spared from the North to be sent to the South—even if the northern government shall still persist in carrying on a war of invasion on the southern confederacy.

LETTER LV.*

Washington the seat of the southern federal government. Free negroes expelled from the District of Columbia.

WASHINGTON, —— —, 1868.

* * * * As soon as could be arranged after the capture of Washington, and its occupation by troops of the southern confederacy, the southern congress, in concert with the state government of Maryland, adopted

---

* The two preceding letters are wanting—but their contents, as to matters of importance, may be inferred from the references made in this and succeeding letters.—EDITOR.

the necessary measures to make that city again the seat of the federal government for the South. This was soon arranged. Within a short time after the frustration of the attempt to excite servile insurrection in Maryland, the federal government for the southern confederacy was regularly and completely fixed at Washington, and all its departments and central functionaries were in regular operation. For the safety of this capitol of the South, (which is inconveniently near to the northern frontier and to the enemy's territory,) the garrison is strengthened, and will consist in part of 2000 soldiers of the new regular army of the southern government. But a still stronger defensive force, and which, if alone, would be amply sufficient to guard against any successful *coup de main*, or even insult to the capitol, from the northern enemy, is offered in the volunteer companies and the general warm zeal and public spirit of the city of Washington and the remainder of the District of Columbia. Every consideration of vital self-interest of the inhabitants comes in support and futherance of their public spirit and patriotism. The previous removal of the northern federal government from this city, and its ceasing to be the capitol, (if things had continued as they then were,) would have been the death-blow to the prosperity of this district, and the ruin of every property-holder, and even of the business and daily earnings of every tradesman, mechanic, and laborer. The re-occupation of the city as the seat of federal government for the southern confederacy, offered the only possible hope for safety from the impending and almost consummated ruin. Therefore, there was every reason operating strongly on every inhabitant to preserve and defend the safe possession of the District, as the seat of the federal government to the southern power, which now promises not only to substitute the former general government in this occupancy, but to rival it in strength, and exceed it in duration. For these reasons and motives, the military spirit of the District of Columbia was especially ardent and active, and the organized force of volunteers is unusually numerous for the population, and already in good military condition. Every volunteer company has been carefully drilled once or more in each week; and the whole force can be arrayed under arms and proper command, within a few hours after any call that may be made for defensive service.

Still earlier than the re-establishment of federal administration in the District of Columbia, there had been there commenced, and are still in progress to full completion, important new measures of policy, to reverse the northern and former federal action, by which negro slavery had been deprived of all support, and was virtually abolished, and all the negroes of the District made free—and any others permitted to come there for refuge and security. Now, the former and legal protection of slave property was re-established and enforced, according to the laws of Maryland. All the free negroes of the District of Columbia were banished, and compelled within a limited and short time to move beyond the northern border of Maryland, or elsewhere to the northern states. This order was forthwith obeyed by many, and by all who, whether as free or enslaved, might have been troublesome as residents. But the greater number preferred, and adopted, the alternative course, of resorting to the legal facilities afforded by the laws of both Maryland and Virginia, to re-enslave themselves to masters of their choice. This could be easily effected, by entering the close adjacent territory and jurisdiction of either of these two states, and complying with the legal forms required. Thus, after a short interval, the District of Columbia was again the seat of the federal government of the section of states by which it is surrounded, and was always identified with in interest and in institutions, as well as locality—and also, is again slave-holding territory, cleared entirely and permanently, of its former dangerous nuisances of northern abolition agents and free negro population. * * * *

LETTER LVI.

A truce. Effects of the war, and present condition of the two sections.

RICHMOND, September 20, 1868.

The truce which had been agreed upon, in the conference of commissioners of the hostile northern and southern confederacies, while negociating for the restoration of peace, is to continue for thirty days after the close of the conference, (should it not bring about peace;) and hostilities are not to be renewed then, or later, without notice, within less than five days after such notice for the renewal of active war shall have been given by either government to the other. The existing cessation of actual operations offers a suitable occasion for me to take a hasty view of the effects produced by the war, and the present condition of the two now different and opposed peoples, and their respective governments.

The northern government, as early as it could act, began

and continued to make strenuous efforts to subdue the seceding states, speedily and effectually. Every means of war, which had previously been supposed available and likely to be effective—blockade, invasion, and servile insurrections attempted with preparations and accessories that had been, before trial, deemed the most formidable, mischievous, and certain of effect—all have utterly failed to produce any important effect, in weakening or humbling the seceded states; and all these effects have produced much more loss and damage to the aggressive than to the assailed party. The continuation of aggressive hostilities by the northern power, with equal vigor, was prevented, first, by the impossibility of conveying reinforcements and supplies to the seat of war, and next by all the regular soldiers then enlisted and not sent abroad, being suddenly and imperatively demanded to suppress and keep down insurrection and massacre, if not more extended civil war, in the northern states.

The whole of the present northern regular army, including 8,000 prisoners released on parole, (and which must be exchanged or accounted for, if the war is renewed,) is now thus employed, and required, to protect the northern cities from insurrection and domestic violence and civil war.

When active operations could not possibly be carried on, a breathing time became desirable even to the aggressive power. And, as a matter of policy, and for present objects, the most violent and implacable members of the war party, in the northern section, were as ready to agree to this truce and conference, as were those who sincerely desired that the negociations might lead to permanent peace.

The great and almost uniform success of the southern people, through the war in defeating and repelling the aggressions of their northern enemies, was not owing to any superiority of courage, or military talent of the victorious party—but to the inevitable disadvantages of invaders, and of opposite advantages of a people attacked by an invading army on their own soil. These respective disadvantages and advantages are especially great in this southern country—and still more because the powers engaged are communities under republican governments. If the southern people had been so foolish, and blinded by hatred or fanaticism, as to invade, and make a war of aggression on the northern people, the latter would doubtless have been found as brave defenders of their soil and homes, and as indomitable, as they, when invaders, found the southerners to be at home. But, fortunately, a republican and still more a federative government, which, while well conducted, is the strongest of all for defence, and at home, is, under all circumstances, the weakest for aggression abroad. Therefore, in any future wars between these parties, if other circumstances approach equality, the aggressive and invading party will be much the most liable, if not absolutely sure, to be defeated.

The people of the southern confederacy, and their federal government, are all heartily desirous of peace. But they have gained, from the events of the war, greatly increased confidence in their means and ability for military defence, and are assured of the impossibility of there being any serious impression made on the South by any future hostile attempts of the northern government or people, or indeed by any more powerful nation. The existence of negro slavery had been deemed, even by many southerners, and by all northerners, as the vulnerable and very weak and assailable point of the South. This has been fully tested, and by operations as extensive as they were unjustifiable and shameful, and with results that completely refute the before prevailing opinions on this subject. Even with the extraordinary measures used to deceive and excite the slaves to insurrection—less than which would have made insurgents, and robbers and murderers of the most destitute class of any great city of the northern states, or of any country in Europe—the general failure was so complete, that it is not probable that such atrocious and detestible measures of war will be again attempted.

While the presence of numerous slaves has not produced the anticipated dangers and evils to the South, it has been found in other respects a most valuable aid to military strength. For the speedy construction of fortifications, and for any other labors incident to military service, which demand neither courage nor experience, or skill, the resort to the use of negro slaves, which could be obtained to any desired amount, has served to leave all the soldiers for military services only; and so every laboring negro slave, thus employed, supplied the full service of a white soldier. Further, and which is much more important—a slaveholding people can supply a much larger proportion of the whole population, and of better character, and material for military service, upon a sudden emergency, than a hireling or free and laboring population. For one-half of all the men of the dominant class of whites may go abroad to repel invasion, and thereby scarcely cause any of the labor of the country to be abstracted, or the superintendence and direction of the negro laborers to be greatly lessened or impaired. There have been many recent proofs of this proposition, in the service of military companies for some weeks together, without much inconvenience or loss. If like calls had been made upon the people of the northern states, and had been as promptly and fully obeyed, the abstraction of so many laborers would have been ruinous and intolerable to any community so burdened. And so sensible was President Seward of this condition of the northern people, that he has not authorized a call of volunteers at all for any distant service—nor for any other than to oppose riot and insurrection in their own neighborhood. The only other militia force used was obtained by draught and legal compulsion; and no volunteers offered their services for distant localities, and for invasion of the South—except fanatical abolitionists, for exciting and leading in slave insurrections. But abundant as was their zeal, their judgment, and views and capacity for this peculiar military service, were as deficient as those of Peter the Hermit, and his followers, for conducting the first crusade.

The commercial and general loss and distress in the northern states, and especially on the Atlantic border, have been very great. No class or condition of people has escaped heavy losses, or severe suffering, because of the deprivation of southern trade, and of demand for commodities, and of southern employment—and also, directly and indirectly, for the postponement of payment of the debt of ninety millions of dollars due from southern to northern merchants and manufacturers. But the laboring and most destitute classes have been the greatest sufferers—for want of employment, reduced wages, and the increased prices of necessaries of life, previously drawn mainly from the South. These wide-spread sufferings have led to the plundering of great cities, the entire destruction of New York—and the rich inhabitants, and even poorer property holders, now live in continued terror, dreading and expecting like future attempts. To guard against the renewal of such atrocious acts in the great cities, the states to which they belong have been compelled to strengthen their police forces and measures, and also the general government of the North, to maintain strong military garrisons.

But the plundering and sacking of cities, or countries, by mobs and insurgents, with the usual incidents of fire and massacre, however disastrous and fearful, and even when ever so resistless and unrelenting, is not the only, nor the most effective mode by which the poor and destitute of these cities and states may, and hereafter will, plunder the rich, and all the possessors of property. Every ignorant, destitute, and desperate wretch, who would be willing to resort to robbery and murder to obtain his richer neighbor's wealth, has a vote, and an equal share in the election of all representatives and public officers, and of the direction of public affairs—and by the (even peaceable and legal) exercise of their votes, the members of this class, when they are the majority of any community, may rob property holders by law, and to any extent, for the benefit of the legal robbers. And this malignant influence had already been operating with fatal effect in the old northern states, and especially in the city of New York, long before the lowest classes of inhabitants had become the most numerous voters. For long in advance of that condition of culminating political evil and wo, where universal suffrage exists, (and the palliative in negro slavery does not exist,) the layers and disbursers of taxes and the payers of taxes are different and antagonistic classes. The richer citizens who must pay the larger amount of taxation, are too few to control the disbursements. The poorer majority, (including all the destitute,) who pay either little or nothing of the taxes, direct the disbursements, and as much as possible to themselves, and for their own gain. Every waste and misdirection of public money goes (or is expected) to aid some of the necessitous class—and therefore for this class, it is soon understood and acted upon, that the greater the amount of taxes on property, and the greater the abuses and waste of their disbursement, the better will be the chances of some gain or benefit to the poorer majority of voters—and who, moreover, lose nothing by the extravagance and waste of public money. This class too receives early and great additional strength, and efficient guidance in the worst acts, from demagogues of superior grade, and even of the higher and wealthy classes, who hope to wield the votes and influence of the ignorant and brutish multitude to build up their own political advancement and power. This inevitable result of universal suffrage, in free states, (if democratic government itself shall last long enough for working out the political problem,) cannot be prevented by any employment and action of city police, state volunteers, or regular troops of the general government—however effectual these means may be to restrain and prevent the more summary mode of the poor seizing or destroying the property of the owners, by forcible robbery, arson and wide-spread massacre. The same future dangers would threaten the southern states also, but for the existence there of negro slavery, by which (notwithstanding the ultra democracy and universal suffrage, of whites, and in their constitution of government,) the great body of the most ignorant and destitute, are, as slaves, necessarily and completely excluded from all political power. This safeguard, (for which the southern states owe nothing to their constitution makers,) possibly may secure to the southern people the continued blessings of honest and conservative magistrates and good government. And in this point of view, the states having the largest proportion of negro slaves, if equal in other political advantages and disadvantages, will be most justly and discreetly governed, and will be best able to preserve the principles and benefits of free government.

The wretched condition of the finances of the northern government, which I have before mentioned, and stated the causes of, has continued to grow worse. In addition to the great decrease of receipts from customs, (the only important source of revenue of the general government before or since the disruption of the Union,) the payments for public lands, in the new western states and territories, have entirely ceased. The settlers readily avail themselves of the doubts as to the rightful and eventual ownership of the vacant public lands, to refuse all payments for the present time—and the northern federal power, though claiming all these lands, is now too weak to attempt to enforce its claims. It is thought, too, that this refusal to pay, by all previous purchasers on credit, and of all later "squatters" on the public lands, is favored and secretly encouraged by the authorities of the north-western and Pacific states, in their anticipations of benefit, in their own particular political positions, in future time.

Very different is the present condition of the southern states and people—whether political and general, or private and economical. The southern people have indeed been subjected to many disagreeable privations of enjoyment, by the blockade, and the interruption of trade, and the partial cutting off, and enhancement of price, of the accustomed supplies of foreign articles of luxury and comfort—as well as of the greater profits from products and sales which otherwise would have been obtained. Also, there have been heavy and costly burdens, (however readily and cheerfully borne,) in furnishing the military services required, and incurring the incidental and heavy expenses for their support. But this is all. No state or city, and scarcely any individual, (except from the military licence and abuses, or plunderings of the invading armies,) has suffered any loss because of the war that will leave any abiding privations or discomfort. Neither has the southern confederacy incurred more expense, in debts or otherwise, than can be easily repaid by the operations and profits of a few years of peace; and that too entirely out of such sources of the public revenue as had heretofore been paid by the South to the former general government, and mainly to aid or sustain exclusive northern interests. If the war shall end now—or even, otherwise, if the North shall still refuse equitable conditions of peace, yet shall be restrained from invading southern territory, or interrupting southern trade by blockades, in either case, the prosperity of the southern confederacy must be advanced by a new and powerful impulse, exceeding, beyond estimate, the measure of prosperity and of progress, when united with and tributary to the North.

Whether the last of the two named contingencies, or a third, in the resumption and further invigorating of hostile action, shall succeed this truce and negociation, it may be counted upon with certainty that England and France will not longer permit the northern confederacy to maintain its system of nominal blockade of southern ports, when it has barely enough naval force to watch them irregularly, and to compel the obedience to their commands of unarmed trading vessels. In the early uncertainty of the persistence of the southern states in their revolt, and as to the ultimate establishment of their independence, it may be presumed that the European powers were unwilling to meddle, and to incur the hostility of the stronger party, (which was then expected to be victorious,) because of a temporary and not very important inconvenience. But as prospects changed, and no early termination of the blockade system seemed probable, both France and England signified their objections, and their implied determination not to submit much longer to this pretended right of enforcing blockade, exercised merely to obstruct trade, without the force for, or any intention of, attempting to conquer, besiege, or even to invest any other of the approaches to a city, whose distant outlet to the sea, only, was thus guarded and obstructed. These great European powers, and, following their example, all other naval powers, fortified by the laws of nations, can rightfully, and certainly will require, and, if necessary, compel, the raising of the blockade as to their respective vessels. Of course this will defeat all the important objects of the blockade, as all the exports and imports of the southern states will be carried in European ships, and as European property—and on either of these grounds will be secured from capture by the northern vessels of war. The only remaining service of the blockade, to prevent the passage of, or to capture, any of the very few vessels owned in the South, would not be worth a tithe of the cost of the means used for the purpose. Even if aggressive war is persisted in, clearly it will be necessary for the northern government to withdraw its various squadrons and single vessels from the vain effort to blockade southern ports. If any naval aggressions can be successful, (even if counting all damage to the South as profit to the aggressor,) it can only be by a powerful concentration of naval and land forces, to conquer and hold, or pillage and burn, some one or more of the large sea-port cities of the South.

If the war shall continue—with the blockade broken up, (as it must be,) the independent nationality of the southern confederacy recognized by the world, and commercial treaties made between it and the chief European powers, (which the commercial interests of France and England will especially need, and cannot dispense with,) then there must soon follow another operation of war, of the most serious importance. The southern confederacy, owing to the former political connections, has almost no shipping—and will have none for commerce, and for ocean navigation, while the continuance of this war shall make such possessions hazardous and unprofitable. The northern section, before this war, was, next to England, the most extensive ship-owner of the world. And even now, reduced in employment and profit as they are, northern vessels are still on every track of the ocean where profitable commerce or gain can be pursued. But however destitute now, the southern people can soon build, equip, arm, and send to sea, hundreds of privateers—and will be at no loss to obtain able commanders and veteran crews for them, if not of natives, of volunteers from all the commercial marines of the world. Still more speedily, and to any needed extent, can privateers' commissions be given to foreign vessels, which, if permitted, will come into southern ports for this purpose, manned, armed and equipped for immediate service, and will merely require to obtain authority to assume the nationality and flag of the southern confederacy. A few hundred privateers will sweep the northern ships and commerce from the ocean; while neither northern privateers nor navy can inflict any such evils in return, because the South will have no vessels at sea to be captured or destroyed, except the privateers. And these, necessarily swift sailers or steamers, and desperate fighters, will be difficult to overtake in flight, or to overcome in combat—and will offer no booty or profit for their capture.

LETTER LVIII.*

Conditions of peace required and denied. The truce extended. State of Military preparation.

CHARLESTON, October 10, 1868.

It was not expected by many persons that the northern government would agree to such terms of peace as the South required. But though peace was not formally made, its virtual existence was continued by the extension of the truce for six months longer, and it is not then to cease, or hostilities to recommence, until one month's previous notice shall have been given by either government that may desire to renew hostilities. In the meantime, the negociations for peace have been continued, but very languidly, as it seems. Trade and all peaceful relations are renewed, and have been from the first truce—but only as between two foreign and separate nations, suspicious and watchful of each other.

The terms of peace required by the southern confederacy, of the northern, were these: 1st. Mutual recognition of

---

* Letter LVII is wanting.—EDITOR.

separate nationalities of the two powers. 2d. Equal division, in value, of the vessels, and of the arms, munitions, and moveable materials for war, of the navy, and contained in the fortifications and arsenals of the former general government of the United States, and of the surplus funds, then in the treasury, as they were at the time of the first secession. 3d. Equal division of the net value of the public lands, wherever situated, or an equitable and general composition for this claim of the South. 4th. The landed or other fixed property, in buildings, forts, dock yards, &c., to be released to the government within whose territory they were severally included. 5th. The certificates of debt, given by officers of the northern army in Mississippi, for provisions and other property seized, to be paid by the northern government. On the forgoing terms being agreed to, then, 6th, the southern confederacy to assume the payment of one-half the former public debt of the United States, at the time of the first secession, with the interest since that time. 7th. The southern confederacy will pay to the northern creditors all the sums received into its treasury for the sequestrated private debts—and authorize the southern debtors to pay all the remaining amounts to the creditors—and to allow the use of its courts of law to creditors to enforce such payments from all debtors who shall withhold them. 8th. The foregoing conditions being carried out, the southern confederacy will agree to a commercial treaty, for ten years, (for trial of its operation,) of perfectly free trade between the people and territories of the two powers, or of entire freedom from all duties on either the exports or imports transmitted between the two countries.

These offered terms were rejected by the northern commissioners, because of the claim of the South to share in the value of the public lands, and other public property, now in possession of the North. This share the southern confederacy certainly never can obtain, and never will seek to enforce the claim for, by military action—and no one imagines the possibility of recourse to any such means for coercion. But though unable to enforce its demands by war, the South has still stronger commercial means for redress than war can furnish—and can well afford to wait for the operation and results of these means. The events of the late war have shown that the North, though much the stronger power at home, is as little able as the South would be to enforce its demands abroad by arms, and by a war of invasion. If the North persists in rejecting (by refusing the connected conditions,) the priceless benefit of free trade with the South, then the trade and vessels of the North must continue to be burdened, in southern ports, at the least, and as now, with as heavy duties and charges as all other foreign trade is subjected to. This will be enough to shut out northern productions, if not also all employment of northern ships—and to encourage the substitution of the use of the cheaper European products and shipping. Even this state of things will go far to exclude the northern states from their best customer, and heretofore the almost sole consumer of their manufactures. But the entire exclusion of northern trade may be at once effected, by the southern congress doubling the duties on the commodities of the unfriendly northern states, or lowering to one-half the duties and charges of all other countries, with which treaties of amity and commerce shall be formed. It is understood that such mutual and equal reduction of duties, by treaty, have already been offered to the commercial countries of Europe.

The disagreement of the negotiators, upon the proposed terms of peace, led to the continuation of the truce, as stated. There is very little probability of active hostilities, or any war measures, being renewed for the want of any inclination thereto on the part of the South, and because of the inability of the North. And so long as the truce shall continue, and its permanency is trusted to, it will be even more beneficial for the South than the obtaining its required terms of peace.

Even with the remaining burdens and charges on northern (as foreign) trade in the southern confederacy, and the new impediments of police regulations on all the border lines, the return to peaceful and trading relations was a great benefit to both sides, and especially to the northern section. Still more beneficial was the renewed intercourse, and the truce as the cause thereof, to the north-western states on the Ohio, and other upper waters of the Mississippi river. As nearly all the products of these states are agricultural, they are not among the taxed articles in the last United States tariff law—which still remains the present tariff law of the southern confederacy. Therefore the exports of these states are free of duty, whether sold in New Orleans, or transmitted thence to any foreign mart. Their imports, in return cargoes, if of southern production, are also free from duties; and if of European production, they will only pay on them (in increased price,) such duties as are charged by the tariff law, and are imposed, and enhance prices, at the North, as well as the South. But the fabrics and manufactures of the north-eastern states being now taxed as foreign productions, will all be too high-priced in southern marts, (if found there at all,) to be bought there for consumption in the north-western states. Therefore, these states must substitute such commodities by the like kinds imported from Europe—or otherwise procure them by the northern route from the north-eastern states.

Since the extension of the truce, the southern garrisons of military posts along the lines bordering on the North, have been still more reduced in number. Stronger garrisons are as yet maintained in the principal fortresses on the sea-coast. But all these garrisons, (and which are deemed amply sufficient for safety,) amount to no more than 10,000 men. The greater number of these are regulars and artillery men. This number is not greater than half the former United States peace establishment of regular soldiers, and the expense is far less than half. Therefore, even now, the military expenses of the southern confederacy, as an independent power, are much less than was the share paid by the same states for the whole military expenses of the former joint army. This small standing army is deemed sufficient, even for this time of uncertainty as to the duration of the truce, because the facilities of communication offered by the telegraph lines, and of transportation on the railroad, enable reinforcements of from 3000 to 8000 volunteers and minute men to be sent within four days after notice of their being needed, to almost any threatened point. And, if it should be made necessary, by the renewal of war, the whole southern armed forces, in the field and in garrisons, can thus be increased to 40,000 men within ten days. It is deemed better, and is far cheaper, to rely upon such speedy reinforcements, than to maintain a larger standing army in service. The northern section also maintains military posts along its side of the dividing lines. But a much larger military force is required, and so used, to keep strong garrisons of regulars in or very near to all the great cities of the

North, to guard against the unceasing and permanent danger of the renewal of insurrections of the rabble and "rascal multitude." These city garrisons alone, and required for this purpose, are more than double the whole number of troops deemed necessary to be kept by the South, to guard against foreign open or secret foes. Against internal foes or dangers, in all the South, there is kept no permanent military guard, except one company in each of a few great cities, and no more are wanting, for perfect security and tranquility.

The Congress of the South has continued in session to this time, with but a few short intervals of recess. The organization and putting in operation of a new government, even with all the aid of the existing forms of the previous general constitution and laws, have required much time and deliberation. Since the suspension of hostilities, and the consequent raising of the blockades, much of the care of the southern government has been given to military arrangements and to naval preparations. Though most anxious for the establishment and permanence of peace, the southern confederacy is not the less determined to be sufficiently prepared for war.

LETTER LIX.

Effects of the truce on North and South. Reasons and prospects for its continuance.

CHARLESTON, February 24, 1869.

The renewal of commercial intercourse and of peaceful relations between the North and South, under this long continued truce, has given a wonderful impulse to trade and business, and caused also a renewal of much of the former mutual kind feelings of individuals of the two lately hostile sections. The fanatical abolitionists have lost much of their former credit and influence at home, and they dare not now venture to enter on southern territory, and so to work to keep alive or rekindle animosity against the whole people of the North. Also, southern merchants have entirely ceased going to the North, (as was universal formerly,) to purchase goods of any kinds. For all northern fabrics being now subject to high duties, would thereby be so much enhanced in price, that but few kinds can be sold in southern markets, in competition with European articles subject to the same rates of duties only—or of southern manufactures, now protected by the same tariff law which had formerly been enacted by the superior political power of the North, and to operate exclusively for the profit of northern industry and capital. Being thus deprived of their former chief customers—and almost their only customers outside of their own present boundaries—the northern ship-owners, manufacturers, merchants, salesmen and mechanics, and even common laborers in every branch of mechanical industry, are now crowding to the South, hoping to recover there, as residents and citizens, the southern custom or employment which they had lost at home. Many of these persons are possessors of large capitals, which will thus be transferred from the North to give more rapid growth to the mechanical, manufacturing, commercial, and shipping business of the southern cities. All these new immigrants from the North, and designed permanent settlers, are (or profess to be) altogether friendly to the people and institutions of the South. The present intercourse serves to awaken and cherish kindly feelings on both sides. The main business now going on in the southern cities is incidental to or connected with the continual transference to the South, of northern capital and operatives, in every department of industry, which had been formerly sustained by protecting duties and bounties, and by southern custom and employment, thereby secured, under the legislation and policy of the former general government.

* * * * * * * * *

The earlier indications in the northern Congress of hostilities being vigorously renewed, have become more faint as the session advances, and as discussion serves to elicit opinions. The fanatical abolitionists, and insane haters of negro slavery and of the southern people, are still urgent for renewing the war. But this rabid and malignant sect has so lost credit and influence by the events of the war, and their consequences, that they can no longer control political action or popular opinion, except in the six New England states. Elsewhere, (and even there with an increasing minority of opposers,) there has been a strong and growing revulsion of the popular mind against the policy and the persons of the fanatical abolitionists. The majority of the northern Congress are certainly against renewing aggressive war on the South—and no one has supposed that the South will desire to become the aggressor, or to invade the northern section, unless as part of a general system of compelled defence against dangerous aggression. But though indisposed to renew the war, pride and fear of shame prevent the northern power from agreeing to the terms of peace insisted on by the southern government. In addition, the north-western states having virtually the possession, and the prospect of all the benefits, of the vacant public lands, prefer the continuance of the truce, which maintains that state of things, to any definitive treaty of peace. Under these several considerations, the northern government seems content to do nothing to renew active war, or to establish peace, but to let the present state of political relations continue. This would be still better policy for the South—whose government, in its offered conditions of peace, would surrender more of advantage now possessed (if the truce continues unbroken,) than would be gained in the claims now denied by the North. In truth, the claimed property in half the public lands (ill and wastefully managed as they always have been, and must be,) with half of the small navy, &c., are not equal in value to the present and prospective net revenue of the southern confederacy (which formerly all went to swell northern gains,) for five years—and are of less value than the amount of half the debt of the former general government, and the private debts due from southern to northern merchants, both of which are now held by the South as securities to obtain justice from the North. Indeed, the southern government does not care to retain so much security. The sequestration of private debts was a hard and unjust measure, reluctantly resorted to, and which could be justified only by the exigencies and wrongs of the southern states. The southern Congress has withdrawn the previous prohibition of payment of these debts to the creditors. All honest and responsible debtors will soon, of their own will, pay their creditors. The government will postpone the repayment of its receipts from this source to the conclusion of peace.

LETTER LX.

Political aspects, and commercial changes—North and South.

CHARLESTON, March 19, 1869.

The debates in the congress at Albany on the various subjects connected with the continuance of war, or of peace, have served to draw more distinctly the line of separation between the two new parties or interests of the North. One of these, mainly composed of and led by the rabid fanatics, and which makes up the majority nowhere now but in New England, still, in this disregard of all experience and reason, is vehement for war with the South—and still adheres to the first ideas of invasion, re-occupation, and complete subjugation of the southern states, with the excitement of insurrection, and the general emancipation of the negro slaves. The opposing and much larger party includes those of every shade of variant opinions, who are opposed to renewing the war. One branch of this party, of which the strength is in New York, Pennsylvania, New Jersey, and Delaware, are for concluding a treaty of peace, even if it be necessary, for that end, to accede to the terms offered by the southern government. But this policy is directly opposed, not only by the war party, but indirectly by the north-western states, the people and members of which prefer, for their peculiar condition and interests, the continuance of the present truce, to definitive terms of peace. And well may they prefer inactivity, and letting things remain as they are. Under the existing tariff law, (which however may be changed at the will of the southern government,) the north-western states enjoy all the benefits of trade with the southern states, and indirectly, through them, with Europe, that could be obtained from a treaty of peace. And, in the present unsettled state of claims and possessions, the north-western states indirectly derive all the profit now accruing from the settling by squatters, and filling up of the population of the vacant public lands on their western frontiers. But very different is the state of things with the Atlantic northern states, and especially with their manufacturing and commercial cities. Their losses, and distresses, both public and general, or private and individual, had continued to increase with the continuance of the war, and have been even more aggravated by the change to and the continuance of the truce. These evils have been adverted to before, and may be all classed together, as the various sources of gain formerly derived from the southern people, by operation of the former bounty and monopoly system, of which the northern states, and more especially the New England states, enjoyed all the former benefits—and which sources of profit have been all cut off by the independence of the southern states. And either continued truce or final peace will induce and enable most of the remaining capital and industry, thus left profitless, to move to the South, if permitted, for profitable investment and employment, And if such is the manifest progress of injury to northern trade while its burdens are only equal to all other foreign trade, by the southern tariff and navigation law, how much worse may it not be made by taxes discriminating against the northern states? And that this will be done, no one ought to doubt. When the negociations now in progress with England, France, and other commercial European states shall end in commercial treaties of these several powers with the southern confederacy, there will doubtless be exchanged between these several contracting and friendly powers, commercial benefits, and special favors, that will be withheld from others—and which neither policy nor magnanimity can operate on the South to offer to the unfriendly and half-hostile North. These confidently expected new relations of the southern confederacy with European countries, when established, must serve to deprive the northern states of even the present poor remnant of trade with the southern states.

In the meantime, and in advance of these aids of more profitable commercial regulations of foreign trade, the commercial prosperity of the southern confederacy is growing with a force and rapidity exceeding any previous anticipations of the most sanguine early advocates for the independence of the southern states. Nearly all the trade with Europe is still carried on by European vessels—but at lower charges than were formerly paid for northern vessels. The business of ship building is pursued actively, and with much spirit, in every sea coast state, and in some of the western. And very much faster than the building of vessels can be commenced, are northern vessels, and their owners, officers and crews offered to be naturalized in the southern states, and the men and property are so admitted.

The before established southern factories, now protected by the existing duties, are thriving, and many new establishments, for various fabrics, are in progress. Northern capitalists, merchants and manufacturers, and numerous mechanics and former operatives in northern factories, now closed, (all with good vouchers of opinions, character and conduct,) are seeking investments or employment in the South—and beginning the pursuit by taking the required oath of allegiance to the new government. Every such transference, from the North to the South, of either capital, industry, knowledge or skill in mechanical labor, is as much a gain to the one community as a loss to the other. On account of these and all other previous and greater losses, the industrial and commercial interests of the northern cities are obviously and rapidly declining. Already many northern residents predict and believe that grass will grow in the streets of Boston, and that the site of New York will remain, as now, overspread by the ruins left by the conflagration.

Financially, and in public affairs, the prospects of the southern confederacy are as bright as those of private and commercial interests. Heavy as were the expenses of the war, and as are the still continuing expenses of the military establishment and naval preparations and constructions, all will be paid for, and in a short time, out of the ordinary and present sources of revenue. The present receipts of customs amount to three-fourths as much as were obtained, under the same tariff law, by the former general government before the separation and war. And the estimated annual peace expenditures of the southern government, will not amount to one-fourth of the latter ordinary expenses of the general government, even before the beginning of President

Lincoln's administration, and while the democratic party was still in power. But it is true that a large portion of that expenditure was unjustly wasted, and corruptly squandered, and especially under the democratic administration of Buchanan.

For obvious reasons, it has been the policy of the southern confederacy to treat indulgently, and to conciliate, the north-western states. For this reason, no new duties have been charged upon their products or their imports, and no unnecessary restraints imposed on their foreign trade, carried down and through the Mississippi river, or by any other route. In consequence of this liberal policy, the people of the north-west have not sought, nor desired, to open direct communications with Europe, and are content to continue to trade principally with New Orleans. They not only find that city the best market, for the sale of their heavy agricultural products, but also their cheapest mart in which to buy foreign commodities, having, as they do, the benefit of draw-back of the duties on all imported commodities in unbroken bales and boxes—but paying duties, in increased price, on all purchases of smaller quantities of European and duty-paying goods. The latter supplies, while still cheaper to the buyers than would be the manufactures of the north-eastern states, by whatever channel brought, still are burdened with the cost of the duties paid on their importation—and so far, the north-western states voluntarily pay so much of the import tax to the treasury of the southern confederacy.

* * * * * * * * *

LETTER LXI.

Conflicting views of policy in different portions of the northern section. Common interests of the north-western and southern states.

CHARLESTON, April 7, 1869.

The differences of opinion and views of policy between the north-eastern states on one side, and the north-western and Pacific states on the other, are becoming more marked, and threaten to become irreconcilable. The former, and especially the New England states, desire to maintain the protective system, and as much as possible the forcing or indirect bounty policy of the former general government for supporting manufactures and navigation. By that system, these states were enriched at the expense of the agricultural states; and they still aim at retaining as much as may be of the like gain, under the present less favorable circumstances. As the southern states, which formerly paid most of the exactions of this bounty system, have withdrawn from its operation and oppression, such burdens as can now be maintained must be borne by the north-western and Pacific states only. When thus reduced in application, the working of the system is more clearly seen, and it is obvious that the north-eastern and Atlantic states will receive all the benefits, and the western and agricultural states (if submitting to the restrictions,) will endure all the evils. Hence the latter interest becomes more and more inclined to the policy of free trade, or low duties—while the former adheres to its old and strong advocacy for high protecting duties and the bounty system. The still abiding tariff (and other former United States) laws, were sufficient for these purposes, while the southern states remained in the Union. But now the northern states on all the upper waters of the Mississippi have entirely free trade with the separated southern states, and so far are freed from paying protecting duties through northern custom houses, or being compelled to buy the manufactures of the Atlantic northern states. It would be impossible to prevent this new free trade with the South, even by a cordon of interior custom houses and revenue officers along the separating line, for some 2000 miles. But the north-western states are not inclined to try any such restrictions. Besides this great and growing subject of alienation between these two sections of the North, the fanatical abolitionists still influence and lead the majority of the inhabitants of the New England states, while the majority of the people of the north-western and the Pacific states have been taught, by the events and results of the war, much more correct views on the subject of negro slavery. These states are now indifferent as to this important domestic policy of the South, and desirous that it shall not be meddled with by their laws, or by any of their citizens. Indeed, very many politicians, and others, and some newspapers, openly maintain the southern doctrine of the benefits of the institution of negro slavery, not only for the South, but also for their northern region, (for domestic and menial services,) and argue in favor of slavery being permitted and protected in their states. An early result of this change of sentiment, (and also an indication of the supposed necessity for conciliating the South,) has been seen in the recent repeal by the several north-western states of their "personal liberty" laws, formerly enacted to damage the security of property in slaves, and to encourage and aid their absconding from their masters. Self-interest serves much to quicken the perception of truth in these, as in all other cases. The north-western states find that their natural and chief trade is, or ought to be, with the slave-holding states on the lower waters of their great common river. This beneficial and all important commercial intercourse with the South, though now open, and as free from restrictions as the slavery question and differences now permit, is still much hampered and impeded by the police regulations of the South, which are necessary to watch, exclude, or promptly to punish, the detected emissaries and agents of abolitionists. Now all these vexatious, and costly restrictions would have no existence if there was complete extinction of the fanatical spirit and action of abolitionists of the north-western states—which extinction now seems to be in progress. If the supremacy of sound sense and good state policy, aided by state laws made in conformity, shall remove all danger and fears of the southern people of interference with this delicate subject, (of vital importance to them, and to the North, of scarcely less indirect benefit, and no detriment,) then all the present restrictions on free intercourse would be removed. The discussions of these questions, and of others in connection, is becoming common; not only in conversation, and in publications, but it even intrudes upon the latter debates of the northern Congress, in questions of conflicting interests of the Atlantic and western portions of the northern states.

But all the present inconvenient restrictions and police regulations, are of little moment, compared to what would be the awful consequences of the complete obstruction of that trade, which would be certainly caused by the renewal of the war, and by every future occurrence of war, with the southern power. The recent cessation of trade, for but a few months, was sufficiently injurious to show that the cessation for some years, by a war of ordinary duration, would be utterly ruinous to the north-western states. All these subjects for consideration and reasoning have latterly more and more occupied the minds of the thoughtful men of these states. It is easy to see to what conclusions the investigation of the whole subject ought to lead. But as political action is rarely directed by sound reasoning, it may be difficult to predict the issue.

Among the many subjects of public economy and regulation that have been arranged by the Congress and administration of the southern confederacy, has been the placing the post office and mail department on proper footing as a southern establishment. Like arrangements have been made, and with less difficulty, in regard to the communications to and connections with the northern states by mail roads, and by the magnetic telegraph lines. The obvious common interests, in all these subjects, of the now separated political communities, has induced the ready concurrence of all parties in equitable and proper arrangements.

LETTER LXII.

Commercial treaties with European powers.

CHARLESTON, April 14, 1869.

The report of a commercial treaty having been concluded between the southern confederacy and England, was soon followed by the like news in regard to France. Both treaties were speedily ratified by the Senate and President.

These treaties are precisely alike in their general provisions, and also in one novel and particular article. This provides that neither of the contracting parties shall impose duties on imported products or manufactures of the other, exceeding twenty per cent. on the home value of any article. This important approach to free trade, being a new experiment of treaty obligation, may be put an end to, by notice, at any time after ten years duration. While it continues, it will operate as an important benefit to the southern growers of tobacco, which 'export had before been taxed very heavily both in France and England. A still more important effect will be produced on the northern confederacy. For while its commodities when brought to the South, will continue to be charged, under the existing tariff, duties equal to forty per cent., the like commodities from England and France cannot be charged more than twenty per cent.

But this is not all. As soon as these two treaties were ratified, the southern Congress enacted the imposition of duties of twenty per cent. or more, on all commodities previously free of duty, and coming from any country not having a treaty of amity and commerce with this government. At the same time, the provision of a reciprocal restriction to the rate of twenty per cent. of maximum duty, is offered to every friendly power that may conclude a treaty of commerce with the southern confederacy. These measures must utterly destroy all remaining trade of the north-eastern states with the southern states. They will not effect the states west of the Ohio, as their agricultural productions have been especially excepted from duties. This exception, or any other special provision, this government has a right to make, in the absence of any general treaty of commerce with the northern government. This exception, while it is a favor of incalculable value to the north-western states, is at the same time a very significant hint to them that this favor may be at any time withdrawn, and consequent and inevitable ruin be thus brought upon the productive and commercial interests of that region. At the same time, and as in previous practice, the southern government has offered every facility, consistent with maintaining its police regulations, to the free passage of all products of the upper states (when at peace) bordering on the navigable waters of the Mississippi river, along its channel and out to the ocean. These several measures, adopted only after long delay, will operate as a reminder to the north-eastern states of the necessity for making a definitive treaty of peace, and also of commerce—and to the north-western states of their dependence on the forbearance of the southern confederacy, and the good policy of cultivating its good-will, if not of entering into closer political relations. * * * * * *

LETTER LXIII.

State of the two sections. Prospects of disruption of the Northern Union.

CHARLESTON, January 27, 1870.

The economical and commercial results, to this time, in both the northern and southern confederacies, are such as might have been anticipated from the operation of the previous and existing causes. Especially have causes rapidly been working out effects since the commercial treaties were made, eight months ago, between the southern confederacy and England and France respectively—and which were soon followed by treaties containing like general provisions, with most of the other commercial nations of Europe. The progress of improvement in every branch of industrial and commercial business, in the South, is manifest, and in most cases, very remarkable. The improvement is especially striking in the growth and increased business of the sea-ports and cities of the South which have succeeded to the possession of more than all the trade which the northern Atlantic cities formerly enjoyed, and nearly all of which they have now lost. Norfolk has received the most powerful impulse. This city (including Portsmouth) has already, in the short time since the truce begun, had its population more than tripled, and its commercial business increased five-fold. This city is fast advancing to the position which its great natural advantages, and its recent release from political disadvantages, demand—that of being the chief sea-port and commercial mart on the Atlantic coast. Charleston, Savannah and Mobile, also, are improving rapidly, as is every other southern city, in proportion to its late increase of capital and business. New Orleans maintains its former progress of rapid growth and prosperity. The northern Atlantic states, and still more their cities, have continued to decline. Indeed so low already are the rates of profits on capital and industry, that no enterprising man of commercial or manufacturing business is content to remain there, (and scarcely any working man in New England,) if not confined by circumstances to his local position. The north-western states, subsequent to the close of hostilities, (by the forbearance, and the favoring policy of the South,) have lost nothing in progress by the political changes—and since the truce, have resumed and continued their former rapid growth and general prosperity. But, still, there prevail general anxiety and uneasiness lest war should again occur, or the southern confederacy should withdraw its existing exceptional favors so far granted to the trade of this region. These fears alone serve to depress the price of lands to half of what it would be if these fears were entirely removed—which they can be only by these states being annexed to the southern confederacy. It is a powerful inducement to seek this object, however difficult of attainment, when, in addition to all other inducements, every proprietor believes that both the market price and intrinsic value of his land would be doubled by the attainment of the object.

Before the first secession of the southern states occurred, it was predicted, by "conservatives," and advocates for submission to the then long existing evils and wrongs, as one of the sundry and certain disastrous consequences of disunion, that the separated southern states would soon be further divided. For this result, there is no cause or inducement seen operating, or in prospect. There are no important conflicting interests of the southern confederacy, composed as it is entirely of agricultural states, and also slaveholding states, on which to found any motive for further separation. But in the now distinct and northern section, there are strong causes and inducements in operation, (besides the particular one just referred to,) which can scarcely fail to produce further and speedy secession, or more extensive disruption. The interests, and preferred public policy, of New England are peculiar, and different from those of all the western co-states. In these respects, and in other matters of public opinion, &c., there are existing, and fermenting, subjects of difference, and of future discord, even between the New England states, and the other northern Atlantic states of New York, Pennsylvania, New Jersey and Delaware. Yet, passing these by, and considering all these states as concurring in political views and public policy, (as they have usually acted,) this Atlantic section, taken as a whole, is separated in interest and policy from the north-western states, (on the upper waters of the Mississippi river,)—and both these sections are no less separated in interest, and far more in local position, from the remote western states near the Pacific ocean.

New England had lived and fattened upon the bounty and protecting duty system, and had every reason of interest for advocating that policy, while the great and rich agricultural South remained in the Union, and mainly paid the costs of the system which supported New England. The manufacturing and navigation interests of the other northern Atlantic states were also benefited by that system—and, though mistaken as to the supposed benefit to their other and general interests, these states also concurred with New England in supporting the general protective policy. This Atlantic section of the northern states therefore now urges the maintenance, and increased stringency, of the before existing high tariff and bounty policy. But the former operation of that system, even for the benefit of New England alone, would be now impossible to renew. Not only has the secession of the southern states withdrawn the payers of three-fourths of all the profits formerly received by the North from protecting duties and bounties, but even the Atlantic northern states cannot now pay their former share of the tribute. These states, which formerly imported foreign commodities for the supply of the whole former

United States, now import barely more than are needed for the consumption of their own limited section—and even that supply is greatly reduced, because of the recently much reduced capital, income and profits, and even productive or useful population of that section. At present, the southern states import all needed foreign commodities for themselves entirely—and also for the wants of the north-western states, which can obtain them much more conveniently and cheaply from the southern than from the northern importers. Under present circumstances, these north-western states pay almost nothing in duties on importations to the treasury of the northern confederacy—but, instead, prefer to pay the tax on their consumption to the southern treasury, in the much lower taxed, and therefore lower priced, southern importations. Of course the north-western section will not consent to the urgent demands of the Atlantic co-states to maintain and increase the stringency of the tariff and bounty system, to support northern manufactures—and still less to aid in cutting off the present free and profitable trade of the north-western states with the South. The Pacific states have still looser bonds of connection with the other two sections of the whole northern territory—and other and distinct motives for separation. Even before the first southern secession, it was as certain as anything of the future of political events, that California and the other new states of the Pacific slope would not remain as part of the then general union, any longer than their youthful and feeble condition required the guardianship, aid, and support of the general government, and defence by its army and navy. Separated in local position from the other states by barren deserts and high mountains, also usually barren, and rarely free from snow, for an intervening space of more than 1000 miles in breadth—and the broken navigation to the northern Atlantic cities as long as 6000 miles—these natural difficulties made the union of the very remote and far separated western and eastern states, under one government, as a permanent policy, both unnatural and inexpedient—and the disruption of their then political connection, would have been but a question of time. But now the reasons for disruption, and for hastening the measure, have been much strengthened by the southern secession. The Pacific states, their products, their commerce, the duties received in their ports on imported commodities, all are growing nearly as fast as the northern Atlantic states have been latterly declining. They are already strong enough to defend themselves from any power whose enmity and aggressive hostilities can be deemed in the least probable. And even if needing military and naval aid, the northen Atlantic states are now too poor and weak, as well as too remote, to afford any worth consideration. Further—both the Pacific and the north-western states wish to retain to themselves the vast extent of vacant public lands lying nearest to their respective localities. The northern Atlantic section, in loudly and continually asserting its claim to the joint property and benefits of these vacant lands, (while denying the like claim and right of the seceded South,)—as well as in its required policy as to restrictions on trade—has come to be considered, by the two western sections, as an importunate and troublesome pauper, rather than a profitable member of the present political co-partnership. It is a growing opinion in the West, that the eastern states are a political incumbrance, (and mainly because of New England,) of which the disconnection and riddance would be an unmixed benefit to the western states. In addition to all these causes of growing alienation, the fanatical abolitionists, and their doctrines, are becoming more and more disliked, or abhorred, by all persons who are not now included in that much diminished sect—which now is scarcely strong or bold enough to speak aloud, except in New England, throughout which, abolitionism is still dominant and raving. To the misguiding by this sect, and to its iniquitous hostile aggressions on the interests of the slaveholding states, the secession of these states, and all the latter misfortunes and difficulties of the northern section are justly ascribed. And no persons are more strenuous in charging and denouncing these offences, and expressing hatred of the fanatics, and of the New England states in which they still rule, than the many thousands of their former misguided followers in the north-western states, who have since changed their opinions as to the evils of the institution of negro slavery.

With such separation of opinion, and of interests, and of business pursuits, and connections—with such discordance of views of policy, and in their remote localities, it is impossible that these three minor sections can remain long united in one political body. When the time shall come for such results, the probable course of the section on the Pacific slope will be to declare its independence as a separate nationality. The north-western states, on all the upper navigable waters of the Mississippi, will desire re-annexation to their natural and proper partners, as co-states with the present southern confederacy. This re-union may be made, under the existing provisions of the constitution of the southern confederacy, upon the one condition, that the legal recognition, and secure protection of negro slavery, shall be enacted and maintained by every state to be so annexed. In requiring this indispensable condition, it is not expected (or desired) that the north-western states shall become actually slaveholding to any notable extent—nor is it supposed that negro slaves can be cheaply used for field labor in a cold climate. The most free permission and perfect legal security for holding slaves, at most, would only serve to introduce them as house and menial servants, for which places slaves would be very useful even in the coldest of the new north-westhern states, where labor is scarce and high priced, and domestic and menial service not to be hired. The great and essential object of this condition required by the southern federal constitution, of the legal recognition and secured position of slavery and slaves in every state admitted to its union, is to prevent any renewal of abolition or hostile action against slavery where it now exists. For if the rights of all slaveholders are legally and amply protected in the border states, having few or even no slaves, their residents, or emissaries from them, could not easily invade and damage these rights in the states where slavery is general.

The presence of the rich southern section in the former general union was the strong link that bound all the other parts together—the abundant aliment on which each necessitous and hungry northern interest fed and fattened. That link of connection is broken—the foundation and support of the former union removed—and the remaining states are in three parts, separated in interests, pursuits, and in locality, having no common bond of coherence, and which will fall apart, even if without the aid of any new or extraneous force. But the pressing financial difficulties and growing necessities of the northern government, will furnish new reasons and stronger motives to hurry the inevitable disruption. The revenue of the federal government, derived entirely from customs paid on imported foreign commodities, is now, by the diminution of imports to the north-eastern states, reduced so low, that it cannot defray the ordinary expenses of the government, exclusive of the interest of the public debt. The improvements of the navy, in repairs and new constructions, which were in progress, have been suspended, most of the vessels before nearly or quite ready for service, have been laid up in ordinary, for want of means to keep them in use. The recruiting for the regular army has been stopped. All the regular army in service has been kept, and cannot safely be dispensed with, to guard the great Atlantic cities from outbreaks of their destitute and dangerous classes. The Atlantic states are urging the laying of direct taxes to supply the deficiency of the revenue, and provide for the wants of government. To this necessary measure the two other sections demur—and complain that the present outlay, and especially for military expenses, is made mostly for the defence, and the other burdens imposed by the protective tariff are for the gain, of the Atlantic section—and that the products of direct taxation would be mainly used for the same purposes. The Atlantic states complain that under the present system of indirect taxation, by imposts, the north-western states pay scarcely anything—and that they are opposed to any mode by which they would be made to pay their fair proportion. They also complain that the settlers and squatters on the public lands no longer pay any of the purchase money to the treasury, and that the western states, indirectly profiting by this abuse, will not concur in enactments stringent enough to correct it. The Pacific states, already and always having the possession and use of the public vacant lands, and of the immensely rich products of gold yielded by mining, have come to consider these as their own exclusive property—and regard the claims and efforts of the north-eastern states to obtain their share as attempts of actual usurpation and robbery.

Under these circumstances, it is safe to predict that this ill-assorted union under one general government of all the non-slaveholding states will fall asunder, and speedily, by the mere force of its own elements of repulsion and discord. Whether before or after this disruption, there will be utter inablility for the resumption of war against the southern confederacy—and, even if the northern people were as strong as at first, there would be now no desire to make war, except by fanatical New England. In any contingency, the whole northern section, while yet united, and still more, apart, after disruption, will be entirely unable to make aggressive war on the South; and even the still raging madness of fanaticism in New England will scarcely dream of renewing the practical efforts to emancipate negro slaves, or to assail with any success the institution of slavery. When the disruption shall take place, it will probably be begun by the assertion of the independence of the Pacific slope—which will be a judicious and safe policy for that thriving and growing section. And if, after being independent, there shall be made a treaty of perfect free trade between the Pacific section and the southern confederacy, and perhaps also with the remaining section of the North, that arrangement will be better for all parties than the former or the present close political connexion of regions so far separated in geographical position. Better, I would say, even for the Atlantic parties, whether retaining or forfeiting the claimed and rightful, or equitable shares of the yet remaining golden treasures of the mines, or of the vacant lands of the whole Pacific territory.

The geographical position and relations of the north-western states unfit that great section for independent political existence. Its interests will be best promoted by re-annexation to the southern states, under one general government.

As to the predaceous and troublesome New England states, with their pestilent fanaticism, no political community or power will be willing to accept their annexation, by union or allegiance. Greedy as England has always been for territorial acquisition and extended dominion, and anxious to retain even the most costly and unprofitable colonial possessions—even England would now refuse to receive, as a free gift, the voluntary annexation of New England to British America. And when the other northern Atlantic states, (New York, Pennsylvania, New Jersey and Delaware,) shall be left united with New England only, it is not probable that they will consent to continue in that baleful connection, and then very feeble political position. These four states, bordering upon the great confederacy of not only the southern but the north-western states, will doubtless desire to be re-annexed to the great and prosperous body, even if yielding, as the necessary condition, all power for the future action of anti-slavery fanaticism. Then New England will be left alone, as it ought to be, without any political associates to rob of their wealth, or to hate and annoy or persecute, because of their diverse opinions, or preferred policy.

In the meantime, the offer of peace from the southern confederacy, with the equitable arrangement of all the claims of opposite parties, remains open to the acceptance of the still united northern power—and of course will be so to either and all of the fragments made by future disruption. Whether this offer shall be still rejected, or accepted—and whether accepted soon or late—is of but little practical importance, or interest, to the southern confederacy—which, in either of these contingencies, must go on to thrive and flourish, drawing growth and vigor and wealth from nearly all the sources which heretofore had supplied the whole former United States, and of which the former benefits were retained mostly by the northern portion, and especially by New England. And should New England be left alone, thenceforward its influence for evil on the southern states will be of as little effect, and its political and economical position scarcely superior, to those conditions of the present republic of Hayti.

APPENDIX.

CAUSES AND CONSEQUENCES

OF THE INDEPENDENCE OF THE SOUTH *

FIRST PUBLISHED IN 1856-7.

SECTION I.

The sectional abolition party barely defeated in 1856—and the causes.

In the late presidential election a victory has been achieved for the constitutional rights of the southern states. The northern abolitionists and their auxiliaries have been repulsed, and their strongest assault has been foiled and defeated for the present time. But though defeated, our enemies are neither weakened nor discouraged. They have seen that with even their present numbers, if more adroitly marshaled and directed, they might have been victorious. And with their growing and certain gains, from the hordes of future ignorant immigrants from Europe,

[* This argument, which consists so largely of "Anticipations of the Future," and therefore is appropriately appended here, will be reprinted from the first publication, which was made in the Richmond Enquirer in December, 1856—and which was republished in De Bow's Review, in 1857, with the addition of the concluding section. The only changes now to be made, from one or both of

(most of whom will be ready tools for the service,) the abolition party will be relatively stronger for the next contest, in the next presidential election.

And what is this victory that the South has gained, and its value? And by what means was it secured?

Even if Maryland had not been an exception to the otherwise unanimous vote of the slaveholding states, their unanimous vote would have been overpowered by an united vote of the states under abolition influence, and all of which will be ready hereafter, under different circumstances, to follow the lead of abolition to put down slavery, and to crush the rights and the vital interests, and the very existence of the slaveholding states. The recent victory for the South was gained only by the southern people sustaining a northern candidate for the supreme magistracy. And the democratic party was victorious, only by adopting as their candidate one who differs from that party on some important questions of public policy, and still more from the southern portion of that party. If Mr. Buchanan had been a southern man, and even had equal or superior abilities and claims, he could not have been elected, because he would have failed to obtain the necessary additional aid of northern votes, adverse in feeling and interest to the South. Therefore, however much we may rejoice for our victory, it affords but slight ground for triumph, and still less for assurance of safety, or even of a like temporary defence

these early publications, will be in some merely verbal and trivial corrections, the addition of section headings, and in the form of words of the general title. Any new addition, required for explanation, will be distinguished by being enclosed in brackets. Both the date and place of the earliest publication should be borne in mind by the reader at this later time, when the lights of subsequent events have served still more to sustain the positions which, in this article, were so much earlier asserted and maintained by the writer.—1860] hereafter, against the renewed and better concerted attack of our enemy. It has been truly said that this victory has given to the South, not peace, but only a truce from active hostilities. Let us of the South use this time of truce to thoroughly examine, understand, and strengthen our position, and so be prepared to meet and repel every future attack on our constitutional rights and our rightful interests.

SECTION II.

The rights and liberties of a people may be effectually destroyed, without violating the letter of their constitutional safeguards.

It is often asserted, and is admitted by many among ourselves, that so long as the northern people and states use only their constitutional power to assail our interests, the sufferers have no just right to complain, and still less cause to resort for defence to extra-constitutional remedies. No position is more false or dangerous. The forms or letter of the constitution may be so used as to destroy its spirit and substance, and the very benefits that the constitution was enacted to secure. When one, and the much more powerful section of a country and people is entirely opposed to and arrayed against the other section, in interest or principle, or in fanatical sentiment, the constitutional forms and literal restrictions of the government may be respected, and yet the weaker section and party may be subjected to the utmost extent of injustice, wrong, and oppression. The right of representation granted for Ireland in the British Parliament, even if entirely fair and equal in proportion to the respective populations of Ireland and England, would have done nothing to guard the weaker from the oppression of the stronger country. If the plan had been adopted of allowing to the former American colonies of England representatives in the English Parliament, it would have been futile and contemptible, as a measure of defence. Our ancestors would have scorned to accept, as protection for their assailed and threatened rights, a representation in Parliament, even if then greater in proportion to population than that of the far more populous mother country. And, as the people and the states of this confederacy are now divided, by sectional lines, in sentiment, opinion, and supposed interests, and are standing adversely, and in still growing opposition and hostility, the representatives in Congress of the Southern and weaker section, being a fixed minority in both houses, are no more a safeguard to the section they represent, than would exist if it were deprived by the constitution of all right of representation. In the lower house of Congress, that result is already seen fully exhibited. In the Senate, the majority of members from the non-slaveholding states is smaller, and, owing to the longer term of service, and slower changes of members in that body, the cause of right and justice has not yet been trodden under foot by the brute force of a fixed and sure majority of voters. But the same end must be reached there also in good time. The senators of the sixteen non-slaveholding states must hereafter truly represent the opinions of their constituents, as now do their fellow representatives in the lower house, and then both legislative bodies will concur in controlling the fixed minority of the fifteen slaveholding states. And, even without this certain, though slow change of voice of the

Senate, and long in advance of its completion, there will be admitted other senators from four or five new non-slaveholding states, which increase will make the abolition party as irresistible in the Senate, as it is already in the other branch of Congress. When this party is thus supreme, it will, of course, elect a President of the United States of like sentiments. And then, without the need of infringing the letter of a single article of the constitution, the southern states, their institutions, property, and all that is dear to them and necessary for their very existence, will be at the mercy of their fanatical and determined enemies. Under these circumstances it would be very easy to destroy, by legislation, all the value and security of the institution of slavery, and so lead to its necessary abolition, and the consequent inevitable ruin of the southern states and people. But these would not be the only means to reach this end. If more power were needed for more complete victory and success, and the constitution (even as construed at the North) stood in the way, that instrument, in accordance with its own provisions for amendment, may be altered and put in any required shape. Owing to the actual much faster settlement and filling up of the non-slaveholding territories, (mainly by foreign immigrants,) and their greater extent, and even if no unjust preference were given by Congress, it will not be long before the non-slaveholding states will be so increased as to make three-fourths of the whole number of the members of the confederacy. Then the federal constitution may be legally altered in any manner, by the votes of the northern states only. Negro slavery may be thus abolished, either directly or indirectly, gradually or immediately. Can any man doubt that the full power and constitutional right, then possessed, will not be exercised as directed by the already existing fanaticism and hostility of the northern people? The man who can entertain a hope of the contrary course may be, (indeed must be,) too virtuous to know or believe in the extent of the violence of fanaticism, or the baseness of party spirit. But he will be a poor judge of human nature, a novice in political history, and altogether unfit to be trusted to guard and protect our rights and liberty.

SECTION III.

Some of the ruinous injuries which may be inflicted on the South, without infringing on the federal constitution.

The present contest between the northern and southern states, in regard to negro slavery, has been growing in violence for a long time. It was begun with the iniquitous aggression of attempting to exclude Missouri from the Union as a slaveholding state, and in the successful exaction of the Missouri compromise, in relation to which, both the general enforcement and exceptional violation of its principle by the North have been exercised and varied, the more to wrong and injure the southern states. But it has been only since the (falsely so-called) compromise enactments of 1850, that abolition has been hastening towards its object with gigantic strides—and also that the South has been partially roused from its sleep of fancied security. Unfortunate it has been, that this sleep had not been effectually shaken off thirty years sooner, and that all the means had not then been used for defence, that were abundantly possessed by the South at that time. If, when the Missouri compromise was submitted to, the proposed restrictions had been resisted by the South at all hazards, there would have been no further trouble about slavery. And if the fanaticism (or, more truly the unholy grasping for political power) of the North, had then been so unyielding as to permit a separation of the United States, the southern portion would now have double of their present wealth and power—and the northern states would not have attained half of their present greatness and wealth, which have been built upon the tribute exacted from the South by legislative policy. But no separation would have been produced. If, at the time of the Missouri compromise, the northern members and states had been firmly resisted, they would have drawn back, and the spirit of political abolition would have been crushed in the bud. The sincere abolitionists, who are actuated by what they deem moral and religious considerations, are but the simple and deluded tools of the hypocrites and knaves who are using them to further their own objects of personal ambition and political power.

Without looking even as far as twenty years into the future of the effects of the northern crusade against southern slavery, let us see what might have been the speedy consequences, if the contingency had occurred, which was so near occurring, of an abolitionist being elected President—he being the candidate of the northern states only, and on the abolition question and principle. It is true that a more conciliatory policy would probably have been adopted at first, because the victorious party would not have risked the driving their conquered opponents to desperate and revolutionary measures of resistance. But it is fair to suppose that a party so fanatical, greedy, and unscrupulous, would have used every means to reach its object, that could be used safely and successfully. Let us, then, see what means, and all claimed as constitutional by the North, could be used by an abolitionist administration of the government of the United States. If elected, it would have been supported by a majority of the people of the states, and of the House of Representatives. It would not have required much time, or management, (by corruption or other influences,) for the President to have also at his command a majority of the Senate—representing states that were already his supporters. Then, the President, with a majority of both Houses of Congress, might adopt any or all of the following measures, to weaken and destroy the institution of slavery:

The first and greatest measure, is already openly avowed by the abolitionists, and the majority of every northern state, as their designed policy and plan of action hereafter. This is to admit into the Union no new territories as slaveholding states. This alone, even if nothing else is done, will soon increase the non-slaveholding states to three-fourths of the whole, so that the constitution can be changed, and slavery abolished. But, in advance of the consummation of this great and effectual measure, various other auxiliary means might be used to hasten the end, as thus:

Each of the largest non-slaveholding states, with its own consent, might be divided by act of Congress, so as to make two states of each, and so have four abolition senators in place of two.

Every office and emolument in the gift of the federal government might be bestowed on abolitionists only, and in all the southern states on northern abolitionists, until corruption and fear, or despair, should induce conversions, or professions and acts of abolitionism in southerners, as offering the only road to office or gain.

The zealous and active exertions of all these many thousands of government officials and employees, down to the lowest laborers on any government work, would be counted on and secured, to operate against the institution of slavery and the interests of slaveholders. This open, unassailable, and powerful influence, would be added to, and serve to increase a hundred-fold, the existing secret influence and concealed operations of the many abolition agents, male and female, lay and clerical, who, in various ostensible business employments, have long been operating on our slaves, often under the hospitable shelter of our own roofs, and as our pretended friends.

Every military and naval officer hereafter to be appointed, might be an abolitionist, and all now commissioned, and not abolitionists, might be dismissed from service on other pretexts, or otherwise not entrusted with any command.

The various lands held by the federal government, for forts, dock-yards, arsenals, light-houses, &c., in the South, and every national ship in southern waters, would be made places of secure refuge for fugitive and even rebellious slaves, and secure positions for any other incendiary action.

The District of Columbia would be made non-slaveholding by law, and soon in sentiment. It would be openly and entirely what it is already partially, (by northern and government influence,) ground, within the southern and slaveholding territory, where the enemies of the South have the greatest facilities for their most effectual and dangerous action. Already under the protecting shield of the federal government and its administration, at a former time, the agents of the abolitionists have been able there to effect more injury to slaveholders, and with more of impunity, than anywhere even in the abolition states.

The removal of slaves by sales from states where they were in excessive numbers, to other states or new territories where they were most deficient, would (as long threatened) be forbidden by an early law under the complete supremacy of a northern administration. This alone would prevent the making of any new slaveholding states in the small extent of the remaining territory in which climate does not forbid slavery; while the increase of slaves in the old states, from which they would have no sufficient outlet, would render them an unprofitable burden and a dangerous nuisance to the whites. The condition of the slaves would thereby be made much worse, in regard to their own happiness, and the institution of slavery would be hastened toward its doomed extinction.

Some of these measures might require that liberal mode of construing the federal constitution which is general at the North, and especially on this subject. But even the strict construction of that instrument might be conformed to, literally, and yet an abolition administration, in a little more time, could as effectually extinguish the institution of slavery, and the prosperity and existence of the southern states as independent communities.

Such might have been, and to great extent, such would have been the earlier or later effects and operation of an abolitionist's election to the Presidential office. Such, and with more sure and extended operation, will be the effects of the future election, by a much stronger constituency, of a Seward, or some other northern abolitionist, or of another southern renegade and traitor, of more ability than the one who was lately raised so nearly to the height of his ambition, only to be let fall and sink in an abyss of contempt.

Will the southern states wait for the completion of these surely coming results, or will they take the warning so plainly to be read in their enemies' acts and avowals, and save themselves from the impending ruin? The fast growing strength of the abolition party, and the signal success of that party in the next Presidential election, may cause every southerner to regret that its candidate was not elected in the recent contest, when the south was relatively stronger for defence than it will ever be hereafter.

SECTION IV.

Obstacles to resistance.

In such a contingency as we have just now barely escaped, the election of a President by abolition and sectional votes, there will remain no chance for the slaveholding states to preserve their property and their political rights, unless by another declaration of independence of, and separation from, a despotic party, whose wrongful and oppressive acts have already far exceeded, and threaten to exceed much more in future, all the acts of actual and prospective oppression of our mother country, against which our brave and patriotic fathers revolted—preferring a struggle for freedom, with all the certain disasters and incalculable dangers of a war with a nation of ten-fold their power, to submission or unjust oppression.

We, the sons of those fathers, eulogize and glorify their act of separation from the previous glorious and happy union of these colonies with their mother country. Their act of separation and disunion we deem a noble and patriotic devotion to freedom, worthy of all praise. We the children of those fathers, in maudlin love of, and devotion to a union with those who were formerly deemed our brethren, but now are our most malignant and dangerous enemies, have submitted to oppression and wrong incalculably greater than ever England inflicted, or thought of inflicting on her colonies. And still many of the South continue to recommend patience, and endurance, and submission to every wrong and evil, rather than meet the evil of disunion!

SECTION V.

Separation of the Union no ground for war.

If Fremont had been elected, the consequences would have been so manifestly and highly dangerous to the rights and the safety of the slaveholding states, that they would scarcely have waited to be completely shackled, and powerless for defence, before they would have seceded or separated from the victorious and hostile states of the present confederacy. It is proposed here to inquire what would have been the results of such separation, and especially to consider the question of the danger of war, which it is so generally believed would necessarily ensue between the separated communities, and the results of any war.

If the necessity was manifest to the people of the South, there would be no obstacle to their deliberate action, and no probability of opposition by the northern states, nor by the then remaining fragment or shadow of the federal government of the previous confederacy. The legislatures of the offended states would call conventions, and these conventions would declare their separation and independence, and, by subsequent acts, make a new confederation. If all the fifteen slaveholding states united in this action, they would be far stronger, at home and for repelling invasion, than would be the northern states as invaders. Even if but five or six adjacent southern states alone seceded, no remaining power of the federal government, or of all the northern states, could conquer or coerce the seceders.

But, contrary as is the opinion to that which generally prevails, I maintain that such act of secession would offer no inducement or occasion for war; and that there would be no war, as the immediate or direct result of secession or separation.

The malignant hostility of feeling that is even now entertained by the abolition party, and perhaps by a majority of the northern people, towards those of the South, is not here overlooked or underrated. If they could, by merely willing it, they would ruin us, even while united with them under one government—and still more readily if we were separated. If the mere wish of abolitionists could effect the destruction of our system of negro slavery, even by the destruction of the entire white population of the South, I would fear that that consummation would not be a remote event. But *to will* and *to do* are very different things. And even northern fanaticism, (to say nothing of northern self-interest and avarice,) would prefer to forego these gratifications, if they were to be purchased only at the cost, to the North, of hundreds of millions of dollars, and hundreds of thousands of lives. Even if admitting, what is so arrogantly and falsely claimed by the North, that it could conquer and desolate the South, any such victory would be scarcely less ruinous to the conquerors than the conquered.

But there would be no such war, and no movement towards it—because war could not subserve or advance any interest of the North. It is unnecessary to maintain the like proposition in regard to the South, inasmuch as it is universally admitted. No one, of either side, has ever asserted, or supposed, that the South would assail, or make war upon the North, in consequence of their separation. Whether this peaceful disposition is ascribed to a greater sense of justice, or to the weakness, or the timidity of the southern people, all concur in the belief that the South would desire peace, and would avoid war, unless necessary for defence. Then, passing by this contingency, deemed impossible by all parties, we have only to examine the supposed inducements for offensive war and attack by the North on the South.

SECTION VI.

The interests of the South not endangered by separation from the North. Means for peaceful retaliation and indemnity for injuries.

"But," it is urged by many among ourselves, "even if the North refrained from making war, still it would retain the direction of the federal government, and exercise its right and remaining power—and also hold possession of the seat of government, the army and navy, the fortifications, and the public lands. How could the public property be divided peaceably? And, without resorting to war to enforce our right to a fair share, would not all be necessarily lost to the South?" I answer that, even if admitting all these premises, still there would be no need, and no advantage, for the South to seek justice through war—and no benefit to the North would be gained by withholding our just dues, either by war, or in peace. Nations, in modern days, do not often go to war, and never in advance of negotiation, to recover debts, or to settle pecuniary accounts and obligations. There are other means, in many cases, to induce, and even constrain nations to render justice; and, luckily, in our case, the means available for the South would be of the most cogent influence. These will presently be discussed. But first, I will say, that even if the result of separation to the South was, indeed, the loss of every value named above, (except the few spots of southern ground, heretofore ceded to the federal government, and which would necessarily go finally to the states in which they were situated,) the South would still gain, by separation, much more than it would lose by this great spoliation. As to the army, it would, probably, like the present federal government, cease to exist, as soon as the Union was dissolved. The public buildings, fortifications, and navy, and all other material values held by the government of the Union, and the annual revenue, have been mainly (at least two-thirds of the whole) acquired from the contributions of the southern states—while the much larger proportion of all disbursements of government, and pecuniary bounties and benefits of all kinds, have as regularly gone to enrich

the northern people. If, then, this regular and very unequal apportionment of the burdens and bounties of government were stopped, as it would be by separation, the South would gain more in retaining, for the future, its own resources for its own benefit, than the actual pecuniary value to the South, in the Union, of its share of all the present national property. And these retained resources, within a few years, would amount to a fund more than sufficient to replace the forfeited values of army, navy, and all the public edifices. As to the public lands, vast as is their extent, and enormous their value, the South has already been virtually deprived of them. No southerner can safely remove with his slaves to any new territory. The people of the South were thus unjustly and illegally shut out from the rich fields and richer mines of California, by the action of the North and the federal government. The conquest of Mexico was achieved by men and money supplied (as of all other contributions) in much the larger proportion by the southern states. By their much larger expenditure of both blood and treasure, California and New Mexico were acquired. Yet the people of the South, as slaveholders, were excluded from the whole territory; and southern men have had no access to or benefit from the rich mines and lands of California, that were not as open to, and equally enjoyed by, the semi-barbarians of China and the Sandwich Islands, the former convicts of Australia, and the needy and desperate outcasts, attracted by these benefits, from every foreign land. A like virtual exclusion of slaveholders will be effected hereafter as to every other new territory. And even from the sales of public lands, and through the federal treasury, it can scarcely be expected that any considerable benefit will hereafter accrue to the South, or serve to lessen its greater share of the burden of taxation. For nearly all the resources from the public lands have, in latter years, been squandered by Congress, and mainly to benefit northern men and northern interests. So little revenue from the public lands will hereafter reach the treasury, that the amount will probably not more than defray the great expenses of the land surveys and sales, and the much greater expenses incurred in governing and protecting the new territories. If the gigantic and much urged and favorite scheme of either one or three railroads to the Pacific ocean should be adopted by Congress, (as seems probable,) all the net proceeds of future sales of public lands, and that amount doubled by additional grants from other funds of the government, will not suffice to construct and to keep in use this work of unexampled magnitude and unheard of national folly or extravagance.

According to these views, the entire loss to the South, and at once, of all the public property, would be no greater damage than the former and present and prospective unjust apportionment of contributions and disbursements. Still, this is no reason why, in the event of separation, the South should submit to lose its just rights in the common public property. And in this respect, the independent South would be more able to obtain redress for spoliation, or to save something out of the general wreck of the present public property, than will be possible if remaining united to and governed by the stronger northern states. As a separate power, wronged by spoliation, the South would negotiate for redress, calmly and peaceably. And, if necessary, until redress was obtained and an acceptable composition made, a prohibition should be enacted against the introduction or sale of all northern commodities, and the employment of northern vessels in the southern states. These peaceful means would soon produce satisfactory redress, or, otherwise, ample retaliation, for any amount of previous injury. These measures would be far more potent than war, and yet entirely peaceful, and such as could not be opposed or countervailed, or even complained of by the northern states.

SECTION VII.

Fanatical and political abolition. Superior political talents of the slaveholding states.

The picture which has been sketched of the ruin of the South, which will surely result from the present and continued efforts of our "northern brethren" and fellow-citizens to extinguish negro slavery, has nothing in it to moderate or discourage any abolitionist of the fanatical school of Garrison, Giddings, and Beecher. Fanaticism has no moderation, no reason, no mercy. The true abolitionist—an abolitionist for the sake of conscience and what he deems religion—would welcome all the evils and horrors that would come, if these were the necessary consequences of the consummation of his great measure and object. But these men, the only sincere and honest members of the great anti-slavery party, are comparatively but few, and they are but the tools of the more selfish and cunning and baser Sewards, and Sumners, and Greelys, who know full well the folly and falsehood of their professed doctrines, and who advocate them merely to acquire political power or personal gain. These and all of the most intelligent leaders, and the greater number of their followers in the abolition party, are not in the least actuated by the alleged sufferings and sorrows of the "poor slave," or by the other evils generally imputed to the institution of slavery. These charges are but pretences to delude their own followers, and induce their obedient following and zealous support. Many of the more candid men of the party admit that they are not deceived, or directed by sympathy for the "poor slave," whose condition they know to be better than it would be if the "poor slave" were made free. But they say (and truly) that notwithstanding the larger population and vote and decided majority of the North, and its greater wealth and more extended education and intelligence, (as claimed,) that the government of the United States has always been, and still is, generally directed by men of the South, or by men and measures of their choosing. This greater influence of the South is denounced as the "slave power;" and to overcome and prostrate this "slave power," and transfer its rule to the North, is the true and great object of the political and hypocritical abolitionists who now lead the great northern party.

It is true, (and almost the only great truth that the abolitionists have yet arrived at,) that the intellect of the South, in most measures of high importance, has influenced and directed, and controlled the much greater numerical power of the North. And it is also true, that this superiority of influence is a direct consequence, and one of the great benefits of the institution of domestic slavery. In the United States, it is only where negro slavery exists that many men of the rural or agricultural population can have enough of leisure and opportunity to cultivate their intellect, and especially, by social intercourse and the instruction thence derived, so as to become qualified to teach and to lead in public affairs, instead of being mere "hewers of wood and drawers of water," (slaves, in effect, politically,) to a few of the better instructed of their fellows. In the southern states, the greatest men who have been sent to Congress, or who have occupied still higher public stations, were for much the greater number, always residents of the country. Washington, Henry, Jefferson, Mason, Bland, Lee, Calhoun, Cheves, and hundreds of other able statesmen, were all slaveholders and country residents. For any such cases of representatives of distinguished talents that can be stated of the rural portions of the non-slaveholding states, in recent times, the South, from its much scantier numbers, can adduce fifty of equal or greater political knowledge and ability. In cities, the case is different. In all great cities there are operating inducements and also facilities for mental culture and improvement, much greater than anywhere in the country, or than we can have in the southern states, where there are very few large cities, and none to compare in these respects with Philadelphia, New York, and Boston. Therefore, in the great cities of the North and especially in the learned professions and scientific pursuits, there are more of highly educated and scientific professional men, than are to be found in the southern states. But even of these shining lights of learning and science, but few seem to be fitted for, or at least are entrusted with political offices and duties, by the votes of their fellow-citizens. Even the great cities of the North, with all their learned and able men to select from, more frequently elect representatives of the lower than the higher order of education and intellect. Still, almost the only distinguished statesmen who have appeared from the North have been the residents and representatives of cities. Of all the far greater number of northern members of Congress from the strictly rural districts, and even including in such the villages and small towns, scarcely any deserve to be distinguished for superior education, talent, or statesmanship. This is notoriously the fact. And though the workings of the caucus or convention system, (a political iniquity and curse borrowed from New York) and also of the evil changes of state constitutions, (in regard to suffrage and popular elections,) have served greatly to lower the grade of the representation of the South, yet, even now, any ten southern representatives, taken at random, will probably possess more political talent than one hundred from the rural districts of the old northern states, where the stultifying operation of the absence of slavery on an agricultural population has had the longest time to show the sure consequences. Under these different circumstances, it necessarily follows, that the greater superiority of intellectual power, more than the mere brute power of greater numbers, will govern in most questions of statesmanship and profound national policy. And such has been the case in this federal government for a long time, and such will be the case, and increasing in degree, so long as one portion of the confederated states enjoy, and the other is without the refining operation of slaveholding on the superior race.

A very marked statistical illustration and evidence of my position has come under my eye since writing the above. It is a passage in the noted abolition article in the number of the Edinburgh Review for October, 1856. This infamous piece of elaborate calumny on the South is doubly a fraud, in its source and authorship, besides being a tissue of inventions in its general statements and argument. It appeared in a British publication as if by a British author. And when this fraud was exposed, and it was known that the author was an American both by birth and residence, it was as falsely claimed that he was a southerner, because he was born of northern parents during their sojourn in the South, though he is a northerner in education, residence, and principles. This writer, to prove the supremacy of the "slave power," adduces these facts: that of the sixteen successive Presidents of the United States, eleven have been slaveholders; and that for five-sixths of the duration of the government, southerners by birth, or northern men elected by southern votes, have occupied the presidential office. And of the other higher federal offices, there have served from the southern states,

> "Seventeen out of twenty-eight Judges of the Supreme Court;
> Fourteen out of nineteen Attorneys-General;
> Sixty-one out of seventy-seven Presidents of the Senate;
> Twenty-one out of thirty-three Speakers of the House;
> Eighty out of one hundred and thirty-four Foreign Ministers."

Now, it is very true that high official position, even in a free or popular government, is not often obtained by the greatest fitness for the service. But, when so much the larger proportion of the highest offices of government have been, during a long time, filled from the South, there can be no stronger proof of the fact, that in the scanty population of the South, there was a very far greater amount of political talents of high order, than in the more populous northern states.

SECTION VIII.

Superior southern intellect contrasted by northern self-interest.

But though the superior southern intellect has generally guided the national councils in important matters, it has only been, and can only be, in questions of general policy, requiring great abilities to investigate, and in which the pecuniary interests of members, or those of their constituents, are not concerned. In all questions in which self-interest or sectional aggrandizement is supposed to be involved, the highest intellectual power must be governed by the power of numbers—and even by the most obtuse understandings, if of greater numbers who have, or believe they will have, their personal interests affected by the decision. In questions of foreign relations and policy, of war or peace, or in the selection of chief magistrates, and in supplying or choosing subjects for other high offices, the South has had the main direction of the federal government. But in all questions of money, or the means for acquiring gain, either for northern members or their constituents—as by protective tariffs, bounties, direct or indirect, to navigation and commercial interests, pensions, construction of public works, wasteful, or corrupt expenditures from the treasury, bribery, &c., &c., the northern members have always exerted and enforced their greater numerical power. Thus, southern intellect was generally free to direct all matters of policy for the public good alone. But in legislative contests between southern and northern interests, the South has had to submit to a fixed numerical majority, and to any degree of injustice and outrage which that irresistible majority was interested in inflicting. It is on this ground, and by this latter power, that the great question of slavery, and all minor questions incident thereto, have been judged and decided—because the great body of the northern people have been so deluded by their unprincipled leaders, as to be made to believe that their personal interests would be promoted by extinguishing slavery in the southern states. If they knew the truth of the reverse proposition, then the northern people would quickly become as indifferent to the existence of slavery, as those of the city of New York are to the continual fitting out, in that city, of vessels to carry on the African slave trade in all its present horrors. This enormity, and infamous breach of both moral and statute law, is a matter of notoriety, and frequent occurrence; but which seems neither to shock nor disturb the Greeleys and Tappans, and the other numerous abolitionists or fanatics —and indeed seems to be of no concern to but a few of that community.

SECTION IX.

Mistake of northerners as to their interest in southern slavery.

If, then, as is here charged, the people of the North are so much governed by self-interest, it may well be asked, why do they oppose the institution of negro slavery in the South, in the products of which they are so deeply concerned? It has already been said, that the great body of the northern people are deluded by their leaders. But that is not sufficient. It still is required to be explained why any of the great northern party, if knowing the truth, should still advocate a policy which, if carried out, would be destructive to northern interests? To this question, there are different answers for different portions of the great abolition party. As to the few honest fanatics, of course, they neither consult reason, nor regard consequences. Of the politicians, such as Seward and Hale, they merely aim to join in, and to get the full benefit of the popular clamor against slaveholders, to promote their own personal advancement and gain. Such men would oppose, as injurious to the North, the working of their own present measures, if these measures did not promise still more to serve their private ends and interests. Further—the political leaders of the party would not be willing to meet the consequences of their own complete success, if they expected complete success, and intended to go so far. But they, and all the people of the North, have been taught, by the long continued submission of the South, to believe that no repetition or increase of oppression by legislation will induce the South to secede, or to offer any other effectual resistance. Some renegade southerners have, in substance, re-asserted this opinion, and thereby established it in the confidence of the North. Our heretofore and our expected future submission are imputed to our dread of certain ruin, in the destruction of slavery, as a result of separation and war. Therefore, our enemies deem that their best policy, for the purpose of ensuring our submission and complete humiliation, will be continually to threaten and to encroach, but still to withhold entirely from striking the final and fatal blow. It is also a general belief at the North that the southern people, by their inferiority of numbers, and the supposed enfeebling operation of the institution of slavery, are too weak to resist, and too timid to incur the risk of the hostile and warlike action of the stronger North. Hence, impelled by these different considerations, the North supposes that it may vilify and wrong the South to any extent that interest or passion may invite, without danger to the North. And, therefore, the leaders and the most powerful of the party, (who, in opinion or principle, are not real abolitionists at all,) may push the movement as far as necessary to attain their personal ends, and crush the political power of the South, (which stands in the way of their supremacy,) and yet stop short of that extremity of injury to the property of the South which would react disastrously on northern interests.

SECTION X.

No danger to the South from war, unless for want of preparation.

Southern men have met all past violations of their rights by threats of resistance or separation, and then submitted, until no such threats are believed, or will be believed, unless unmistakable action shall have commenced. This well-founded incredulity is the secret of all the recent and present abolition movements and designs. And even if, by possibility, and when driven to desperation, the insulted and oppressed South should secede, it is confidently believed by the North that its own stronger military and marine force, and greater wealth, would serve, speedily and easily, to subdue the southern states. Never was there a greater mistake, or one which, if acted upon, will be corrected more effectually. It is only this mistaken idea of southern weakness, together with the absence of all military preparation in the South, that can possibly produce war, as the direct and immediate result of separation. If, when separating, we shall be, as now, unprepared for defence, we may surely expect to have war. But due preparation for war will as certainly ensure the maintenance of peace.

It is assumed by most persons that war between the separated portions would be a necessary and immediate consequence of separation. Even if no other ground for war existed, one certain and unavoidable cause is apprehended in the fact of the separate ownership, by the separated communities, of the upper and central waters of the Mississippi, and of its lower waters and their outlet to the sea. And one great consequence of war, (as generally believed in the North, and by very many also in the South,) it is supposed would be, that successful insurrection of the slaves would be invited and produced by war and invasion, and thus their general enfranchisement effected in the mode most disastrous and afflicting to the whites. Sure and sufficient reasons have already been offered to show, in reference to other and general grounds, that war would not be either a necessary or probable result of separation. Other reasons will now be offered to invalidate this particular cause of war, and afterwards will be considered the particular and worst possible consequence which has been anticipated.

War, in any mode, is an enormous evil, which it is far from my intention to deprecate. And war between separated portions of the same people, and previously long of the same community, would be the most deplorable and calamitous of all wars. A war between the southern and northern states, embittered by every growing cause of hostility and mutual hatred, and if waged to extremities with such balanced alternations of success and defeat as might be expected between foes so nearly equal, would be scarcely less destructive to the ultimate conqueror than to the conquered party. The prosperity, wealth, and as yet happy condition of both powers, would be engulphed in one abyss of complete industrial and political ruin. The possibility of these awful consequences should be well considered by all. But, as admonition and warning of the most solemn import, it is for the aggressive and offending party to heed, and by stopping and restraining its course, to avoid these consequences, and not for the aggrieved and heretofore always yielding party. The South, if still remaining in the Union, can do nothing except to submit entirely and unconditionally to every present and coming measure of aggression, which will be but another way to reach certain ruin. Rather than entire submission, we should prefer any hazards of war and its consequences. For all the calamities of war should be risked, and met, if necessary, by freemen who deserve to enjoy freedom, rather than to yield their rights without struggling, to the last ground of hope, in its defence. If, then, we are such men, the threat of war, with all the necessary and horrible consequences, will have no influence to induce the South to purchase peace by entire submission.

SECTION XI.

Joint occupancy of the Mississippi not a cause for war. Law and usage of nations in like cases.

The supposed inducement, or necessity, for war in the geographical character of the Mississippi river, is as groundless as any other of the anticipated causes for war, in the incidents of the separation of the present confederacy. Moreover, this result from this particular cause of divided possession of the course of a navigable river, is opposed by the laws of nations, and the usages and experience of the whole civilized world. As, however, the fallacy in question has met with very general admission, it may be necessary to examine and expose it at more length than its importance would otherwise require.

Before coming to the particular matter of the navigation of the Mississippi, when under separate proprietors, it will be necessary to look to general principles, as furnished by the laws of nations, and to the past history and present usages of Europe, in respect to the general subject.

When the Roman Empire was extended over the whole of the known civilized world, and much of the barbarian world, the Roman law, as to the rights of different countries and dominions, was the only law of nations. It not only was recognized and obeyed then, but its main and manifestly good principles were preserved and respected, if not always obeyed, in the understood commercial and political regulations between the many succeeding dominations of Europe in the middle ages. The ancient Roman law and the modern acknowledged laws of nations, both maintain the right of every nation, possessing one or both sides of the upper waters of a navigable river, to use the lower waters and outlet of the river, for navigation, and to transport its commodities to the ocean, or to foreign markets. The vessels, and their freights, of the upper country, so using the waters of a lower, while enjoying the benefit of a free passage, are, of course, bound to respect the municipal laws of the country through which the lower navigation passes, and to bear any reasonable charges (of inspection, &c.,) necessary to prevent violation of these laws. Except for these necessary restrictions and safeguards of defence, the passage would be entirely free to vessels and people of the upper country, so long as the two countries were at peace. War between the neighboring powers, only would alter these, as it must alter all the other relations of peace.

It is true, that with the general recognition of this law of nations, there had been many attempted violations of its principle; and some of them, for a time have been successful. But at the Congress of Vienna, in which all the great powers of Europe acted for themselves and for all the minor powers also, this great principle of the laws of nations was formally recognized and definitely explained, and made obligatory by treaty stipulations. The particular violations of this law of nations, whether before the congress of Vienna or subsequently, would be no reason for general disregard, or for deeming it null and of no obligation. There is scarcely any provision of the laws of nations and especially of the laws of war, which has not been violated. Yet, the laws so infringed continue to be respected and deemed obligatory, and are generally obeyed. These exceptional violations are more and more rare as the world advances in wisdom and in civilization, and governments and communities learn better to understand their own true interests. There will be little reason to expect future violations of this rule of free navigation by any civilized country; and, least of all, in regard to the common right of the Mississippi, which both the proprietary powers would be so deeply interested in preserving.

The law of nations in this respect, and the rights claimed under this law, are of less importance in this discussion than the actual practice and usages and the experience of Europe, and of the civilized world. All the great rivers of Europe, except a few in Russia, are, and mostly have been since the overrunning and dissolution of the Western Roman Empire, in precisely the situation which, for the Mississippi, is generally supposed would be an inevitable cause for war. If this doctrine is true, or worth anything, as to the Mississippi, then it would be as true of every other navigable river, of which different portions passed through different dominions. Now, precisely such divided property is held by different sovereign states in the upper and lower navigable waters of the Danube, the Rhine, the Po, the Elbe, (which passes through no less than seven separate dominions,) the Weser, the Vistula, the Niemen, the Dniester, the Scheldt, the Meuse, (or Maese,) the Moselle, the Douro, and the Oder in connection with its navigable tributary the Warta. Among the sovereign powers to which these divided properties of soil, and joint rights of navigation belong, are Russia, Turkey, Austria, Bavaria, Prussia, Hanover, Piedmont, Lombardy, (before being Austrian,) Belgium, Holland, Portugal, and Spain, besides other smaller powers. If then the mere condition of two or more powers, possessing severally the upper, or middle and lower waters of a navigable river, were sufficient and sure cause of discord and war, all these countries would have been involved in war for ten centuries, or throughout the whole time of their separate political existences. Yet, many as have been the wars, and trivial their causes in most cases, not one is remembered to have been produced by this cause alone. Some temporary difficulties have indeed occurred—and some wrongs have been inflicted, in this as in numerous other cases of supposed conflicting interests, by the strong on the weak. But though connected with these joint rights of navigation, these difficulties and injuries have in no case amounted, (at least in recent times,) to a permanent denial, by the power on the lower waters of a river, of the navigation and passage of the vessels of the upper country, to foreign markets. An exception to this position may appear to be presented in the noted case of the long continued closing of the lower Scheldt, where it passes through the territory of the former Dutch republic to the sea, against the vessels of the then Spanish and afterwards Austrian Netherlands, (now Belgium,) on the upper waters. And when Joseph II. of Austria, becoming the master of the before Spanish Netherlands, attempted to re-open this passage, the vessel sent by his order was fired upon and stopped by the Dutch fort on the Scheldt—and the Austrian power had to submit to be thus thwarted by a much weaker nation, whose right was sustained by the approval of Europe, and the faith of treaties. For this restriction, absurd as it was in a commercial aspect, was a solemn stipulation of the treaty of Westphalia, agreed upon for political considerations, by all the powers that concurred in making and maintaining that memorable treaty. This exceptional departure from the acknowledged general law of nations, was neither designed as a violation or abrogation of that law, nor a denial of its obligation by, in this case, suspending its operation in favor of Holland alone. As such, it would have had no force, and no power would have dared to attempt the course. But it was an agreement made by all the great powers of Europe, demanded by one part and acceded to by the other, as necessary to protect Holland, and in Holland, the protestant interest of Europe, by preventing the continual and easy ingress of the inimical and dreaded power possessing the upper waters. Besides, there were other important considerations. This was not the only passage, though the most convenient for the trade of the Spanish Netherlands. And further, the Dutch claimed that the navigation of the lower Scheldt was an artificial passage, opened formerly by their own industry. Thus, the Scheldt remained closed for some one hundred and fifty years, until the French republic, after becoming possessor of Belgium, forced and kept open the passage. But this act was deemed a cause of war, and was so counted in the war which soon followed between France and Great Britian and Holland. But even this long respected restriction has since been removed, and the lower Scheldt, as all other rivers in Europe held by different powers, under both the law of nations and the treaty of Vienna, is of free navigation.

For centuries past, as now, Denmark has collected the "sound dues," or a tax levied on all vessels entering the Baltic sea—and Hanover in like manner levies the "stade dues" on all vessels entering the Elbe. But wrongful and extortionate as these charges are, (and as such, our government has done well in resisting them,) they were originally demanded, and paid, not because of ownership on the lower waters, but on the ground of supporting light-houses and beacons, and paying other expenses for facilitating the safe passage of vessels.

Perhaps unjust and vexatious claims may have been set up to obstruct or to tax navigation and trade in many other cases, where might defined right. But it is believed that, at this time, nowhere is the possession of the outlet of a river claimed, *per se*, as ground of right, and exercised as such, to exclude or to obstruct the passage of the vessels of a power owning the higher waters of the river. In stating this proposition reference is had to civilized nations and to recent times, and not to such exclusive policy as was adopted by Spain for her former American dominions, (and of which both the policy and the dominion have long been at an end,) and which would still be enforced (if such cases existed) in China and Japan. Even the government of Brazil, narrow-minded as it is, and both jealous and fearful of the entrance of foreigners, and strong, too, compared to all the neighboring dominions, does not pretend to oppose the passage of the vessels and freights of Ecuador, Bolivia, and Peru from passing from their own upper and tributary waters down the Amazon to the ocean, or returning, through thousands of miles extent of Brazilian territory on both sides of the river. All that Brazil has claimed is, that the countries on the upper waters shall be the carriers of their own trade through Brazil, and that the route shall not be opened to all foreigners who may desire its use, to trade with the upper countries, or for any other purpose.

At this time Russia is striving to keep possession of the Isle of Serpents, near the mouth of the Danube, and the other great powers and parties to the late treaty of Paris are as anxious and determined to exclude Russia from the possession. Both parties understand that the possessor of this island, if able to hold it, will, in time of war, command the outlet and control the navigation of the Danube. This, indeed, would only be available during war. But it would then be a most formidable advantage to be possessed by a power so strong as Russia, and which has very little territory on or very near the Danube, and therefore would not suffer materially by closing its navigation. This case is entirely different from that supposed of the Mississippi; and yet, with all the danger to the dominions on the Danube, of the Emperor of Russia occupying merely the mouth of that river, even he would not dare to close or obstruct the navigation, except in war, and to his enemy in arms.

In applying the foregoing views to the particular case of the Mississippi, it is clear that, in the event of separate proprietorship, the lower occupant would have no right either to close or to obstruct the passage of the vessels and freights of the upper occupants. But there is still better assurance that there would be no such attempt, because, in time of peace, there can be no possible inducement for such a course, even if to be effected with certainty, and without danger of war, or reprisals, from the upper country.

The city of New Orleans derives nearly all its immense trade and wealth from the purchasing, or forwarding, and furnishing commodities in exchange for the products of the higher waters of the Mississippi, and (it may be and must be hereafter) mainly from the non-slaveholding region. Now, under any peaceful circumstances, what inducements can possibly operate on the city of New Orleans, or on the state of Louisiana, or on any of the states bordering on the lower river, to exclude or to discourage, by burdensome exactions, the free passage of the vessels and products which brings all the business and profits of the city, and is so greatly beneficial to the whole neighboring country? On the contrary, would not every reasonable facility be afforded for this trade, to prevent its being diverted, as much as possible, to New York and other northern markets? And if there were no such action, and no motive for the proprietor of the lower waters to obstruct the trade of the upper proprietor, what ground would the latter have for complaint? And on what possible ground could either the upper or the lower power go to war with the other, for the benefit of a navigation and trade already fully enjoyed, and which enjoyment could only be prevented, and certainly would be prevented, by the very act of war? The contrary assumptions, or the equivalent assertions of the danger of and even necessity for war, merely on this ground, are so preposterous that they would not deserve to be answered, but for their extended currency.

If a government or private association constructs a canal, or a new artificial passage for navigation, through the territory belonging to the proprietor of the work, the proprietor has undoubtedly the right to forbid the passage to all foreigners, however beneficial to them the new facility might be. But was there ever such a prohibition, or even discriminating and heavier tolls and charges on foreigners, adopted in such a case? Or has any one ever feared such impositions? No such obstructions can possibly exist, until self-interest shall cease to direct the conduct of man. The state of New York, and Canada, have both opened canals to unite the navigation of the great lakes with the Atlantic. Each of these artificial passages may be used to great benefit by the people of the other country. And, so far from obstructing these uses, New York desires and strives to be the carrier for Upper Canada, and the Canadian canals are as open to convey American vessels to the lower St. Lawrence. But lately a vessel laden with flour sailed from Chicago, and without unlading or trans-shipment of cargo, passed through the Welland canal, around the cataract of Niagara, and from Lake Ontario through the Rideau canal to the Utawas, and thence into the St. Lawrence, and across the Atlantic to Liverpool.

In former times there was much diplomatic argument and conflicting claims, between the British and American governments, as to the right of navigation of the St. Lawrence by American vessels. Probably each party claimed too much—the American government for the perfect right to navigate the river, and the British government the right to exclude American navigation. All these theoretical difficulties were finally settled by the recent "Reciprocity Treaty." But previous to that treaty being made, and in time of peace between the two countries, American vessels were (as now) as free to navigate the river as Canadian vessels. From Lake Ontario to near Montreal, the downward navigation is so difficult, because of the numerous rapids, that it is of little use to freight and sailing vessels, or to any that could venture to cross the Atlantic. To ascend the river it is necessary to use the Canadian canals.

SECTION XII.

The ownership by two nations of the upper and lower waters of a great river is a bond of peace between them.

It is very true, and is so obvious as scarcely to need being stated, that the occurrence of war between two nations occupying the upper and lower navigable waters of a river, or the different places of production and of sale thereon, would necessarily shut out either party from navigating the waters of the other, and would prevent the continuance of the previous friendly trade. But the prospect of this sure and heavy penalty for war, and of the certain and great losses which would thence accrue to both nations, would serve as the strongest possible reason and inducement for the preservation of peace. Therefore, if the Mississippi was held in separate occupancy of its upper and lower waters, instead of this great river being then a continual provocation to war, it would be the strongest possible bond of peace between the respective proprietary powers. For neither power could break the peace, without immediately and entirely cutting off the trade which had been the chief source of its prosperity and wealth.

In cases of war between two powers, thus holding the upper and lower portions of a navigable river, though both countries would suffer greatly, it would not be equally. Undoubtedly, for military or naval operations, the holder of the lower waters, or of their outlet to the ocean, would have a great advantage over the upper proprietor. Hence, it is fortunate for the South, and for the better preservation of peace, that in every case of such prospective divided proprietorship of navigable rivers or straits, the weaker southern states will hold the lower, and the northern, which is the stronger, and also the aggressive power, will possess the upper navigable waters. The most noted and important case is the Mississippi river. But, though much the strongest, it is not the only such bond of peace. There are other cases, presented in the Ohio river, and in the Delaware, and still more the Chesapeake bay. These facts offer most important subjects for consideration, for the states and cities most interested in these future relations, which need not be pursued here.

Of course, all independent states are liable, at some times, to have causes of war with neighboring powers, or to be involved in war, whether with or without good cause. From this universal liability, the separated and independent northern and southern confederacies would not be exempt. Either, indeed, might make war on the other, at any time, if choosing the hazards of war, in preference to the benefits of peace. So the United States might have gone to war, (and as then deemed, for just causes,) in a dozen cases, with England, France, or other powers, where no war occurred, and where all differences were subsequently settled by peaceful negotiation. If the northern and southern states were two separate and independent powers, each would gain more by cultivating and preserving peace with the other, and each would lose and suffer more by being at war, without any possibility of gain, than would be in regard to any other two nations in the world. Under such circumstances may we not safely anticipate that peace would be maintained?

SECTION XIII.

The great danger of the South is from northern emissaries and agents of abolition.

Among the evil consequences to the South of a separation from the North, it is supposed by most persons that the abolition action of the North would be thereby stimulated and increased, and the effects would render the preservation of our slaves and the existence of slavery much more precarious than while the relation of union, under one government, continues. There is no ground to expect an increase of this evil action, or of its effects, whether in the state of war or of peace, and good reasons for the reverse.

The main cause of the ability of the abolitionists to operate on our slaves, to infuse discontent, and to seduce them to abscond, or to rebel, is to be found in the existing relation which the hostile incendiary agents from the North bear to us, in being also our fellow-citizens. The worst enemies of the South, even the regular and the most mischievous agents of organized associations for stealing slaves, and exciting insurrection and massacre, have now every facility to enter the country, and to sojourn wherever they can best operate. Any pretext of business is enough to serve to account for their presence; and there is no neighborhood in the southern states into which Yankees have not penetrated, and could freely operate as abolition agents. Under the federal constitution, they are citizens of any southern state in which they temporarily reside, and their conduct and proceedings cannot be questioned, so long as there is cautious concealment from white witnesses of any felonious or incendiary acts. Not only have these agents, as our fellow-citizens, the protection of the constitution of the United States, but we, the people of Virginia, and of all the southern states, afford to these most dangerous of incendiaries the far greater protection of our own laws, by forbidding the evidence of negroes to be heard against any white person. In these cases of incendiary attempts to seduce slaves, or to plot with them to excite insurrection and massacre, it is next to impossible that any other than negroes should have heard their communications, and be able to inform of their proceedings. Consequently, not one case in the hundred, of which negroes could and often would readily testify, is detected and punished. A still stronger reason for changing this policy is, that, with the existing impunity, the abolition agent knows that he may safely attempt to delude or seduce any negro, as no statement of the negro can convict him. Even if suspected, at the worst he has only to shift his residence to some other place where he is not known, and then to operate as before. If the northern agent was subject by our laws to be tried and condemned for this offence on the evidence of negroes, (as he would be at home for any other felony,) he would not venture to incur the great risk of communication. Thus, and by other measures of caution, nearly all such action by foreigners would be prevented.

Thus protected by the federal constitution, and our own mistaken legal policy in regard to evidence, it is no wonder that abolition agents are numerous and efficient in the slave-holding states. They are numerous in the southern cities, especially, where they may be safe from suspicion in their various ostensible or real employments, of traders, mechanics and laborers, or sailors. In every county they have probably entered, and many have remained to operate as pedlars and sellers of northern commodities and patent-rights, solicitors for subscriptions to northern publications, beggars for societies of various moral and religious pretensions, teachers, both male and female, and even ministers (so esteemed) of the gospel of love and peace. Until within the last few years, and after numerous discoveries of such incendiary action and many convictions, (among them two of northern preachers, and two at different times of the same northern lady,) these agents had the most unrestrained access to all our country habitations, and to our slaves.

There had previously been no suspicion entertained of such a system of villainy. The primitive and general hospitality of our country served to admit every apparently decent stranger to our houses, as a welcome guest. And thus, as inmates, they had every facility afforded them for deceiving our slaves, and implanting discontent, as well as for aiding their escape, when any fit subjects were found. With such facilities for agents, and with the instigation, and aid of money, of the northern organized associations, and with the general spirit of the northern people and their state governments to encourage such acts, and to screen the criminals, it is not surprising that these offences against the South have been every year increasing. The counties of Virginia bordering on Pennsylvania, Ohio, and even on the Potomac above Washington, have lost so many slaves, and their possession is so hazardous, that but few remain, and property in slaves is there of such uncertain tenure, as to be of but little value. The city of Norfolk, and its close vicinity, in one year, (preceding the late state law affording partial protection,) lost about one hundred slaves, of the most valuable description, all of which were doubtless forwarded by northern agents, and taken off in northern vessels. In and near Richmond, the losses have not been so numerous, but still very many. There, several agents have been convicted and punished.

But these pecuniary losses in slave property, and even the delusions and discontent produced in many more slaves than the actual fugitives, are as nothing compared to the other evils which abolition agents have the like facilities for encouraging and abetting, and which they are equally ready and zealous to bring about, in insurrections of the slaves, with all the horrible results of the attempts, however unsuccessful as they all must be, in reaching their great object, or indeed any considerable effect in general and political affairs. The continual efforts to excite mutiny and insurrection, even if failing to produce any open or violent act, cause discontent and unhappiness, and a spirit of insubordination in the slaves, and much injury to their owners and to the commonwealth. If actual rebellion, or plotting to rebel, is attempted, it must always end in utter failure. And the worst and most deplorable consequences of such plots, or actual outbreaks, have been, and will be, (and the only spilling of blood, except in the single and peculiar case of the Southampton insurrection,) in the heavy punishments which have fallen upon the deluded victims of the abolitionists; while the far more criminal, and immediate instigators, have generally escaped—and their employers have remained safe in their northern homes, to continue pharisaically to thank God that they are free from the sin of slaveholding.

Even since the writing of these pieces was begun, there have been more cases of discovery of these iniquitous operations, and of more wide-spread extent, than has ever been known before—but not more than might have been expected from the ample means and facilities at command. Plots for simultaneous out-breaks or insurections (which rumor said were to occur at Christmas) have been discovered at several remote points in Virginia, in Kentucky, Tennessee, and other southern states. All, doubtless, were instigated by abolition agents, and induced by their delusive representations; and some of these instigators luckily have been secured, though others have escaped. Probably all these alleged plottings and their incidents have been much exaggerated, as usual, by false reports, and some of them may have had no existence. But there is enough certainly true to produce much uneasiness and extended panic among many of the whites, and to cause much suffering, whether deserved or undeserved, by the implicated negroes. These are dreadful and most deplorable results of these abolition efforts, and the only results they can ever have, save one, which will be also the only good result. This is, that these numerous and far extended designs will be universally and truly inferred to have been instigated and forwarded by concerted abolition action, and to have been the result of, and connected with the recent sectional effort to elect an abolition president.* And the greater the immediate effects may be of this most recent incendiary instigation, the more will be the beneficial ultimate result, of inducing the southern states to ward off, by the only effectual mode, all such future and effective operations of hostile northern abolitionists.

SECTION XIV.

Separation would lessen the mischievous operations of abolition agents.

The power of the abolition agents for mischief, and their security from detection and punishment, and all the evil consequences of their incendiary actions, are owing mainly to their privilege of citizens in the South. If the southern

* Before the election by the people had taken place it was known that slaves had been informed of the northern motives of action, and had received the impression that the election of Fremont would cause the extinction of slavery. It

and northern states made two separate political communities, these agents would be deprived of all their present free access to our slaves, and of the facilities for their operations. Neither the agents nor their employers could find any substitutes for these facilities, in their new relation to us, of foreigners in peace, or enemies in war. It is true, that then, a fugitive slave who may pass the line of division will be safe from pursuit. But it is nearly so now—and the legal remedies, or means for recovering fugitive slaves within the northern states, are null in fact, even when not expressly made so by state law, as is the case in Massachusetts. A mode of redress which cannot be obtained once in a hundred cases of wrong, and which, even when most effective, costs more than the value of the object sought, is clearly worthless. Therefore, the South would lose no more by the immediate and entire repeal of the present delusive "fugitive slave" law of Congress, and by the cessation of all future attempts to recover fugitive slaves from the North.

As a certain result of an independent dominion and government, the South would guard against such future action of emissaries by a strict examination of northern immigrants, and a proper investigation of the objects and proceedings of those newly arrived and unknown. If incendiaries would be safe on the northern side of the line of division, on the southern they could be far more easily watched, detected, and by more stringent laws, speedily hung, as soon as found guilty. If the same disposition to interfere and agitate remained, (which would not be,) there would be much less

---

is said that in the recent (designed) insurrection in Tennessee the poor wretches were deceived and encouraged by the belief, that they had only to fight their way to the north side of the Cumberland river, where Col. Fremont and his army would receive and protect them.

opportunity left for it to be exercised. The new and severe policy of the South, in regard to incendiary action, would at once restrain the efforts of the pious and gentle incendiaries, and greatly restrain the mercenary and boldest. If all such emissaries and agents were shut out from intercourse with our slaves, and deprived of their present facilities for deluding them, it would be very rare for any slave, without influence from abroad, to attempt, or desire, to escape permanently from his home and his condition of slavery. And the spirit of discontent which northern abolitionists have produced by false representations, and the consequent spirit of insubordination—and the new and more stringent measures of discipline for repression of insubordination thus rendered necessary—all being the direct results of abolition action—are the only serious disadvantages, and sources of suffering, to the slaves, and the only thing to prevent their being the most comfortable, contented, and cheerful laboring class in the world.

The means for holding slave property, safely, would be so much increased by separation, and especially near the border lines, that the slave population of the border land would soon increase and extend, where it has been long decreasing, and, at this time, can scarcely exist, because of the inability of the proprietors to shut out northern incendiaries.

So much for the supposed and expected relations of peace. But the great power of abolition action, and its greater, if not complete success, it is usually inferred, will be exhibited in the condition of war between the separated North and South. This branch of the subject will be next considered.

SECTION XV.

Results of war considered—and especially as affecting slaves of the South.

If the northern and southern confederacies were at war, and it were possible that the former could succeed in completely subjugating the latter, then, indeed, the conquered people would be at the mercy of the conquerors, who might abolish negro slavery, or do any thing else. But it is unnecessary to argue on the assumption of such impossible premises. In the very improbable event of any war occurring, the invasion of the southern territory, if attempted, would not likely be successful—or allow more than transient occupation of a small extent of country. If admitting the North to be the stronger power on its own territory, and still more on the water, all its power for invasion and offensive warfare, would be far less than that of the South for repelling and punishing such aggressions on southern ground. Under such circumstances, and with any thing like equal action, and balanced successes, the North would have much less chance for producing successful insurrection and enfranchisement of the slaves, than had the more powerful enemy in both our wars with Great Britain. In the war of the revolution, at different times, the British forces were the masters over lower Virginia, and even extended their incursions to the middle country. They remained in possession of the neighborhood of their encampments for months together. In the farther South, the hostile occupation by the British forces was much more extensive, and continued for years. Encouragement was held out to the slaves, in offers of freedom and protection, to desert their masters and to rebel against and oppose them in arms. In the very commencement of the war in Virginia, the royal governor, Lord Dunmore—while still possessing all respect of the vulgar, and the authority of the representative of the King, and esteemed as a King, and the only known supreme power in the minds of the ignorant slaves—in command of a regular military and naval force, raised together the royal standard, and the banner of negro insurrection—calling upon the slaves to side with the King, and to receive protection and freedom as the reward of their loyalty. Even this invitation, proceeding from the only known previous, and highest legal authority, and backed by the military power and the government of Britain, was a signal failure. Throughout the war of the revolution, and in all the South, there was no such occurrence as even a partial insurrection of slaves, or of the negro deserters to the enemy being embodied for military service. There was no approach to or the least apprehension of any danger of the abolition of slavery. That there were numerous losses sustained in the desertion or the stealing of slaves, is indeed true; as well as that our brave and patriotic fathers incurred numerous other and much greater losses, and risked the loss of everything, in their struggle for freedom and independence.

In the war of 1812, the many facilities for slaves to desert, or mutiny, and the attempts of the enemy to seduce them, were still less successful. At that time many of the old negroes remembered, and all the younger had learned from the older, the inducements offered for the desertion and rebellion of slaves in the revolutionary war, and the treatment and various sufferings of many of the deceived victims; of whom many escaped from the British camps or ships, and returned to the masters they had been induced to desert. Probably it was owing to these recollections and traditions, that very few of the slaves of Virginia deserted or left their homes voluntarily, to go to the enemy during the last war, though British ships occupied permanently, portions of our waters during nearly all the time. Finally, finding that invitation and seduction had no effect, Admiral Cockburn and other officers of the British naval force resorted to compulsion. Then, on the borders of the Rappahannock, and other most accessible places, many slaves were taken by force from the farms, in marauding incursions of the enemy, and driven at the point of the bayonet to the boats of the British shipping. Thence, they were afterwards sent to Trinidad and elsewhere, and, as was reported, settled as slaves, or in bondage much worse than slavery in Virginia, on sugar plantations of the captors, or others. That the abduction of these slaves was effected by force, admits of no doubt. For, on that admitted ground, in the subsequent treaty of peace, the British government agreed to pay for these slaves, and the owners were so paid their full estimated value.

So much for the chances of voluntary desertion of our slaves to an enemy in arms, and of supposed superior force, and desiring and inviting such desertion. But even if counting this danger as nothing, it may still be feared that without the voluntary desertion of individual slaves, there might be produced, by the encouragement of a neighboring abolitionist enemy in arms, a general spirit of insubordination, mutinous conduct, and results leading to revolt. The writer is old enough to have had some personal experience of the like causes, and of the actual results from the beginning of, and through the war of 1812; and what he saw and heard then, bearing on this argument, may be new and of interest, and of weight as evidence, to readers of the present day and generation.

In the beginning of 1813 British ships of war first occupied Hampton roads, and began the blockade of Chesapeake bay and of the rivers of the whole Atlantic coast south of New England, which blockade was strictly maintained to the end of the war in 1815. During all this time, all the rivers emptying into the Chesapeake, and also other accessible shores of the great bay were frequently visited by portions of the British marine force, and the bordering lands were subjected to the incursions and depredations of the enemy. Numerous and great depredations were committed in Virginia, including the forcible abduction of slaves mentioned above. There was no defensive force except hasty levies of the residents, acting as militia, and nearest to the places invaded, or deemed in most danger of attack. And all the men of the tide-water counties, then, (before the introduction of steam vessels, and of railroads, and of the electric telegraph,) would have been a very insufficient defence against an enemy having possession of and command on the water, and therefore able to change the points of attack, or feints of attack, in a few hours, to other points far removed from the previously assembled force, summoned for hasty defence, and this for many hundreds of miles length of the exposed river and bay shores. Along all these shores were the richest farms and the most dense slave population in Virginia; and wherever the British landed they were complete masters for the time, and usually the only white occupants of the place. Therefore, they had every opportunity and means to operate on the slaves, by deception and seduction. Yet, only by force did they carry off any slaves—and in no manner or place did they induce any act or produce any indication of insubordination, then or thereafter.

In the tide-water county of the writer's then residence, the entire body of the militia was called out, in mass, on several different occasions of alarm, because of movements and expected incursions of part of the enemy's force. Each of these general and hasty unexpected calls for immediate service lasted for but a few days, except once, in 1814, when the service was continued for some weeks. During that time, the British vessels were much higher than usual in the river, and every man of military age in the county, and the overseers as well as the proprietors of the slaves, were encamped at one point, where the enemy was expected. Further, the most important operation and heaviest labor of our region, the wheat and oat harvest, was commenced and completed during this time when almost every farmer was from home, and unable to give the slightest attention to his farm, or to procure any fit substitute for the proprietor. Yet, not a single case of insubordination among the slaves was heard of, nor had there been any apprehension thereof. Our wives and children, and all our moveables, were left at home, surrounded by and all in the power of the slaves, and all in perfect security. In the actual absence of all superintendence on the farms, no doubt the harvest and other labors were performed more slowly and carelessly, than would have been under different and ordinary circumstances. But I did not find in my own case, nor hear from others, of any important and serious loss on this score. Suppose that the entire male population, of military age, in a county of the non-slaveholding states, had been thus and so long removed from their farms and employments—or even all except the hireling farm laborers—would not the losses and evils have been very far greater?

The like general circumstances as here stated, to greater or less extent, attended every tide-water county in Virginia and Maryland, and also every accessible river in the more southern Atlantic states. And every resident now living who then had reached the military age, can confirm the general facts, and especially what is here asserted of the obedience and good conduct of the slaves and their almost universal resistance to all attempts to delude them by offers of freedom and promises of gain and benefit. An invading force from the northern states, whether coming by land or by water, will not be likely to have as free communications with slaves, or as great facilities to remove them, whether by fraud or by force, as had the British liberators, and will scarcely meet with more success.

Judging of the whole southern Atlantic states in these respects by the known experience of eastern Virginia, it seems probable that all the slaves induced to desert or to go off voluntarily, in all these states and throughout all the war, did not amount to as many as in late years our northern fellow-citizens have seduced and stolen within a single month.

SECTION XVI.

Comparative capacities of the North and South for carrying on war.

In the foregoing pages it has been maintained that war would not be either a necessary or a probable result of separation; and also, in the improbable or remote event of war, for any cause, that the injury to be thereby produced to the South, in regard to its slave interests, would be less than will be suffered under the present union. But there is still another question to consider. This is, if war, from any cause, should occur hereafter between the severed North and South, what will be the comparative abilities of these parties to carry on the war—it being supposed (as is anticipated by all who predict its certain occurrence,) that the North would be the aggressive and offensive, and the South the defensive party.

Our northern fellow-citizens are so accustomed to scoff at the alleged weakness of the southern states, in military matters, and to ascribe the supposed weakness to the institution of slavery, that the belief is well established among themselves. Should an occasion require, this opinion will be found to be as much mistaken, as any other of the false positions of abolition fanatacism. With the Greeks and Romans, and all other of the most military of ancient nations, and all of them slaveholding nations, slavery did not impair, but on the contrary, increased their military force. Yet their slaves were of the same white race with their owners; and as men, in mind and education, often equal, or, in many individual cases, superior, to their masters. Yet history has nowhere shown that the holding of slaves was deemed a cause of national weakness in war. Among hundreds of slaveholding nations, and in the course of thousands of years, there have been some insurrections of slaves, and some few servile wars, of sufficient importance to be recorded in history. Of all these, the only one which was not quelled by their masters, was the servile war of St. Domingo; and that was both instigated and reinforced by the abolition fanaticism of the Jacobin government of revolutionary France, and the then political madness of the ruling class of that country. Such instigation and encouragement, and, indirectly, the promise of the future aid of armed support, are offered to our slaves by our "northern brethren." But they have a very different people to deal with; and they will equal the emancipators of St. Domingo only in intention and effort.

Where, in all past time, there has been one mutiny, riot, outbreak, or rebellion of domestic slaves, there have been a hundred of as great importance, of the so-called free subjects of the governments of the world. But for the deluding precepts, and stimulation, from our "northern brethren," there would be less of discontent among our slaves, and less of disposition as well as less inducement to rebel, than there is among the laboring class of England, almost the only free and certainly the best government of all Europe —or than there soon will be among the most needy and vicious population of the free northern states of this Union. And there will be much less probability, after a separation, of any important insurrection of our slaves, with even temporary and short-lived success, than there will be of the great cities of Boston, New York and Philadephia, and others, being sacked and burnt, and their wealthiest inhabitants massacred, by their own destitute, vicious, and desperate population. And such horrible atrocities in the northern cities will not be very improbable events, after the severance of the present union, and the cessation of the protection of the present general government, and of the conservative influence (exerted through the federal union) of the slaveholding states—conservative in feeling and action, because of the existence of slavery.*

* Suppose that there existed in the southern states organized, numerous and rich associations, supported and encouraged by public opinion in every southern

The scoffs and contemptuous opinion of the North, in reference to our military weakness, should come in aid of other and stronger considerations to admonish us to be well prepared for war. The only possible danger of the occurrence of any warlike aggression, or invasion, from the North, will be the effect of belief in the weakness or timidity of the southern states. Offer to the abolition states a sure and easy victory, or allow them confidently to expect it, and they will, in that case, and that only, attempt armed coercion and conquest. Therefore, to preserve peace most effectually and certainly, we should be well prepared to meet any contingency of war.

In comparing and balancing the respective advantages (and especially in new countries) of slave and hireling labor, while claiming superiority for the former in most things, it is readily conceded that there are some superior advantages, as usually understood, in the latter. Under the

---

state, whose avowed object and whose continual action and effort through secret emissaries, were to persuade the destitute and suffering people of the North that they had equal rights to the riches and luxuries of their cities and of the world—that they were defrauded of their just rights and starved and made wretched by the actual possessors of wealth, and that they ought, and easily and safely and honestly could, take their full shares of the wealth of others, and quietly and peaceably, if the possessors did not resist this new and just distribution; and that in case of resistance to this act of justice, by the possessors of property, all the probable consequences of massacre, conflagration and irregular appropriation of the property in dispute, would be the fault of the previous property-holders, and not of their former destitute victims, who could in no other way obtain their rights. In the case supposed of such infernal teachings, and of measures so sustained and so propagated and urged, what would the people of the North think, and how long would they submit to such action of their southern "brethren?" Yet, if this atrocious conduct was that of every southern state, and even in advance of all the actual enmity, or of the actual injuries inflicted by the North, it would not be worse in intention or consummation than the abolition action of the North, and of the stronger portion of every northern state, towards the South, in relation to our institution of slavery, and the vital interests founded thereupon.

system of hireling or free labor, there will be a denser population, more labor on the average of each individual hireling or laborer, and more individuals, as capitalists or employers of labor, closely engaged in and confined to their daily business, than in slaveholding countries. Consequently, in the absence of domestic slavery, there will be more production from each individual, both poor and rich, more of general wealth will be produced and accumulated, and more population kept together in a certain space of territory. The system of slave labor requires more space for population—more of comfort and ease for the laborers—than want and suffering permit to the destitute laborers of free society—and it obtains less labor from the slave than the free laborer of countries densely populated must perform to obtain bread. If there are disadvantages to the whole political community, as giving less labor, production and accumulation of wealth, and less population to a slaveholding country, there are some compensating benefits also in each individual member of the community, bond and free, enjoying more space, more comfort and repose, and security against extreme privation; and the proprietary class have more leisure, and use it more for social and intellectual improvement or enjoyment, than can be approached in the class of property-holders where slavery does not exist. But these very defects (as they are estimated by others) of our system of slavery, besides other much greater benefits, provide a numerous class of the best possible material for military service, without drawing much from the productive labor and resources of the country. In every southern county in which slaves make one-third or more of the population, one hundred men on an average could be raised on any sudden and urgent occasion, ready to march at a day's notice, and able to continue in military service a month, if needed, without any important loss to the persons so engaged, or to the productive values of the country at large. And if the danger of the country required, or the want of government supplies, at first, half of all such hasty levies would be volunteers, mounted on their own horses, carrying their own private arms, and with enough of their own provision, or money to buy it, to serve for a week, without any aid of the government. In the busy, frugal, and hard-working North, there is no such class of worthy (and trust-worthy) citizens, able to leave their daily labors and employments, or who could do so without great loss, and suffering to families. If, in case of need, a sudden call was made by the North for 50,000 men only, they could not be supplied, for the shortest time, without stopping the daily and necessary labor of nearly as many. It would be more destructive to the prosperity of any portion of the northern states to furnish one-fourth of its men of military age, for a short service, than it would be for like portion of the South to furnish all for equal time. An army of volunteers from the North to invade the South, will be as likely to be recruited from the rich merchants and capitatists of New York, as from the industrious and worthy of the class of artizans and laborers. The number of young volunteer soldiers, of the best material, who could be readily and quickly raised to defend southern soil, or to inflict vengeance in reprisals, would be limited only by the demand of the country, and the means to arm and feed those who could not arm and feed themselves. And if the extremity of circumstances shall ever require offensive reprisals, and invasion of the enemy's country, the South will be able to obtain ten volunteers for such service, where one would leave the North for such distant warfare.

There is, however, one superior military advantage, or nursery for soldiers, which the northern states have, in the many thousands of the vagrant, destitute, and vicious population, and worst nuisances of their great cities. For materials for a regular or standing army, and for a long, protracted war, requiring regular forces, these men, good for nothing else, and dangerous at home, would offer a valuable supply. But such soldiers, would be destitute of every higher quality than mere physical force and obedience (if under the strictest discipline) to despotic military rule. For any moral or patriotic principle of conduct, or as volunteers, the free negroes of the South would be as respectable; and with the like necessary military rule and discipline, perhaps, would be equal in military array and conduct to the northern "loafer" and convict soldiers.

SECTION XVII.

Naval warfare, and effects.

But, it may be said that there would be no need of land forces for invasion, or of military operations on land, because the North, possessing nearly all the mercantile marine, and, perhaps, retaining all the navy of the present Union, could blockade every southern river and sea-port; and thus, safely and easily produce great privation and loss throughout the southern states, and thus compel their submission.

The first part of this proposition we may safely (for the argument) admit to be probable, or even certain—and yet the conclusion will be none the less impossible. They who suppose that the people of the South would succumb to, or even be seriously affected by, the mere privation of superfluities and luxuries, have no knowledge or experience in this respect, of our people, or of the nature of man.

After providing for the necessities and ordinary comforts of our households in food, clothing, fuel, and lodging, nearly all the remainder of the income of the community is used for expenditures for superfluous objects of luxury and display, to gratify the mind, and not required by the body, and designed for the eyes and admiration of other people, much more than for any comfort or benefit to the possessors or to their families. To such useless and ostentatious expenses the southern people are as much addicted as any others. But there are very few individuals who would not cheerfully and readily yield and forego his share of this expenditure and indulgence for patriotic objects; and would even find therein more of pleasurable excitement. I remember well the operation and effects of this state of things, and of the feelings thereby excited during the war of 1812. No blockade of our coast by northern ships, however close and long-continued, could now cause half the privation and loss then suffered from the British blockade. Previous to the declaration of war, the previous restrictive measures of embargo, non-importation and non-intercourse with Europe, had exhausted, without renewal, nearly all the supplies of manufactured articles, and all foreign commodities. Without manufacturing establishments, and without any facilities for transportation, during the British blockade, our southern country became almost destitute of everything but bread and meat, and a very scant supply of coarse home-spun fabrics. It was then accounted most honorable and patriotic to dispense with every luxury; and the wealthy then contended with each other as to who should be most frugal, plain, and extreme in using only simple and cheap commodities and accommodations, as much as they would have contended at other times in the race of extravagant and ostentatious expenditure. As much real comfort was found, and more gratification of public spirit, and also of vanity and self-love, in wearing the coarsest and homeliest of home-spun garments, than there had been when the family used silks and the finest of cloths. There was positive and great enjoyment in pursuing this new course of hard living, in such a cause—as are the severe labors and great hardships of the hunter welcome to him, with the excitement and chances of the chase. And such will be again the state of things, in the event of its being required by a war with invasion or blockade by the enemy.

But there would be no more possibility of an effectual blockade by the North, than of a successful invasion by land forces. All the naval force, and all the revenue of the northern states, could not maintain a close and effectual blockade of all the southern ports—and foreign powers would not respect, or submit to be shut out by a mere pretence of blockade. If foreign vessels entered southern ports freely, and brought in their commodities and bought ours, we, even though excluded for a time from the ocean, would, in a pecuniary point of view, be nearly as well off as now, when northern vessels are our sole carriers. And if war should occur, the party owning few vessels, and carrying no ocean trade, could suffer nothing by depredations on the ocean; while the numerous ships and smaller vessels of the North, would furnish abundant and rich prey to privateers, which might be fitted out and commissioned by the southern confederacy, even if destitute of all other marine force or wealth. In a war of marine plunder, and destruction of merchant vessels, the country owning the fewest ships becomes the strongest for this purpose, and the one richest on the waters is exposed to loss more than in proportion to its greater amount of mercantile shipping.

SECTION XVIII.

Consequences of separation to the North.

When assuming an independent political existence, and afterwards, every consideration of self-interest will cause the southern confederacy to desire to have peace, amity, and also free trade with the northern states, if true and real amity can subsist. And the best possible relation also for the North, would be amity, (and as a necessary condition, the refraining from all the now existing causes of exasperation,) and trade as nearly free as may be, with the South. But, whether with a moderate tariff of duties, for revenue only, or with no duties, northern vessels and imports, in the southern confederacy, would at best stand only on equal footing with those of all other foreign countries. The northern states and their commerce and manufactures and shipping would be deprived of all their former advantages, by which northern interests gained monopoly prices and profits, and which were paid by the South. No more protecting duties for northern manufactures—no more fishing bounties, (in which $10,000,000 have been already paid, mostly from southern taxation, and received exclusively by the northern navigation interests,)—no more bounties to Collins' or other lines of northern steamers, also mainly paid by southern taxes, and by which policy of the federal government, the last remnant of direct trade with Europe has been taken away from the southern states. This new commercial condition of the North, though equal to that of all other nations, would be bad enough compared to the former and present system, by which so much of unjust and iniquitous gain has been made at the expense, and to the great detriment of the southern states. But by resort to war, whether of arms or of tariffs, even the benefit of free, or of equally burdened trade, would be lost to the North, if not also, all commercial intercourse with the South.

The separation of the northern and southern states by secession of the latter, would, by the very act of dismemberment, put an end to the present confederation and its government. But, probably, the northern remnant will claim to be still the "United States," and to have authority to administer the government for all as well as to hold to the national domain and all other public property. In this case, the South has the full means for redress, in commercial restrictions, as has been already stated. But suppose that these measures were ineffectual, for redress, for any cause whatever, and that the South had to suffer the spoliation, without compensation. There would still be, and mainly because of this act of spoliation, consequences for the old northern states, (the leaders and main actors in the abolition movement,) much worse than would be their yielding the unjustly held spoils, by agreeing to a just and fair division of the national property. The new north-western and Pacific states and territories, within which would lie all the public lands to be embraced in the great northern section, would never agree to share the domain in proportion to population with the old northern states. Each new state, and the squatters on each new territory, would claim, and would hold all the vacant land within their respective boundaries. Then the old north-eastern states will have robbed the South, only that the north-western and Pacific states and territories may secure all the most valuable spoil.

SECTION XIX.

Future end of anti-slavery fanaticism at the North.

This will not be the only evil of vast importance to the old northern states. When the separation of the present Union has been consummated, there will no longer remain to northern men any political object or gain for which to agitate the slavery or abolition questions. The Sewards, and Hales, and Wilsons, no longer kept down by Southern intellect and patriotism, would be the established leaders and rulers of the northern confederacy, and they could gain nothing more by denouncing slavery or contending against slaveholders. It would then be seen that the abolition question had been agitated only for political effect and benefit to the prime agitators; and when such agitation could no longer serve their interest, the alleged sin and horrors of slavery in the southern confederacy would be as little noticed by abolitionists, as has been always the case in regard to Cuba and Brazil. Certainly the condition of the slaves in those countries was far more wretched, and more strongly calling for the sympathy of philanthropists, than in these southern states. Moreover, the illegal African slave-trade, of the most cruel and murderous character, (and with many of the slave vessels fitted out in northern cities and by northern capital,) continued to add to the number of slaves, and by such additions to increase the sufferings of all. These worst evils and sufferings incident to the worst condition of African slavery and the forbidden slave-trade, certainly were, and are, as much worthy of the attention of moral reformers and philanthropic abolitionists as the need for more humane treatment and comfortable condition of slaves in these southern states. Yet scarcely have the northern abolitionists noticed the horrors of Cuban or Brazilian slavery, while all their denunciations and hostility have been reserved for the milder slavery in the southern states. This, if alone, ought to have shown, in advance, how false and hypocritical has been the pretence of this abolition party being influenced by considerations of humanity or benevolence—by morality or religion. Separation of political connection will be the certain end of all actual and injurious abolition agitation. The newspapers of the North, after separation, and public speakers, both lay and clerical, may continue to denounce the iniquity of slavery and the atrocious acts of slaveholders. So are we now denounced and abused in Canadian papers and speeches, and in British newspapers and reviews. But, as in these latter cases there has never been sufficient inducement for attempting more active or practical interference with our rights and property, so neither will there be with the people of the northern states, when no political gain can be made, or sought, by aid of such interference. Then the abolition agitation by politicians will die for want of object and aliment—and the deluded people of the North will recover their long lost sanity on this subject.

SECTION XX.

Other divisions of the northern and western states, to follow their separation from the southern states.

When this change shall have occurred, and the now prevailing delusion is at an end, the people of the new north-western states, who are especially connected with the South in bonds of trade by the Mississippi, and who have no such ties with New England, will see their error in following the fanatical course of the latter, to the end of separation from the southern states, their natural allies and best customers. It will be found by them a source of great inconvenience and loss to have no trade with the southern states, or a taxed trade in time of peace, though the passage of the Mississippi to the ocean or to foreign ports would be still open to their vessels and freights. And if the North should force war on the South, then, of course, the navigation of the lower Mississippi will be no longer open to the use of any portion of the hostile country. This would be ruinous to the north-western states. And on this ground, even without the anticipated difficulty growing out of the contest for the public lands, these north-western states, on the upper waters of the Mississippi, would soon secede from the north-eastern and Atlantic states and make a separate community, and also would make a separate peace—if not seek to be re-united to the southern states. This abandonment by this vast and fertile region would leave the north-eastern states in a much more weak and hopeless condition than previously.

And as early, or perhaps earlier, there will be another secession from the first northern confederacy, by California, Oregon, Utah, and all the other territory of the present United States lying on the Pacific slope. This separation will take place as soon as the residents of the Pacific states and territories shall deem the measure more beneficial to their interest, than to enjoy the bounties and have the protection of the present federal government, and the consummation will only be hastened and hurried by the previous separation of the slaveholding from the non-slaveholding states. And even under the present state of things, if such a separation were to take place, and if the parties would maintain perfect free-trade with each other, after their separation, (as while under one government,) it would be no evil to the other portion of the present Union, and especially to the southern states, if all the Pacific territory would at once declare its independence and secede from the United States. The southern people, from the first possession, have been unjustly excluded from their equal rights to California. They will never receive either the value of an acre of land or an ounce of gold from this part of the public domain. And the only pecuniary interest that will accrue to the South, (even if ever so much to the United States) from the possession of the territory on the Pacific slope, will be the southern (and much larger) share of the cost of its government, maintenance, and improvement in time of peace, and of the incalculably greater cost of its military and naval defence in time of war. It would be far better for the South that the Pacific states and territories should secede at once, and even if without conditions or amicable arrangement, before we shall have to incur our legal share of the enormous cost of constructing one or more railroads to the Pacific, or of defending the Pacific coast from a foreign enemy and naval power. Already King Brigham Young is the despotic and secure ruler of the virtually independent Mormon people and country, to which the government and people of the United States pay tribute, (in defraying the expenses of its territorial government, &c.,) and over which, or its ruler, the general government dares not attempt to exerise any coercive control.

SECTION XXI.

Prosperity of the southern states the result of their independence.

While such elements of division, if not of strife, would operate to separate the non-slaveholding states into at least three portions, the slaveholding states would have common interests, and unity of opinion and principles as to matters of general policy. United in a confederacy, they would possess enough of territory, population, and wealth for an independent community—strong enough for defence in arms against any single power whatever—and of more than double the absolute strength of all the thirteen united colonies when they revolted from and defied in arms their mother country, then one of the most powerful nations of the world. But a guaranty of safe defence, and almost of immunity from war, would be found in the important fact that this southern confederacy would supply nearly all the cotton for the factories and the consumption of both Europe and America. The only nations of both hemispheres that could be dreaded as foes, would incur far more injury from being shut out by war from the needed supply of our cotton, than would be compensated by any possible amount of military success in war against the confederacy of cotton states.

The revenue and resources of the southern states, heretofore contributed mainly to aid northern interests, foster northern industry and trade, and increase northern wealth and power, would thenceforward be retained and used to sustain and build up our own commerce, and cities, and general prosperity. In twenty-five or thirty years our population and wealth will be more than doubled, and the value of our products, and their demand by the commercial world, will be increased in still greater proportion. There will probably be no community of more vigorous and healthy growth, or with better prospects of stable prosperity. With the aid of our own annual profits of industry and capital, and the encouragement that the new condition and demands of the southern states will create, manufactures, and navigation and commerce will increase rapidly, even if the growth was stimulated and maintained by southern resources only. But in advance of this natural and slower growth, these branches of industry, and the men to carry them on, and the capital to sustain them, will be transplanted to any amount that may be desired, and permitted, from the northern to the southern states, as soon as they shall have become separate political communities. Plenty of manufacturing capital, and also of captalists and laborers, and plenty of ships and sailors, will come to obtain the benefits of establishment in the South. There would be nothing more wanting for this speedy and extensive transferrence of capital, industry, and also of (at least professed) allegiance, than the sure and simple operation of greatly reduced employment and profits in the northern states, and the great increase of both in the independent and flourishing southern confederacy—then just beginning to use its own funds and resources to build up and sustain its own cities, manufactures, and navigation.

SECTION XXII.

The proper mode for the practical secession of the southern states Conclusion.

In the foregoing pages it was maintained, and I trust established in the minds of all who know the people of the South, and understand their condition, that there is no reason why a separation of the states should cause war between the portions, acting in their new positions as separate political communities. And further, it was maintained that if, contrary to all probability, war should thence arise, that the consequent and necessary evils of war would bear less heavily on the defensive South than on the aggressive North. That it would not promote the interest or welfare of either of the separated portions to make war on the other, is self-evident. And if that premise is admitted, the deduction is inevitable, that aggressive war would not be made by either community because of their separation, and upon calculation and deliberate design.

But still there would be danger of war springing from other sources, though it might be as contrary to the wishes and intentions, as it would be detrimental to the interests, of both the separated communities, and new political states. Immediately at the time of separation of states previously embittered against each other by injuries inflicted and suffered, quarrels and collisions might take place between imprudent, violent, or turbulent individuals of both sides, which would involve other persons, as partisans, and spread hostile feeling and induce avenging action among many others, ready to be misled through their ignorance or prejudices. Or, otherwise, hostilities might be commenced and blood be shed by the indiscretion of a civil magistrate or military officer, or by the calculating self-interest and unscrupulous ambition of some one clothed with legal authority to command, and who might expect to elevate himself on the misfortunes of his country. Therefore, from one or other of these causes, there would be great danger of the commencement of at least partial hostilities, and private and unauthorized acts of volence and bloodshed, along the new border lines. But all such dangers may be effectually guarded against, at the time and in the manner of beginning the separation, by adopting the policy which will be safest and best in every aspect, and which will be here indicated.

The opposers of further submission to wrongs, and consequent advocates for secession, in the more southern states, have been looking to the great state of Virginia to lead in the movement, in which case the large majority of the more southern states would follow immediately, and all others of the slaveholding states soon after. But, for reasons which ought to be manifest to every thinking man, a border state, as Virginia, or Maryland, or Kentucky would be after the general separation, never will, and scarcely can, take the first step in the actual deliberate movement of secession. There will always be in states thus situated, at least a minority, timid, and also numerous enough to paralyze the will and strength of the majority. And such is the case now in Virginia, even though a large majority of the citizens are most earnestly opposed to longer submission to northern wrongs. The proper and perfectly safe and peaceable course to bring about the secession, and subsequent confederation of all the slaveholding states, (excepting Delaware perhaps,) will be for Virginia, and all the other of the northern tier of the slaveholding states, with North Carolina and Tennessee, *not* to move at first, or as early as the more southern states. Whenever the evils inflicted under the present Union, and the usurpations and oppressions by the northern states shall be deemed no longer tolerable, (if that time has not already arrived,) if five or six only of the more southern states adjoining each other, acting in concert, shall declare their independence of, and secession from the present federal government, the movement will be perfectly safe from the danger of producing individual conflicts and border feuds, as well as from attack or war from the northern states, or the still remaining northern federal power. There could be no border feuds, because the people and their magistrates, or leaders, on both sides of the new (and but temporary) line of separation would be alike in interests and sentiments.

And if the government or people of the northern states should be so insane as to make war, and attempt to march an army to coerce or conquer the seceding states, there would be to these an impregnable barrier of protection afforded in the common feeling and friendship, and the position of the slaveholding and (as yet) non-seceding states. And within a few months, or as early as the plan of government of the new southern confederacy shall have been determined on and organized, and the power of the already separated states consolidated, the time will have arrived for the final and practical settlement of the great question—the question which would have been growing more and more intense in interest—as to the subsequent course of the non-seceding and slaveholding states. This question is, would they follow the course and share the fortunes of their friends, or remain in the power, now more than doubled for their injury, of their opponents and worst enemies? Whether the first seceding states were ten or but five in number, they would be equally and perfectly safe from northern hostility or attack. And whether five or ten in number, their secession would equally leave the non-seceding and slaveholding states in a helpless and hopeless minority in their then political connection, and at the mercy of a hostile, malignant, and remorseless majority of their enemies. If now, when the southern states in the present confederacy number fifteen, to sixteen non-slaveholding states, their rights are trodden down, and their dearest interests are in the course of being gradually but certainly destroyed by their barely more numerous co-states, what will be their prospect for defence or safety when they shall number but five or ten to sixteen hostile northern states? Scarcely would a year elapse, or the requisite legal formalities be complied with, before the present provisions of the federal constitution, which authorize slave representation, and protect slave property, would be annulled, and when other enactments would make the complete destruction of the institution of slavery but a question of time. Would Virginia and North Carolina, or Kentucky and Missouri, wait for this certain consummation? Certainly they will not, unless they are already prepared to submit to this extreme measure of outrage and spoliation. As soon as these middle-ground states could act through their legislatures, they would undoubtedly and necessarily determine to unite with their more southern sister states in their common cause and political connection. Not only would all these named states so act, both from preference and necessity, but Maryland also. For, if this state were separated from political connection and friendship with Virginia and the other more southern states, the commerce of Baltimore would be ruined, and with it the great commercial interests, as well as the property in slaves of that state. Unless the people of Maryland are prepared to make these sacrifices, immediate or remote, for the benefit of remaining united with the northern states—ready indeed to submit to certain ruin—they will as certainly concur in and follow the seceding movement, as will the more southern people.

In this manner, without risk of war or bloodshed, the separation of our present Union with our worst enemies may be effected, and the consequent construction of a southern and slaveholding confederacy. Then, freed from the hostile and incendiary action of our now fellow-citizens and "brethren" of the North, the people of the South will be well able to guard against them either as foreigners, or (if they prefer that character) as enemies. Slave property, by being then duly guarded and protected, will become even more secure in the northern border counties of Virginia and Maryland, than now in their southern frontiers. Freed from longer paying millions every year of legal tribute to the North, through the machinery of tariffs, banks, and other commercial privileges, (as in the fishery bounties, exclusive coast navigation, and bounties to lines of ocean steamers,) the southern states would soon rise to the high position of economical, commercial, and political prosperity, which would be the certain result of retaining the products of their industry and wealth for their own use and benefit. On the other hand, if things continue as they are, the outside pressure of fanaticism, and its secret incendiary action, operating more and more to render property in slaves unsafe, will continue to cause (as has long been the case) and to increase the removal of the slave population from the border slaveholding states until these will lose all, and ceasing to be slaveholding, must consequently become more and more assimilated to the North in sentiment and policy. On this account, every year that shall pass before the secession movement is made, will serve to depress still lower the property and slavery interests, and the power for resistance and self-protection of the border slaveholding states. If these states are to be successfully defended in the possession of their property, their political rights, and everything dear to freemen, or if they are to be preserved as a future antegral portion, and the border bulwark of a southern confederacy, it must be secured by the more southern states seceding first, and speedily.

MATTHEW'S DIGEST OF THE LAWS OF VIRGINIA, of a civil nature and of a permanent character, and a general operation, illustrated by judicial decisions, to which are prefixed the Constitutions of the United States and Virginia, by J. M. Matthews, 2 vols. 8vo, sheep, Richmond, 1856-7, $12 00

THE SAME INTERLEAVED WITH WRITING PAPER FOR NOTES, 2 vols.................................. 17 00

MUNFORD'S (WILLIAM) REPORTS OF CASES argued and determined in the Supreme Court of Appeals of Virginia, 6 vols. 8vo, sheep, Richmond and New York, 1812, &c.. 36 00

PATTON & HEATH. A GENERAL INDEX TO GRATTAN'S REPORTS, from second to eleventh, inclusive, by J. M. Patton and R. B. Heath, 8vo, sheep, Richmond, 1856...................................... 3 50

PATTON & HEATH. REPORTS OF CASES decided in the Special Court of Appeals of Virginia, held at Richmond, and a General Index to Grattan's Reports, from 2d to 11th vol., inclusive, by J. M. Patton and R. B. Heath, vol. 1, 8vo, sheep, Richmond, 1856.................... 6 00

PATTON & HEATH. REPORTS OF CASES decided in the Special Court of Appeals, held in Richmond 1855-6-7, by J. M. Patton and R. B. Heath, 2 vols. 8vo, sheep, Richmond, 1855-7........................... 7 00

QUARTERLY LAW JOURNAL, A. B. Guigon, Editor, vol. 1, 1856, vol. 2, 1857, vol. 3, 1858, vol. 4, 1859, 8vo, sheep, Richmond, per volume......................... 5 00

RANDOLPH'S (PEYTON) REPORTS OF CASES argued and determined in the Court of Appeals of Virginia, 6 vols. 8vo, sp. Richmond, Va., 1823, &c....... .... 24 00

RITCHIE'S (THOMAS, JR.) TRIAL. A full report, embracing all the evidence and arguments in the case of the Commonwealth of Virginia *vs.* T. Ritchie, Jr., for the killing of John Hampden Pleasants, to which is added an appendix showing the action of the Court in relation to the other parties connected with the said case, 8vo, paper, New York, 1846.. 25

VIRGINIA. PAY AND MUSTER ROLLS OF THE VIRGINIA MILITIA IN THE WAR OF 1812, 8vo half calf, Richmond, 1851-2.......................... 15 00

VIRGINIA CASES. A Collection of Cases decided by the General Court of Virginia, chiefly relating to the Penal Laws of the Commonwealth, commencing 1789 and ending 1826, copied from the Records of the said Court, with explanatory notes, by Judges Brockenbrough and Holmes, second edition, with abstracts prefixed to the cases, 2 vols. in 1, 8vo, sheep, Richmond, 1826 and 1853 .... 6 00

VIRGINIA LAW OF CORPORATIONS, ACTS OF THE GENERAL ASSEMBLY compiled from the code of Virginia, together with an act passed in 1837, relating to Manufacturing and Mining Companies, 8vo, paper, Richmond, 1853........ 50

WYTHE'S (GEO.) REPORTS. Decisions of cases in Virginia of the High Court of Chancery, with remarks upon Decrees by the Court of Appeals, reversing some of those decisions, by George Wythe, 2d and only complete edition. With a Memoir of the author, Analysis of the Cases, and an Index, by B. B. Minor, L. B. And with an Appendix, containing references to cases in *pari materia*, an essay on lapse, joint tenants and tenants in common, &c., &c., by Wm. Green, Esq. 8vo, sheep. Richmond, 1852........ 4 00

WHITE ACRE *vs.* BLACK ACRE, a Case at Law, reported by J. G., Esq., a retired barrister of Lincolnshire, England, 18mo, mus., Richmond, 1856........ 75

VIRGINIA. RULES OF THE COURT OF APPEALS from its establishment to the present time. Also, Rules of the District Courts of Fredericksburg and Williamsburg. 8vo., paper. Richmond........ 10

GILMER'S (F. W.) VIRGINIA REPORTS. 8vo., calf. Richmond, 1821........ 2 00

GRATTAN'S (P. R.) VIRGINIA REPORTS. 15 vols., 8vo, calf. Richmond, 1845–60. Per volume........ 4 00

LEIGH'S (B. W.) VIRGINIA REPORTS. 12 vols., 8vo, calf. Richmond, 1830–44. Per volume........ 4 00

ROBINSON'S (C.) VIRGINIA REPORTS. 2 vols., 8vo, calf. Richmond, 1843–4. Per volume........ 4 00

HENING (W. W.) & SHEPHERD'S (S.) STATUTES OF VIRGINIA from 1619 to 1807. 16 vols., 8vo, sheep. Richmond, 1823–36........ 13 00

VIRGINIA ACTS OF ASSEMBLY from 1808 to 1860. 8vo, half sheep. Richmond........

SELECTIONS OF THE MOST IMPORTANT PORTIONS OF THE REPORTS OF THE REVISOR'S OF VIRGINIA CODE. With notes by A. H. Sands. 8vo, sheep. In press........

POLITICS.

TUCKER'S (H. ST. GEORGE) LECTURES ON NATURAL LAW, also Lectures on Government, 12mo, muslin, Charlottesville, 1844........ 75

ANTICIPATIONS OF THE FUTURE, TO SERVE AS LESSONS FOR THE PRESENT TIME. Extracts from letters written from Washington to the London Times during the years 1864–5–6–7–8. 12mo, mus., Richmond, 1860........ 1 00

TUCKER'S (H. ST. GEORGE) LECTURES ON CONSTITUTIONAL LAW, for the use of the Law Class of the University of Virginia, 12mo, mus., Richmond, 1843.. 75

VIRGINIA POLITICS. A History of the Political Campaign in Va. in 1855, to which is added a review of the position of parties in the Union, and a statement of the political issues distinguishing them on the eve of the Presidential Campaign of 1856, by J. P. Hambleton, M. D., 8vo, mus., Richmond, 1856.......................... 2 50

VIRGINIA CONVENTION. Proceeding and Debates of the Va. State Convention of 1829–30, to which are subjoined the new Constitution of Virginia, and the votes of the people, 8vo, calf, Richmond, 1830................. 5 00

VIRGINIA STATISTICS. Documents containing statistics ordered to be printed by the State Convention sitting in the city of Richmond, 1850–51, 8vo, calf, Richmond, 1851.. 2 50

VIRGINIA CONVENTION. Journal, Acts and Proceedings of a General Convention of the State of Virginia assembled at Richmond 1850, 8vo, half calf, Richmond, 1850. 5 00

VIRGINIA CONVENTION 1850–51. Register of the Debates and Proceedings of the Virginia Reform Convention, (imperfect,) 8vo, half sheep, Richmond, 1851........... 3 00

VIRGINIA. Journal of the Senate and House of Delegates for various years. Richmond.

VIRGINIA. Journal of the Convention of 1776. 4to, half sheep. Richmond, 1816............................. 2 00

ELLETT'S ESSAYS ON THE LAW OF TRADE, in reference to the Works of Internal Improvement in the U. S. 8vo, mus., Richmond, 1839.. .... 1 50

LETTERS OF CURTIUS, written by the late John Thomson, of Petersburg; to which is added a Speech delivered by him in August, '95, on the British Treaty; to which a short Sketch of his Life is prefixed. 12mo, paper. Richmond, 1804.. .... 1 00

JEFFERSON. Memoir, Correspondence and Miscellanies from the Papers of Thomas Jefferson. Edited by Thomas Jefferson Randolph. 4 vols., 8vo, boards. Charlottesville, 1829.......... .... 5 00

JEFFERSON. Observations on the Writings of Thomas Jefferson, with particular reference to the attack they contain on the Memory of the late Gen'l Henry Lee. In series of letters, by H. Lee. 2nd edition. With an Introduction and Notes, by Charles C. Lee. 8vo, mus. Philadelphia, 1839... 1 75

LONDON (D. H.) ON THE COMMERCIAL, AGRICULTURAL AND INTELLECTUAL INDEPENDENCE OF VIRGINIA AND THE SOUTH. 8vo, paper. Richmond, 1860... 25

VIRGINIAN (THE) HISTORY OF THE AFRICAN COLONIZATION. (This contains, among other documents, portions of the Debate on Slavery in the Virginia Legislature of 1832.) Edited by Rev. P. Slaughter. 8vo, mus., Richmond, 1855.. .:......................... 1 00

RUFFIN'S (EDMUND) AFRICAN COLONIZATION UNVEILED. Slavery and Free Labor described and compared. The Political Economy of Slavery; or, the Institution considered in regard to its influence on public wealth and the general welfare. Two Great Evils of Virginia, and their one Common Remedy, 8vo, pa. Richmond, 1860. Each................................. 10

HISTORY.

BEVERLY'S (ROBERT) HISTORY OF VIRGINIA. In four parts. I. The history of the settlement of Virginia, and the government thereof, to the year 1706. II. The natural productions and conveniences of the country, suited to trade and improvement. III. The native Indians, their religion, laws and customs, in war and peace. IV. The present state of the country, as to the polity of the government, and the improvements of the land, to 10th of June, 1720. By Robert Beverly, a native of the place. Re-printed from the author's second revised London edition of 1792, with an introduction by Charles Campbell, author of the "Colonial History of Virginia." 14 plates, 8vo, mus. Richmond, 1855.......................... 2 50

AN ACCOUNT OF DISCOVERIES IN THE WEST until 1519, and of Voyages to and along the Atlantic Coast of North America from 1520 to 1573. Prepared for the Virginia Historical and Philosophical Society, by Conway Robinson. 8vo, mus. Richmond, 1848. (Published at $5.) 2 50

JEFFERSON'S (THOMAS) NOTES ON THE STATE OF VIRGINIA. A new edition, prepared by the author, containing many new notes never before published.

It is printed from President Jefferson's copy (Stockdale's London edition of 1787) of the Notes on Virginia, with his last additions (they are numerous) and corrections in manuscript, and four maps of Caves, Mounds, Fortifications, &c.

Letters from Gen. Dearborn and Judge Gibson, relating to the Murder of Logan, &c.

Fry and Jefferson's Map of Virginia, Maryland, Delaware, and Pennsylvania—very valuable on account of the Public Places and Private Residences, which are not to be found on any other Map.

A Topographical Analysis of Virginia, for 1790—a curious and useful sheet for historical reference.

Translations of all Jefferson's Notes in Foreign Languages, by Prof. Schele de Vere, of the University of Virginia. 8vo, mus. Richmond, 1853........................ 2 50

SMITH'S (M.) GEOGRAPHICAL VIEW OF THE BRITISH POSSESSIONS IN NORTH AMERICA. 18mo, sheep. Baltimore, 1814.................... 35

VIRGINIA CONVENTION OF 1776: Historical and biographical. By H. B. Grigsby. 8vo, mus. Richmond, 1855. 1 50

OREGON, OUR RIGHT AND TITLE: containing an account of the condition of the Oregon Territory, its soil, climate and geographical position; together with a statement of the claims of Russia, Spain, Great Britain, and the United States. Accompanied with a map prepared by the author. By Wyndham Robertson, jr., of Virginia. 8vo, paper. Washington, 1846...................... 50

HOT SPRINGS. The Invalid's Guide to the Virginia Hot Springs, with cases illustrative of their effects. By Thos. Goode, M. D. 32mo, cloth. Richmond, 1846.......... 25

VIRGINIA. Report on the Soils of Powhatan County. By W. Gilham, Prof. Va. Military Institute. With a Map. 8vo, paper. Richmond, 1857...................... 35

BIRD. WESTOVER MANUSCRIPTS, containing the history of the dividing line betwixt Virginia and North Carolina. A Journey to the Land of Eden, A. D. 1733; and A Progress to the Mines, written from 1728–36, and now first published. By W. Bird, of Westover. 8vo, boards. Petersburg, 1841.................................... 3 00

BLAND PAPERS, being a selection from the manuscripts of Col. T. Bland, jr., of Prince George county, Va.; to which are prefixed an Introduction and Memoir edited by Charles Campbell. 2 vols. in one, 8vo, h'f ro. Petersburg, 1840.. 3 00

VIRGINIA POLITICS. A History of the Political Campaign in Virginia in 1855; to which is added a review of the position of Parties in the Union, and a statement of the political issues distinguishing them on the eve of the Presidential Campaign of 1856. By J. P. Hambleton, M. D. 8vo, mus. Richmond, 1856........................... 2 50

VIRGINIA CONVENTION. Proceeding and Debates of the Virginia State Convention of 1829–30, to which are subjoined the New Constitution of Virginia, and the votes of the people. 8vo, calf. Richmond, 1830............. 5 00

VIRGINIA. Pay and Muster Rolls of the Virginia Militia in the War of 1812. 8vo, half calf. Richmond, 1851–2. 15 00

VIRGINIA STATISTICS. Documents constaining statistics ordered to be printed by the State Convention sitting in the city of Richmond, 1850–51. 8vo, calf. Richmond, 1851.. 2 50

VIRGINIA CONVENTION. Journal, Acts and Proceedings of a General Convention of the State of Virginia, assembled at Richmond, 1850. 8vo, half calf. Richmond, 1850.. 5 00

VIRGINIA HISTORICAL SOCIETY COLLECTIONS, ADDRESSES, &c. (Contents: Stuart's Indian Wars, 1763; Grace Sherwood's Trial, 1705; Address in 1833 by J. P. Cushing; in 1851 by W. H. Macfarland; in 1852 by H. A. Washington; in 1853 by H. B. Grigsby; in 1856 by R. M. T. Hunter; in 1856 by J. P. Holcombe.) 8vo, half turkey. Richmond, 1833-56.............................. 5 00

VIRGINIA CONVENTION, 1850-51. egister of the Debates and Proceedings of the Virginia Reform Convention, (imperfect.) 8vo, half sheep. Richmond, 1851........ 3 00

VIRGINIA. A Comprehensive Description of Virginia and the District of Columbia, containing a copious collection of geographical, statistical, political, commercial, religious, moral and miscellaneous information, chiefly from original sources, by Joseph Martin; to which is added a History of Virginia, from its first settlement to the year 1754, with an abstract of the principal events from that period to the Independence of Virginia, by W. H. Brockenbrough, formerly Librarian at the University of Virginia, and afterwards Judge of the United States Court of Florida, 8vo, sp. Richmond.......................... 2 00

MAURY. Paper on the Gulf Stream and Currents of the Sea, read before the National Institute at its annual meeting in 1844, by M. F. Maury, Lieut. U. S. Navy. 8vo, pa. Richmond, 1844................................ 13

BURKE. The Virginia Mineral Springs, with remarks on their use, the Diseases to which they are applicable, and in which they are contra-indicated; accompanied by a Map of Routes and Distances. A new work—2d edition. Improved and enlarged. By W. Burke, M.D. 12mo, muslin. Richmond, 1853........................... 75

COTTOM'S EDITION OF RICHARDSON'S ALMANAC. 24mo, paper, 6c. Per dozen, 25c.; per gross, $2.50. Containing, besides the twelve calendar pages and astronomical calculations, a Jewish Calendar, Gardener's Monthly Instructor, List of the Virginia Senators, Members of Congress, Senate and House of Delegates; Virginia and North Carolina State Governments; State and Federal Courts of Virginia, North Carolina, Maryland, and the District of Columbia; Conjectures of the Weather, Equation or Time Tables, Receipts, Anecdotes, &c. Published annually.

JEFFERSON & CABELL. Early history of the University of Virginia, as contained in the Letters of (during the years from 1810 to 1826) Thos. Jefferson and Joseph

C. Cabell, hitherto unpublished; with an Appendix consisting of Mr. Jefferson's bill for a complete system of education, and other illustrative documents; and an Introduction, comprising a brief historical sketch of the University, and a biographical notice of Joseph C. Cabell. 8vo, muslin. Richmond, 1856........................ 2 50

JUBILEE AT JAMESTOWN, VA. Report of Proceedings in Commemoration of the 13th of May, the Second Centesimal Anniversary of the Settlement of Virginia, containing the Order of Procession, the Prayer of Bishop Madison, the Orations, the Odes and Toasts; together with the Proceedings at Williamsburg on the 15th, the day when the Convention of Virginia assembled in the old Capitol, declared her Independent, and recommended a similar procedure to Congress, and to the other States. 8vo, paper. Petersburg, 1807........................ 1 00

VIRGINIA. Journal of the Senate and House of Delegates for various years. Richmond.

VIRGINIA. Journal of the Convention of 1776. 4to, half sheep. Richmond, 1816...... .... 2 00

JEFFERSON. Memoir, Correspondence and Miscellanies from the Papers of Thos. Jefferson. Edited by Thos. Jefferson Randolph. 4 vols., 8v, boards. Charlottesville, 1829.. .... 5 00

JEFFERSON. Observations on the Writings of Thomas Jefferson, with particular reference to the attack they contain on the Memory of the late Gen'l Henry Lee. In series of letters by H. Lee. 2nd edition. With an Introduction and Notes, by Chas. C. Lee. 8vo, mus. Philadelphia, 1839.. 1 75

AGRICULTURE.

RUFFIN'S (EDMUND) FARMER'S REGISTER. 10 vols., 8vo, half roan.................................. 30 00

RUFFIN'S (EDMUND) PRIZE ESSAY ON AGRICULTURAL EDUCATION. 2nd edition, 8vo, paper....... 10

RUFFIN'S (EDMUND) AGRICULTURAL ESSAYS: Containing articles on the theory and practice of draining (in all its branches:) advantages of ploughing flat land in wide beds; on clover culture and the use and value of the products; management of wheat harvests; harvesting corn fodder; on the manner of propagation and habits of the moth or weevil, and means to prevent its ravages; inquiry into the causes of the existence of prairies, savannas and deserts, and the peculiar condition of soils which favor or prevent the growth of trees; depressed condition of lower Virginia; apology for "book farmers;" fallow; usefulness of snakes; embanked tide marshes and mill ponds as causes of disease; on the sources of malaria, or of autumnal diseases, and means of prevention; on the culture, uses and value of the southern pea, (Ruffin's Prize Essay of November, 1854,) and especially as a manuring crop. 12mo, half bound. Richmond, 1855............ 1 25

RUFFIN. An Essay on Calcareous Manures. By Edmund Ruffin, a practical farmer of Virginia from 1812; founder and sole editor of the Farmer's Register; Member and Secretary of the former State Board of Agriculture; formerly Agricultural Surveyor of the State of South Carolina; and President of the Virginia State Agricultural Society. 5th edition, amended and enlarged, with plates. Fine edition, 8vo, library style, $2; cheap edition, 12mo, half roan or mus. Richmond, 1852.................... 1 25

PLANTATION AND FARM INSTRUCTION, Regulation, Record, Inventory, and Account Book, and for the better Ordering and Management of Plantation and Farm Business in every particular. By a Southern Planter. "Order is Heaven's First Law." *New edition printing.*

THEOLOGY.

MAGRUDER & ORVIS' DEBATE on the Punishment of the Wicked, and on the Kingdom of God. 12mo, muslin. Richmond, 1855.................................... 75

WALSH'S (REV. J. T.) NATURE AND DURATION OF FUTURE PUNISHMENT. 12mo, muslin. Richmond, 1857.................................... 50

MEMOIR AND SERMONS OF THE REV. WILLIAM DUVALL, City Missionary. By the Rev. C. Walker. With a portrait. 12mo, mus. Richmond, 1854......... 50

STRINGFELLOW'S (T., D.D.) STATISTICAL AND SCRIPTURAL VIEW OF SLAVERY. 4th edition, 12mo, mus. Richmond, 1856....................... 50

FAMILY CHRISTIAN ALBUM. Edited by Mrs. E P. Elam. 8vo, mus. Richmond, 1855.................. 1 50

FLAVEL'S WORKS. Balm of the Covenant. View of the Soul of Man, &c. 8vo, half roan. Richmond, 1828.. 60

BLAIR. Sermons of Rev. John D. Blair, collected from his manuscripts. 8vo, sheep. . Richmond, 1825............ 50

POETRY.

BARTLEY'S (J. AVIS) POEMS. Lays of Ancient Virginia, &c. 12mo, mus. Richmond, 1855.............. 75

MOCK (THE) AUCTION. Ossawatamie Sold! A Mock Heroic Poem; with Portraits and Tableaux, illustrative of the character and actions of the world-renowned Order of Peter Funks. By a Virginian. 12mo, mus. 10 tinted plates. Richmond, 1860............................ 75

CARTER. Mugæ, by Nugator; or Pieces in Prose and Verse. By St. Ledger L. Carter. 24mo, half roan. Baltimore, 1844.......... 75

BETHEL HYMNS. A Collection of Original Spiritual Songs. By Mrs. Elizabeth Sowers, of Clark county, Va. 48mo, sheep. Richmond, 1849............. 25

FARMER'S (C. M.) FAIRY OF THE STREAM, and other Poems. 12mo, boards. Richmond, 1847.......... 50

COURTNEY'S (REV J.) SELECTION OF HYMNS. 24mo, sheep. Richmond, 1831..... 35

SCHOOL.

VAUGHAN'S (S. A.) ABECEDARIAN; OR, FIRST BOOK FOR CHILDREN. Designed to render the learning of the Alphabet, and of Elementary Spelling and Defining, pleasing and intellectual; and to fix in the mind habits of attention to the force of letters in the formation of words, and to the meaning of words, and through their application to their appropriate objects, to inculcate the love of Nature and reverence of Nature's God. 12mo, roan back. Richmond...................... 15

YOUNG (THE) AMERICAN'S PRIMER, OR FIRST BOOK. 24mo, paper. Richmond, per dozen........... 25

SCHOOLER'S (SAMUEL) ELEMENTS OF DESCRIPTIVE GEOMETRY, the Point, the Straight Line, and the Plane. 4to, mus. Richmond, 1853............... 2 00

The paper, type, and plates, are in the finest style of the arts; and the book, altogether, has been pronounced equal, if not superior, to any English, French, or American work on the subject.

GARNETT'S (JAMES M.) LECTURES ON FEMALE EDUCATION, AND THE GOSSIP'S MANUAL. 3rd edition, 18mo, sheep. Richmond, 1825.......... 50

CÆSAR, with English Notes. By Samuel Schooler. *In preparation.*

SLAVERY.

STRINGFELLOW'S (T., D.D.) STATISTICAL AND SCRIPTURAL VIEW OF SLAVERY. Fourth edition, 12mo, mus. Richmond, 1856......................... 50

FLETCHER'S (JOHN) STUDIES ON SLAVERY. 8vo, sheep. Natchez, 1852.................................. 2 00

DEW. An Essay on Slavery. By T. R. Dew, late President of William and Mary College. 2d edition, 8vo, paper. Richmond, 1849.............................. 50

RUFFIN'S (EDMUND) AFRICAN COLONIZATION UNVEILED. Slavery and Free Labor described and compared. The political Economy of Slavery; or the Institution considered in regard to its influence on public wealth and the general welfare. Two Great Evils of Virginia, and their one Common Remedy. 8vo, pa. Richmond, 1860. Each.................................. 10

UNCLE ROBIN IN HIS CABIN IN VIRGINIA, AND TOM WITHOUT ONE IN BOSTON. By J. W. Page. 2nd edition, plates, 12mo, muslin. Richmond, 1853..... 75

WHITE ACRE vs. BLACK ACRE, a Case at Law, reported by J. G., Esq., a retired barrister of Lincolnshire, England, 18mo, mus. Richmond, 1856................ 75

MASONIC.

DOVE'S (JOHN) VIRGINIA TEXT BOOK OF ROYAL ARCH MASONRY. Plates, 12mo, mus. Richmond, 1853, 1 25

DOVE'S (JOHN) HISTORY OF THE GRAND LODGE OF VIRGINIA, AND ANCIENT CONSTITUTIONS OF MASONRY. 18mo, muslin. Richmond, 1854..... 75

DOVE'S (JOHN, M.D.) MASONIC TEXT BOOK. 2nd edition. Plates, 12mo, mus. Richmond, 1854.......... 1 25

NOVELS.

REMINISCENCES OF A VIRGINIA PHYSICIAN. By Prof. P. S. Ruter. 2 vols., 12mo, paper. Louisville, 1849, 50

SOUTHERN AND SOUTH-WESTERN SKETCHES. Fun, Sentiment and Adventure! Edited by a Gentleman of Richmond. 18mo, mus. Richmond............... 60

TUCKER. Gertrude. A Novel. By Judge Tucker, Professor of William and Mary College. 8vo, paper. Richmond, 1845.. 35

UNCLE ROBIN IN HIS CABIN IN VIRGINIA, AND TOM WITHOUT ONE IN BOSTON. By J. W. Page. 2nd edition, plates, 12mo, mus. Richmond, 1853........ 75

SKETCHES OF CHARACTER, (Randolph, Wirt, Kenton, &c.) AND TALES FOUNDED ON FACT. By F. W. Thomas. 8vo, boards. Louisville, 1849......... 25

MICHAEL BONHAM, OR THE FALL OF BEXAR. A Tale of Texas. In five parts. By a Southerner. 8vo, paper. Richmond, 1852............................ 25

EDITH ALLEN, OR SKETCHES OF LIFE IN VIRGINIA. By Lawrence Neville. 12mo, mus. Richmond, 1855.. 1 00

MUSIC.

EVERETT'S (DR. A. B.) ELEMENTS OF VOCAL MUSIC; including a Treatise on Harmony, and a Chapter on Versification. Designed as a text-book for teachers and pupils in Female Seminaries, Male Academies, Singing Classes, etc., etc., and for private study and reference. 2nd and enlarged edition. 18mo, mus. Richmond, 1860, 50

EVERETT'S (L. C. & DR. A. B.) NEW THESAURUS MUSICUS, OR U. S. COLLECTION OF CHURCH MUSIC; constituting the most complete variety of new Psalm and Hymn Tunes, Sentences, Anthems, Chants, &c. for the use of the Choir, the Congregation and the Singing School, ever offered to the American people. Comprising also all the popular old choir and congregational tunes in general use. Music, 8vo, boards. Richmond, 1860...... 1 00

WINKLER'S HINTS TO PIANO-FORTE PLAYERS. 12mo, boards. Richmond, 1847...................... 25

MISCELLANY.

LUMBER (THE) DEALER'S ASSISTANT, OR COMPLETE TABLES OF THE MEASUREMENTS OF TIMBER, &c.—showing the quantity in feet and inches in any number of plank or scantling, from one to fifty; of any length in feet or half feet, from eight to twenty-two feet long; of any width in inches and half inches, from three to twenty inches wide. By George S. Sutherlin. 12mo, half sheep. Richmond, 1849.................. 50

VIRGINIA JUSTICE'S RECORD BOOK OF JUDGMENTS. Cap size, half bound..................... 1 50

PAJOT'S OBSTETRIC TABLES, translated from the French, and arranged by O. A. Grenshaw, M. D., und J. B. McCaw, M. D. 4to, boards. Richmond, 1856....... 1 25

PHYSICIAN'S TABULATED DIARY, designed to facilitate the study of Disease at the Bedside. By a Physician of Virginia. Pocket size. Muslin. Richmond, 1856.... 50

SOUTHERN LITERARY MESSENGER. 29 vols., 8vo, in numbers. Richmond, 1834–59.....................100 00

☞Most of the volumes or numbers are for sale separate.

RANDOLPH'S POCKET DIARY AND DAILY MEMODANDUM BOOK. Richmond, 186—. 18mo, half bound, 35c.; tucks.. 60

RANDOLPH'S POCKET DIARY, DAILY MEMORANDUM AND ACCOUNT BOOK. Richmond, 186—. Half bound, 75c.; tucks................................. 1 00

LIBRARY CASES, OR BOXES, in neat book form, very convenient and useful for preserving valuable pamphlets and magazines. 8vo. roan back...................... 60

SKETCHES OF CHARACTER, (Randolph, Wirt, Kenton, &c.,) AND TALES FOUNDED ON FACT. By F. W. Thomas. 8vo, boards. Louisville, 1849......... 25

EDGAR'S SPORTSMAN'S HERALD & STUD BOOK 8vo, sp. New York, 1833....... .... 1 50

WATER CURE. By Dr. J. B. Williams, and others. With comments and explanatory remarks on bathing for invalids, &c., by J. Timberlake. 18mo, paper. Richmond, 1853.. 25

THE PRACTICAL MINER'S OWN BOOK & GUIDE. By J. Budge. With additions by J. Atkins. Plates, 12mo, muslin. Richmond, 1860.............................. 2 00

THE CARPENTER'S GUIDE IN STAIR-BUILDING AND HAND-RAILING, based upon Plain and Practical Principles, with sufficient explanations to inform without confusing the learner. By Patrick O'Neill, Practical Stair-Builder. Folio, mus. Richmond................. 2 00

www.ingramcontent.com/pod-product-compliance
Lightning Source LLC
LaVergne TN
LVHW021137110826
845150LV00005B/1049

* 9 7 8 1 4 2 5 5 4 8 2 9 2 *